JEWISH THINKERS

General Editor: Arthur Hertzberg

Moses Mendelssohn and the Religious Enlightenment

JEWISH THINKERS

Published

ARLOSOROFF
Shlomo Avineri

BIALIK
David Aberbach

BUBER
Pamela Vermes

ELUSIVE PROPHET:
AHAD HA'AM AND THE
ORIGINS OF ZIONISM
Steven Zipperstein

HEINE
Ritchie Robertson

HERZL
Steven Beller

IBN GABIROL
Raphael Loewe

RASHI
Chaim Pearl

Moses Mendelssohn and the Religious Enlightenment

David Sorkin

PETER HALBAN
LONDON

FIRST PUBLISHED IN GREAT BRITAIN BY
PETER HALBAN PUBLISHERS
42 SOUTH MOLTON STREET
LONDON W1Y 1HB
1996

British Library Cataloguing-in-Publication Data.

A catalogue record for this book is available from the British Library

ISBN 1870015 27 4

The publisher gratefully acknowledges permission to reprint in this publication, in somewhat different form, material that originally appeared in "The Case for Comparison: Moses Mendelssohn and the Religious Enlightenment," published in Modern Judaism 14 (1994), 121–138.

Printed in the United States of America

To Phoebe, Gideon, Isaac, and Naomi,
who often took their meals with talk
of Mendelssohn, without complaint and
apparently without ill-effect on their
digestion.

Contents

Preface

The reader wearied, if not bewildered, by the endless flood of literature on Moses Mendelssohn may justifiably ask: why a book? The answer is the need for a succinct and accessible interpretation of Mendelssohn's Jewish thought. The authoritative biography by Alexander Altmann is so vast and vastly learned as to tax even the specialist's abilities. This volume is intended to provide a serviceable introduction for the interested layperson or undergraduate, Judaica scholar or historian. Unlike Altmann's study, this is neither an intellectual biography nor a comprehensive study of Mendelssohn's oeuvre.

While I explain my method in the introduction, one prior observation belongs here. It has become a time-honored practice to study Mendelssohn primarily, or even exclusively, from his German works. In attempting to understand Mendelssohn as a philosopher of the German Enlightenment this practice is appropriate. But in attempting to understand Mendelssohn's thinking about Judaism it is untenable. Mendelssohn's Jewish thought has been studied time and again on the basis of a narrow body of evidence, the political/philosophical essay *Jerusalem, or On Religious Power and Judaism* and one or two other German works. That Mendelssohn wrote on Jewish subjects in Hebrew throughout his career has long been neglected. There is in English little if any scholarship on many of these Hebrew works, nothing that succinctly treats the entire Jewish corpus, and certainly nothing that concisely analyzes that corpus in relation to Mendelssohn's general thought. One object of this book is to survey Mendelssohn's Hebrew works in order to introduce them into the discussion of his Jewish thought. One contention of this book is that if we read his better-known German pronouncements on Judaism as part of the larger corpus, a different understanding of them emerges.

I discuss Mendelssohn's German and Hebrew works in order to analyze his Jewish thought and delineate its place in the eighteenth century and its relationship to the medieval Jewish tradition. This volume will have discharged its duty if it serves as a map that enables readers to explore his thought further on their own.

I would like to thank Peter Halban and Arthur Hertzberg for inviting me to write this book for the series "Jewish Thinkers," and I am grateful to Arthur Hertzberg for judiciously editing the manuscript. Through a fortunate turn of events the American edition is being published by the University of California Press. I am grateful to Stan Holwitz for his interest in this book and for expertly shepherding the manuscript through the various stages of publication. My thanks to Michelle Nordon for overseeing the production process and to Amanda Clark Frost for excellent copy editing.

A book such as this would be unthinkable without the splendid edition of Mendelssohn's works begun by the Berlin Academy for Jewish Studies in honor of the bicentennial of his birth (1929), resumed in 1971 under the editorship of the late Alexander Altmann, and now being completed by an international team of scholars. It would also be unthinkable without Alexander Altmann's monumental scholarship, which has immeasurably enhanced our understanding of Mendelssohn.

A number of individuals deserve my gratitude. I am deeply indebted to my friend and former colleague at Oxford Daniel Frank, who helped to make this a better book by generously putting his knowledge at my disposal. Larry Dickey has brought relevant literature to my attention and happily discussed arcane points of eighteenth-century philosophy and political thought. Gabriel Sanders, a gifted undergraduate with an interest in Mendelssohn, was the first to cast a critical eye over the entire manuscript. Klaus Berghahn gave the manuscript a thorough reading and brought additional sources to my attention. Steven Beller encouraged me to sharpen my arguments. Michael Meyer criticized the work with his characteristic rigor. Edward Breuer gave the chapters on exegesis a close reading. Shmuel Feiner improved the manuscript with his expert knowledge of the Haskalah. David Myers far exceeded the call of collegiality or friendship in the time and energy he devoted to this book.

I wrote the first section of this book during the last of the six years I spent in the congenial setting of the Oxford Centre for Postgraduate Hebrew Studies and St. Antony's College. A semester at the Institute for Research in the Humanities at the University of Wisconsin offered an ideal venue in which to study Mendelssohn's exegesis. I would also like to thank the British Academy for a grant that enabled me to read some rare publications at the Bayerische Staatsbibliothek and the Graduate School of the University of Wisconsin, which supported a visit to the Hebrew University and National Library, Jerusalem.

Chronology

1671   Jews readmitted to Berlin

1672   Jews officially permitted to reside in Dessau

1719   Christian Wolff publishes the first of his German philosophical treatises

1729   Mendelssohn born in Dessau, September 6

1733   Publication of Reinbeck's *Considerations on the Augsburg Confession*

1741   Publication of Israel Samoscz's *Netsah Yisrael* (Glory of Israel)

1742   Publication of Siegmund Jacob Baumgarten's *Interpretation of Holy Scripture*

       Republication of Maimonides' *Guide of the Perplexed*

1743   Mendelssohn arrives in Berlin

1750   Mendelssohn appointed tutor to the Bernhard family

1753   Publication of Robert Lowth's *The Sacred Poetry of the Hebrews*

1754   Mendelssohn appointed a clerk in the Bernhard silk factory

       Publication of *Philosophical Dialogues*

1755   Publication of *Letters on the Sensations*

       Translation of Rousseau's *Discourse on the Origins and Foundations of Inequality*

       Joins "Learned Coffeehouse"

Publication of *The Preacher of Morals* (probable date)

1756 Contributes to the moral weekly, *Der Chamäleon*

Publication of Naphtali Herz Wessely's *Levanon*

1760 Publication of *Logical Terms*

1761 Appointed manager in Bernhard silk firm

German works published as *Philosophical Writings*

1762 Marriage to Fromet Gugenheim

1763 Berlin Academy awards him first prize for *Treatise on Certainty in Metaphysical Philosophy*

Exempted from taxation by Jewish community

1767 Publication of *Phaedon*

1768 Appointed joint owner of Bernhard silk firm

1769 Intercession in Altona

Lavater affair

Writes *The Book of the Soul*

1770 Publication of commentary to Ecclesiastes

Begins to translate Psalms

1771 Elected but not appointed to Berlin Academy

1772 Intercession in Mecklenburg-Schwerin

1774 Begins translation of Pentateuch (probable date)

1775 Intercession in Switzerland

1777 Intercession in Königsberg

1778 Publication of prospectus for Pentateuch translation and commentary

Publication of *Ritual Laws of the Jews*

1779 Begins work on commentary to Exodus

1780 Publication of Genesis translation and commentary

Intercession in Alsace

1781 Publication of Dohm's *On the Civic Amelioration of the Jews*

Publication of translation and commentary to Exodus and Leviticus

1782 Introduction to Menasseh ben Israel's *Vindiciae Judaeorum*

Publication of introduction to Pentateuch ("Light for the Path")

1783 Completion of *The Book of the Paths of Peace*
      Publication of translation of Psalms
      Member of Berlin "Wednesday Society"
      Publication of *Jerusalem, or On Religious Power and Judaism*
1784 Publication of "What Is Enlightenment"
      First issue of *Ha-Me'asef* (The Assembler) published
1785 Publication of *The Morning Hours*
1786 Mendelssohn dies, January 4

Introduction

Moses Mendelssohn numbers among those rare figures who are a legend in their own lifetime and a symbol thereafter. Yet so rare a status has distinct liabilities. Two relentlessly eventful centuries of history have shaped the myriad versions of the legend and symbol as well as the diverse uses made of them. Those two centuries dominate our field of vision and obstruct our understanding of Mendelssohn's thought.

The legend and symbol present a Mendelssohn with two faces. The one is the man of the German Enlightenment, immortalized in the appellation "the Socrates of Berlin," after the publication of his Socratic dialogues, the *Phaedon,* in 1767. The other is the Jew, Moses Dessau (which is how he signed many of his letters and works in Hebrew), enshrined in the phrase "from Moses [Maimonides] unto Moses [Mendelssohn] there was none like Moses," which made him *the* Jewish thinker of modern times, the legitimate successor to the Moses of antiquity and the medieval Moses Maimonides.

In the innumerable descriptions and analyses of these two faces since Mendelssohn's death, the inescapable question has been the relationship between them. The answers to this question comprise a veritable index to modern Jewish thought since such an answer has been integral to virtually every modern Jewish philosophy and ideology. The answers range between two extremes.

The one extreme is that Mendelssohn's faces were of a piece and at peace, that he was the exemplary modern Jew in his ability to harmonize European culture with Jewish belief and observance. Isaac Euchel took this position in his study of Mendelssohn published in 1788 (appropriately, this work was the first book-length biography in modern Hebrew). Euchel called Mendelssohn "singular in his generation, unique in his nation" and made him a model for all Jews: "His life should be our standard, his teaching our light."[1] In the mid-nineteenth century another biographer, Meyer Kayserling, could celebrate him as the creator of a German-Jewish symbiosis, the man who "wished to foster jointly Judaism and German education [deutsche Bildung]," who as a "sincere religious Jew and a German writer" was "a noble model for posterity."[2]

The other extreme interpretation sees the two faces of Mendelssohn as ill-suited and at odds, making him the false prophet of assimilation and denationalization. The late nineteenth-century Hebrew publicist Peretz Smolenskin put this graphically: "R. Moshe ben Menahem held to the view of the love of all humanity, and his household and friends followed him. But where did it lead to? Almost all of them converted."[3] In a critical spirit the twentieth-century philosopher Franz Rosenzweig wrote: "From Mendelssohn on . . . the Jewishness of every individual has squirmed on the needle point of a 'Why.'"[4] Between these two poles are numerous variations, including such memorable ones as that of the poet Heinrich Heine, who saw Mendelssohn as the "reformer of the Jews" who "overturned the Talmud as Luther had the papacy,"[5] or that of the nineteenth-century German Jewish theologian Solomon Ludwig Steinheim (1789–1866), who wrote that Mendelssohn was "a heathen in his brain and a Jew in his body."[6]

Whether one renders Mendelssohn a hero, a villain, or something intermediate, the intractable difficulty of the relationship between the German philosopher and the Jewish thinker remains. Even Mendelssohn's ardent biographer, the late Alexander Altmann, conveyed an unmistakable ambivalence in trying to comprehend this tension. Altmann called him the "patron saint" of German Jewry by virtue of his acquisition of the German language and participation in German culture, his uncompromising loyalty as a Jew, his formulation of a modern philosophy of Judaism, and his advocacy of Jewish civil rights. Yet Altmann could not make this assertion unequivocally. "In many ways Mendelssohn was the first modern German Jew, the prototype of what the world came to recognize as the specific character, for better or worse, of German Jewry."[7] "For better or worse." This phrase reminds us how two centuries of history haunt any investigation of Mendelssohn. This difficulty applies whether we construe the symbol of Mendelssohn narrowly, understanding it only in relationship to German Jewry, as Altmann did, or whether we construe it broadly, seeing Mendelssohn as *the* modern Jew.

Perhaps the first step in a new evaluation is to look at the bare facts behind each of Mendelssohn's two faces. First, the legendary Moses Dessau. Mendelssohn was born in 1729 to a poor if learned family in Dessau. A promising scholar of Talmud and rabbinics with a delicate constitution and a deformed spine, he went to Berlin in 1743 to continue his studies at the yeshiva, now headed by the former rabbi of Dessau. Mendelssohn shared the plight of other yeshiva students, eking out his daily bread through a combination of free meals and odd scholarly jobs. His situation improved in 1750 when he was appointed a tutor to the wealthy Bernhard family and even more so in 1754 when he became a clerk in the family's silk factory (he was to become manager in 1761 and partner in 1768), a position that also gained him the privilege of residing in Berlin. Both these occupations were typical for Jewish men of letters, the clerkship especially for those who also knew the vernacular. In the 1750s and 1760s Mendelssohn served the Berlin community by writing sermons and translating them into German for festive occasions. In 1763 the community elders recognized his contributions by exempting him from taxation. During these years Mendelssohn also published two issues of the first journal in modern Hebrew (1755? 1758?), the *Kohelet Musar*, or *Preacher of Morals*; he wrote a commentary on Maimonides' philosophical primer, *Logical Terms* (Milot ha-Higayon), in 1760–1761, a Hebrew treatise on the immortality of the soul in 1769, and a commentary on Ecclesiastes in 1770. Following the Lavater affair of 1769–1770, in which Mendelssohn was publicly challenged to justify his beliefs or convert to Christianity, he suffered a nervous debility. He subsequently began to translate into German and comment on portions of the Bible, beginning with a translation of Psalms. This endeavor culminated in a translation of the Pentateuch, with commentaries by himself and others, published as the *Book of the Paths of Peace* (the German translation was printed in Hebrew characters). As a result of his reputation Mendelssohn was called upon to speak for and defend the Jews. This activity began in the late 1760s (Altona, 1769; Schwerin, 1772; Switzerland, 1775; Königsberg, 1777; Dresden, 1777; Alsace, 1780) and resulted in the publication of a compendium of Jewish law for use in German courts (*Ritualgesetze der Juden*, 1778), an introduction to a translation of a seventeenth-century plea for the readmission of the Jews to England ("Rettung der Juden"), as well as his *Jerusalem, or On Religious Power and Judaism* (1783).

As for the Socrates of Berlin, Mendelssohn came to Berlin in 1743 entirely unlettered in secular culture. While supporting himself and studying at the yeshiva, he acquired the tools of a secular education: languages (including German, Latin, Greek, English, and French), mathematics, logic, and philosophy. He accomplished this with some help from tutors but largely through great personal exertion. By the time Mendelssohn met Lessing in 1754—and their friendship was, of course, an important symbol of the Enlightenment's ability to surmount religious differences—he was already well oriented in contemporary philosophy (Christian Wolff, John Locke, and Leibniz). In the next decade and a half, beginning with Lessing's help and then in collaboration with Lessing and the Berlin publisher Nicolai, Mendelssohn became a central figure of the Berlin Aufklärung. He wrote important philosophical works such as the *Philosophical Dialogues* (1754) and *Letters on the Sensations* (1755), translated French and English philosophy into German (including Rousseau and Shaftesbury), became a regular reviewer of contemporary philosophy and aesthetics, won first prize in the essay competition of the (Berlin) Royal Academy of the Sciences with his "Treatise on Certainty in Metaphysical Philosophy" (Immanuel Kant won second prize) and received a permanent personal visa from Prussia in 1763 (in the event of his death the visa could not be transferred to his wife or children), and with his *Phaedon* of 1767 gained a European reputation and the designation "the Socrates of Berlin." What is ironic is that Mendelssohn was known and revered as much for the quality of his prose as for his thought. Mendelssohn wrote in a limpid prose and often in a dialogue form that was unusually attractive and readable for German philosophy of the time. Mendelssohn consequently became a landmark on Berlin's cultural landscape. He received visitors from all Europe and carried on a European-wide correspondence with scholars and statesmen. In 1771 he was elected to the (Berlin) Academy of Sciences (though the king exercised a pocket veto) and he was immortalized in Lessing's play *Nathan the Wise* (1779). Mendelssohn devoted his last work (*Morgenstunden,* 1785) to the defense of Lessing and the demonstrability of God's existence.[8]

So cursory and bifurcated a view of Mendelssohn's life conceals as much as it reveals. How could one man have two such different personae? What sort of milieu made this possible? The obvious response is to seek an answer in the setting in which he lived and thought—and the theory of a Socrates of Berlin and a Moses Dessau appears to do precisely that in pointing to the two arenas of German culture and Jewish thought in the age of the Enlightenment. Yet that theory, in all of its multiple and rival variations, lacks explanatory power: it portrays yet is unable to link the two realms of Mendelssohn's activity. It cannot account for both his full belief in revealed religion and his full-scale participation in Enlightenment thinking. The missing link is to be found in a neglected aspect of eighteenth-century culture and religion. Between the face of the Socrates of Berlin and that of Moses of Dessau was the interface of the religious Enlightenment.

Common wisdom has long had it that there was an irreconcilable hostility between the Enlightenment and established religion. One need only think of the anticlericalism of Voltaire and Diderot in France or of the deists' assault on revelation in England. In fact, the relationship of religion to the Enlightenment was more complex and varied. In particular, if we look at the issue from the side of the established religions, then we find that all of them had influential representatives who welcomed the new science and philosophy of the Enlightenment as a means to renew and reinvigorate faith. This attempt to put the Enlightenment in the service of revealed religion was at the heart of the religious Enlightenment, which as a movement represented a kind of golden mean. Thus in England after the Edict of Toleration (1689) a moderate Anglicanism used key notions of the Enlightenment (Lockean reasonableness, Newtonian science, ideas of natural religion and toleration) to provide a broadly Arminian alternative to Catholic fideism on the one side and the inner light enthusiasm of Puritanism on the other. For Catholics in central Europe and Italy the religious Enlightenment meant a middle ground between baroque piety, scholasticism, and Jesuitism on the one side and a highly charged reform movement like Jansenism on the other, enabling Catholics to recover neglected aspects of their textual heritage as well as absorb contemporary science and philosophy. What these representatives of the religious Enlightenment sought was a way to reconcile faith and reason by enlisting substantial portions of Enlightenment thought to support, renew, and reinvigorate belief.[9]

The Haskalah was the Jewish version of the religious Enlightenment and Mendelssohn its preeminent representative. The Haskalah was an effort to correct the historical anomaly of a Judaism out of touch with central aspects of its textual heritage as well as with the larger culture. Throughout most of the Middle Ages in Europe, and especially during most periods of heightened religious creativity, Jews had sustained a balanced view of their own textual heritage as well as a beneficial and often intense interaction with the surrounding culture. In the post-Reformation or baroque period, in contrast, Ashkenazic Jewry had increasingly isolated itself in a world of Talmudic casuistry and Kabbalah, neglecting the Bible, Jewish philosophy, and the Hebrew language within and the vast changes in the general culture without.[10] In so doing Ashkenazic Jews parted ways with their Sephardic and Italian contemporaries, who continued to hold a balanced view of Judaism and to draw on the larger culture to enrich their belief and understanding. The Haskalah was initially an Ashkenazic phenomenon. Italian and Sephardic Jews had no need of such a corrective, and it comes as no surprise that they served the Haskalah, and Mendelssohn, as a model.[11]

The Haskalah began as an effort to revive and to introduce into baroque Judaism those neglected intellectual traditions that promoted a reasonable understanding of Jewish texts and thereby made it possible to engage with contemporary science and philosophy. When the Haskalah emerged as a public movement in the last third of the eighteenth century (1770s), it borrowed many forms and categories from the Enlightenment, but its contents were largely derived from medieval Jewish philosophy and biblical exegesis.

Mendelssohn relied on what one scholar has called the "Andalusian" tradition in medieval Jewish thought. This was not a school that emerged at a particular time or place but a flexible approach to Judaism encompassing the works of many scholars at different times. Its defining characteristic was that it kept philosophy subordinate to piety and observance by refusing to admit a contemplative educational ideal that promoted a search for ultimate truths or secret knowledge. By denying the possibility of a comprehensive science of the divine and thereby limiting the reach of human knowledge, the Andalusian tradition established boundaries to rationalism yet did not reject rationalism itself. Instead, it aimed to create a pietist or practical rationalism devoted to ethics and observance through a broad curriculum that "embrac[ed] several different disciplines that enrich[ed] each other without any one dominating entirely or crowding the others out"—philosophy and biblical exegesis, Hebrew language and rabbinic literature.[12] The nature of this tradition can be seen in its relationship to Maimonides: it prized his legal works and the ethical treatise *The Book of Knowledge* as monuments of scholarship and popular education but questioned the systematic philosophy, and especially the Aristotelianism, of the *Guide of the Perplexed*. The tradition can be traced to Saadya Gaon in the tenth century and includes the works of Judah Halevi (*The Book of the Kuzari*) in the twelfth century and Nahmanides in the thirteenth.[13]

Seeing the Haskalah through the bifocals of Jewish and European history allows us to locate Mendelssohn in the multiple settings that comprised the culture in which he lived and thought: not only the immediate context of the Haskalah and German Enlightenment but also the religious Enlightenment and its specific German Protestant variant on the one hand and the medieval Jewish tradition on the other. Such comparison will shed light on many aspects of his thought and will also give us various correlatives by which to judge it—secular and religious, medieval and modern, Jewish and Christian.

Understanding Mendelssohn as a "religious Enlightener" highlights the complexity of his relationship to the larger culture. His intimate involvement in Enlightenment culture was not exceptional—other exponents of the Haskalah, known as *maskilim* (singular: *maskil*), were similarly involved. What was exceptional was his standing in European culture. Yet such standing was also fairly widespread in the religious Enlightenment. The most gifted religious Enlighteners (such as Siegmund Jacob Baumgarten, Anselm Desing, Ludovico Muratori, William Warburton) were also active in secular pursuits. Many gained considerable reputations from such endeavors yet also managed to make them compatible with, if not subordinate to, religious ones.

For Mendelssohn, as for the religious Enlighteners, the Aufklärung was not a finished product he merely adopted. He had a hand in its development and he created a selective version that he applied to Judaism in a consistent way. He used novel means for conservative ends. Mendelssohn did for Judaism what the "theological Wolffians" (1725–1750) had done for German Protestantism. He used his own version of Wolffian philosophy as a means to articulate his full belief in revealed religion.

In his understanding of Judaism Mendelssohn followed the Andalusian tradition. Despite all appearances, he was not a Maimonidean. Mendelssohn had a detailed knowledge of Maimonides' work and borrowed freely from it. Yet on the most fundamental issues Mendelssohn differed with him. Mendelssohn set greater limits to abstract knowledge and did not aspire to a speculative theology that would include a systematic account of Judaism's beliefs or a thorough rationalization of its laws. Maimonides belonged to the cultural legacy Mendelssohn claimed, but Maimonides was neither its only nor even its dominant figure. Mendelssohn's understanding of Judaism drew heavily on Judah Halevi, his exegesis on Nahmanides, Ibn Ezra, and other "literalist" commentators. As a result of the polemics of the 1780s over Lessing's alleged

Spinozism, it has been commonly assumed that Mendelssohn's chief rival or "archenemy" was Spinoza.[14] In fact, Spinoza did not pose a threat. His position was so extreme that Mendelssohn could even attempt to rehabilitate his thought.[15] In contrast, Maimonides so bedeviled Mendelssohn that in his Hebrew works (especially the *Logical Terms* and the *Book of the Paths of Peace*) Mendelssohn was tireless in trying to distinguish Maimonides' thought from his own. The religious Enlightenment represented a kind of golden mean. Mendelssohn's version was a middle way between the casuistry and Kabbalah of baroque Judaism and the speculative rationalism of Maimonides.

This book will proceed in a thematic order that is also roughly chronological, analyzing Mendelssohn's Jewish thinking in three overlapping phases. The philosophical phase extended from his first publications to the Lavater affair (1755–1770). Mendelssohn attempted to renew the tradition of philosophy in Hebrew by introducing the terms and some of the views of Wolffianism. He emphasized practical over theoretical knowledge by affirming the primacy of law, which he supported with an uncompromising endorsement of heteronomy.

Mendelssohn's endeavor to renew the tradition of biblical exegesis extended from the commentary on Ecclesiastes to the publication of the translation and commentary on the Pentateuch (1768–1783). In his commentary on Ecclesiastes he defended the methods of rabbinic interpretation. In his commentary on the Pentateuch he expanded the method of "literal" interpretation in order to understand the Bible as the font of practical knowledge. His exegesis showed that the basis of his faith lay in history, namely, the authority of the revelation at Sinai. While he espoused historical truth, he also resisted the historicism of contemporary biblical criticism, using oral transmission as a means to defend the authenticity of the biblical text. His approach to history resembled that of some important theological Wolffians.

The political phase reached from Mendelssohn's earliest political pronouncements to his decidedly political work, *Jerusalem* (1783). He worked in the tradition of German Enlightenment political thinking, making the transition from "intercessor" to the advocate of civil rights. Here he reiterated the main tenets of his faith: Judaism was a religion of practical knowledge ("divine legislation") grounded in history, maintained by oral transmission, and based on heteronomy. He used secular and ecclesiastical natural law theory—the latter had also been used by theological Wolffians—to argue that the Jews deserved an unconditional grant of rights as well as that they should reconstitute themselves as a voluntary society without coercive powers.

These three phases of Mendelssohn's thought largely corresponded to the three stages of the Haskalah's development: from a tendency among individuals (1700–1770), to an intellectual circle (1770s), to an organized society with a journal (1780s). Mendelssohn was the only member of the Haskalah to make the transition from the earliest period to its later political phase. Yet his political activity clearly represented a diversion from his original agenda. This was the case for the Haskalah in general. Its reputation as a revolutionary movement resulted from its convergence in the 1770s with the fundamental political and social changes known as emancipation and assimilation. While the Haskalah became identified with these changes, they in fact altered its original course.

In Mendelssohn's thought the relationships of Judaism and Enlightenment, philosophy and revelation, politics and belief were so intricate that they might best be described by the negative and positive versions of a metaphor. The Enlightenment was not a ready-made canvas onto which Mendelssohn merely painted a version of Judaism with premixed paints. He stretched the canvas to his own design, mixed his own palette of colors, and painted directly from his religious and philosophical imagination.

PART ONE

Philosophy

CHAPTER ONE

Foundations

Born in Dessau in 1729, Mendelssohn was named for two illustrious maternal ancestors who personified the kinds of activity he was to undertake and influenced the intellectual world in which he was raised. A distant ancestor who represented Jewish scholarship was Moses Isserles (1520–1572): an eminent scholar, he adapted to the needs of Ashkenazic Jewry the sixteenth-century compendium of Jewish law, the *Shulkhan Arukh*, which had been compiled by a Sephardic scholar. A more immediate relative was Moses Benjamin Wulff, a court Jew and founder of the Jewish community of Dessau, who embodied worldly activity in the service of Judaism. Besides reorganizing the duchy of Anhalt-Dessau's finances and undertaking numerous commercial and diplomatic ventures on behalf of his prince, Moses Wulff also established a study house and a press that were to make Dessau a "city of scholars and writers," if of a particular sort.[1]

Dessau was one locus of the early Haskalah—the effort to recover neglected aspects of Jewish knowledge and to engage with contemporary science and philosophy—and the study house and Wulffian press exposed the young Mendelssohn to its influence. The Wulffian press issued the standard range of legal, kabbalistic, and ethical texts as well as works of a wider intellectual horizon typical of the early Haskalah: medieval Jewish philosophy, Hebrew grammar, and scientific works (in Hebrew).[2] A landmark for the press was the first republication (1742) in almost two centuries of the Hebrew translation of Maimonides' *Guide of the Perplexed,* one of the central texts of the medieval Jewish philosophical tradition because of its systematic effort to reconcile Judaism with Aristotelian philosophy. This cultural event was arranged with the tacit approval of the rabbi of Dessau, David Fränkel. Earlier he had seen to it that Maimonides' legal magnum opus, the *Mishneh Torah,* was republished in order to be available to his students (1739). Fränkel showed the Haskalah to be an integral part of mainstream Judaism. His interests ranged beyond the accepted Ashkenazic curriculum of the authoritative Babylonian Talmud to the neglected Palestinian one, for which he wrote a famous commentary betraying some Maimonidean influence in its method. He also approved the study of Hebrew language and grammar.[3]

Mendelssohn's early education followed the standard Ashkenazic curriculum in its emphasis on Talmud, commentaries, and codes with the method of study heavily casuistic *(pilpul).* Yet at an early age Mendelssohn showed a propensity for subjects that were to be typical of the Haskalah: he read the Bible and committed long passages to memory, studied Hebrew grammar, and tried his hand at writing both prose and poetry in the biblical style. He also began to study Maimonides' *Guide of the Perplexed.* In later life he attributed his deformity (curvature of the spine) to the rigors of this endeavor, though he never regretted it. Maimonides introduced him to Jewish and general philosophy, imbuing him with the philosophical spirit. Yet he was not to become a Maimonidean; instead, he was to display a characteristic independence of mind in reclaiming the medieval tradition. At the age of ten or so Mendelssohn began to study with Fränkel. A demanding teacher, Fränkel had reservations about the casuistic method—though obviously not about the study of Talmud—characteristic of the Haskalah. He taught Mendelssohn new ways to study the legal tradition.[4]

At the age of fourteen Mendelssohn left Dessau. He always ascribed his move to his desire to continue studying with Fränkel, who in the meantime had been appointed rabbi of Berlin and had founded a study house.[5] The Berlin in which Mendelssohn arrived and was to live the remainder of his life was a court and garrison boomtown, the capital of the rapidly developing kingdom of Prussia. Numbering some 20,000 inhabitants in 1690, the population would reach 100,000 in 1747. The Jewish community had been founded in 1671: by 1737 it totaled 1,187 persons and by the 1780s some 3,500. It was a fully traditional community boasting the usual array of pious associations and foundations and would remain so until the end of the 1780s. Berlin was also a center of the German Enlightenment. At court Frederick the Great hosted luminaries of the Enlightenment, including Voltaire. In town the presence of large numbers of educated civil servants—nobles and commoners, laymen and clerics—as well as publishers and writers gave rise to an indigenous intellectual life.[6]

Mendelssohn might also have been attracted to Berlin by figures of the early Haskalah.[7] Israel Samoscz (ca. 1700–1772), an émigré from Galicia, was an autodidact who typified the Haskalah's effort to revive the Jewish philosophical tradition and acquire scientific knowledge. In a 1741 treatise (*Netsah Yisrael*) Samoscz demonstrated the indispensability of mathematics and astronomy for understanding passages of the Talmud. His commentary on a philosophical dictionary (*Ruah Hein*), published by the Wulffian press in 1744, might have brought him or his work to Mendelssohn's attention in Dessau. Once in Berlin Mendelssohn studied Talmud with Fränkel and philosophy with Samoscz. In addition, Mendelssohn benefited from contact with another type of early *maskil*, or exponent of the Haskalah. Jews were admitted to the medical faculties of some German universities from the late seventeenth century (Frankfurt on the Oder, 1671; Halle, 1724); in consequence, doctors played a disproportionate role in the early Haskalah.[8] One medical student, Abraham Kisch (b. 1728), gave Mendelssohn daily tuition in Latin. Another, Aaron Salomon Gumpertz (or Emmerich: 1723–1769), taught Mendelssohn French and English, took him to a course of Latin lectures on philosophy, and in general served as the model of a pious Jew immersed in the larger intellectual world.[9] Mendelssohn's experience highlights the fragmented nature of the Haskalah in this early period: it was a tendency promoted by autodidacts (e.g., Samoscz), doctors (e.g., Kisch, Gumpertz) and rabbis (e.g., Fränkel) who worked largely in isolation from one another and wrote their works for an audience that was difficult to identify.

The intellectual world into which Kisch and Gumpertz ushered Mendelssohn was the early Enlightenment, especially its German version. The Enlightenment represented the highwater mark of confidence in the ability of human reason. The scientific revolution of the seventeenth century, which culminated in Newton's *Principia,* appeared to have solved many of the universe's mysteries. Inspired by such success, philosophers adopted the scientific and mathematical method, though the way they did so depended on cultural traditions. In England the scientific revolution and the Enlightenment put scholasticism and metaphysics to rest, giving rise to a new empirical tradition (represented by Hobbes and Locke, for example). In the German states of the Holy Roman Empire, in contrast, scholasticism endured in the post-Reformation period as the medium of religious disputation between Catholics and Protestants. The Enlightenment here gave scholasticism new life.[10] Some of the earliest philosophers of the German Enlightenment, especially Christian Thomasius, did reject scholasticism and speculative philosophy for an empirical and practical philosophy, and they found adherents throughout the eighteenth century. The bulk of the German Enlightenment, however, followed Leibniz and Christian Wolff.

Leibniz effected a reconciliation of Cartesian philosophy with scholasticism which was to exercise a formative influence on the German Enlightenment until Kant's "Copernican revolution" at the end of the eighteenth century.[11] Christian Wolff, Leibniz's successor, was inspired by Newton and the scientific revolution. His first works were successful mathematical textbooks. He then adopted the mathematical method for philosophy, hoping to attain the certainty of science. Although his philosophy accommodated some empirical elements, it was fundamentally rationalist; he tried to deduce from a few self-evident logical principles (such as contradiction or sufficient reason) an entire system whose truths could be linked one to the other as in an unbroken chain. He wanted philosophical truths to have the same coherence as mathematical ones. Wolff also had an enduring impact on the language and, through it, on the shape of German philosophy; in his early works he created German equivalents for accepted Latin scholastic terms.[12]

When Mendelssohn reached Berlin in 1743, Christian Wolff was at the height of his influence. For that very reason the ground below was shifting. Wolff wanted his philosophy to be comprehensive as well as coherent. With unflagging industry he applied his method to all fields of philosophy. He produced a shelf of books—the early ones in German, the later in Latin—on logic, metaphysics, ethics, politics, law, and nature. Yet because of the premises of his philosophy, Wolff left two major areas untouched: aesthetics and theology.[13] This was the ground that began to shift. The Wolffians who tried to extend the master to these two areas began to alter his system. Mendelssohn would be among these Wolffians.

Wolff refrained from theology because his was a "natural" philosophy. In the Enlightenment's parlance "natural" was the opposite of "revealed," denoting that which was universally accessible to reason. The Enlightenment revered reason as the faculty potentially capable of unifying mankind by providing it with a common foundation. The Christian gospel also had universalist aspirations, of course, but these rang hollow in the late seventeenth and early eighteenth century since religious disputes had divided and devastated much of Europe, especially the Germanys, during the century of war following the Reformation. Like other Enlighteners, Wolff aspired to a philosophy that included a "natural" religion that transcended Christian confessional boundaries in containing only those religious truths universally available to reason: the existence of God, his providence, and the immortality of the soul. These "natural" religious truths supplied a common foundation for morality as well as belief: sin was less tempting if there was an omniscient and omnipotent God who oversaw human action and meted out justice in this world and the next. For some radical Enlighteners, such as the deists in England, this natural religion sufficed. For more moderate figures, such as Wolff, natural religion was the foundation for revealed religion, even if philosophical works were not the appropriate place to discuss the subject.

Wolff was an ardent Christian and saw his philosophy as a tool of belief. He hoped pastors would use his philosophy to expound the faith in sermons, since he thought it harmonized perfectly with revealed Christianity.[14] That he conceived of the world as a machine with all its parts connected and functioning according to law, he thought testimony to God's wisdom. That revelation was possible and must be accepted *in toto*, that miracles were possible, and that God's omniscience set limits to human reason was only more of the same. Yet his philosophy set obstacles to revealed religion greater than the mere absence of a discussion of the Gospel's contents. For example, he placed numerous conditions on revelation. It could contain nothing reason could not comprehend on its own and its contents must also agree with reason. These were some of the difficulties confronting the Wolffians who attempted to utilize his philosophy for theology.[15]

It was certainly auspicious that one of the first books Mendelssohn read in German was a treatise by the foremost theological Wolffian in Berlin. Johann Gustav Reinbeck (1683–1741), who held high office in the church (provost) and ecclesiastical government (consistory councillor), pioneered the use of Wolffian concepts in the sermon, and also wrote a book on the immortality of the soul, the very subject with which Mendelssohn was to gain his European reputation.[16] In his *Considerations on the Augsburg Confession* (1733), which had its origins in a series of sermons marking the centenary of the confession, Reinbeck tried to chart a middle course between the rationalist's exclusive reliance on reason and the orthodox believer's exclusive reliance on Scripture.[17]

Some truths could be demonstrated entirely by reason and revelation confirmed these. Thus Reinbeck proved the existence of God solely through reason (employing the ontological argument and the principle of sufficient reason); he then showed God's existence from Scripture. Other truths he deemed only partially susceptible to proof "from the light of nature and of reason."[18] Reinbeck proved as much as reason allowed about God's attributes (for example, God as spirit), then carried on with scriptural citation.[19] As for the Creation, reason demonstrated the possibility of *creatio ex nihilo* and the necessity of providence, with Scripture providing the details, such as man in the divine image and the origins of the two sexes. Other truths, especially the mysteries of Christianity such as the Trinity, entirely resisted rational demonstration. In sum, for the truths of natural religion (God, providence) reason had its role; for the mysteries of Creation revelation was the primary source; for the mysteries of the Trinity revelation was the exclusive source. Yet Reinbeck insisted that revelation contained nothing at variance with reason, imposing on it the same reasonable conditions that Wolff had.[20]

This work held obvious fascination for a young man who had cut his philosophical teeth on Maimonides. The encounter with Reinbeck was to have a lasting, if unacknowledged, influence. Mendelssohn was to undertake for Judaism what Reinbeck and other theological Wolffians had for Christianity, although in a form consonant with his own convictions.[21] In Mendelssohn's thought Enlightenment philosophy and Judaism complemented and explained each other, yet each retained its integrity and respective sphere. Philosophy presupposed and depended on God, on the one side; on the other, revelation set clear limits to the scope of philosophy. In general, philosophy served Judaism as an instrument of self-articulation. In consequence, Mendelssohn could employ novel means for conservative ends. These relationships were less explicit in Mendelssohn's works first because he maintained an apparent dualism by writing general philosophy in German and Jewish works in Hebrew but also because of the nature of his Hebrew works.

Mendelssohn's reading of Reinbeck aroused his interest in Wolff. He studied Wolff's works diligently, but he also read widely in philosophy in general, from the Greeks onward and in Enlightenment philosophy in particular, studying and translating recent French and English thinkers, such as Rousseau and Shaftesbury. As his work immediately shows, he adopted the dialogue form, fluent style, and practical concerns of French and English philosophy which were incorporated into the German tradition of "popular philosophy" (which had roots in the work of

Thomasius).[22] In Mendelssohn's version of "popular philosophy," Wolffian ideas received a new form and a practical emphasis.

From the outset Mendelssohn was convinced that German Enlightenment philosophy was fully compatible with Judaism. The "editor" in his "On the Sensations" wrote that he preferred German to French philosophy because it valued believing thinking over free thinking.[23] In a passage that some commentators treat as transparently autobiographical, an interlocutor in that same work passionately asserted that Locke, Wolff, and Leibniz had restored him to truth and virtue, describing their effect on him as "edifying."[24] Edification (*Erbauung*) was a key term that denoted the theological Enlightenment's new piety: the building of the whole person (heart as well as head) in a reasonable, tolerant, and devout Christianity. Mendelssohn had used a term resonant with the effort to reconcile faith and reason.

From his first work, the *Philosophical Dialogues* (1754), which Lessing had a hand in publishing, Mendelssohn espoused a version of the Wolffian philosophy notable for its compatibility with religious belief: the entire system—metaphysics, epistemology, ethics—was rooted in the ideas of natural religion (God, providence, immortality of the soul). This was a natural philosophy that both presupposed and tried to prove through reason alone the existence of God.

In Mendelssohn's version of Wolff, God was the source of all perfection and thus also the source of metaphysics and natural theology.[25] All the immutable truths of the universe were present in God's mind and connected, as if in a logical demonstration.[26] For God there was no disparity between possibility and reality, whereas for man there was a "terrible chasm" between the two.[27] His existence was demonstrable from the very possibility of the conception of a perfect being (this was the so-called ontological proof Leibniz put forward and Kant later demolished).

Just as God's perfection was the source of natural theology, so his freedom was the source of justice. Since God had freely chosen this world, it was the "best of all possible worlds." God had devised a "preestablished harmony" that enabled the world's constituent elements, the "monads," to act in harmony with one another. This was also an incontrovertibly Newtonian world. The world was a machine governed by laws, albeit ones divinely decreed. Though God no longer actively intervened in the world, the notion of the "best of all possible worlds" combined with the "preestablished harmony" to constitute a theodicy that proclaimed God's abiding justice.[28]

God's freedom was the foundation of human morality, his perfection its standard. The preestablished harmony included rather than precluded human freedom. Freedom required man to act ethically, which meant to strive for perfection in imitation of God. Perfection was man's vocation.[29]

As the "science of a free being," ethics was grounded in metaphysics, that is, God's perfection.[30] The good was whatever contributed to perfection, the "better" what removed imperfection, "perfection" itself "harmony within diversity."[31] The "primordial urge for perfection" was inherent in man's nature as a thinking being and all nature worked to increase that perfection.[32] In keeping with the concept of the "monad," the perfection of the soul was the extent of its ability to create clear representations, that is, to think.[33] Not only was the empirical element in epistemology decidedly subordinate (sense experience was not the source of ideas but merely the occasion for the soul to raise innate representations to full consciousness) but God had a central part in it.[34] Thinking developed through relations with one's fellowman—and man was by nature a social being—but even more through contemplation of God.[35] Virtue, in consequence, was action in harmony with nature and man's reason. The first law of nature was therefore "Make your and your fellowman's internal and external condition, in due proportion, as perfect as you can."[36]

Mendelssohn was one of the most eloquent exponents of Wolffianism. A recent historian of philosophy has characterized Mendelssohn's contribution to Wolffianism in the "Treatise on Certainty in Metaphysical Philosophy," his prize-winning essay, in words that might apply to all his work:

> It is rationalistic with due place for sense experience; it is dogmatic moving from one well-defined metaphysical concept to another by stately formal arguments; it proves the existence of God and of a Leibnizian world of monads; it is edifying and elevating. It is all very beautiful; it is even interesting; there is nothing else like it, even in Leibniz or Wolff, for lucidity and polish.[37]

Mendelssohn was also critical of Wolffian philosophy. He complained that Wolff's Latin works would have been more useful as a philosophical dictionary than as a system.[38] He also thought Wolff's attempt to give philosophy irrefragable certainty by adopting the mathematical method had been mistaken since philosophy's validity did not derive from method alone.[39]

More important than Mendelssohn's criticism of Wolff was his insistence on the limits to philosophical knowledge: he aimed to ensure that natural philosophy did not trespass on revelation. He rejected as sheer arrogance the claims of any philosophy to omniscience, excoriating Leibniz's critics for so ludicrous an expectation since it virtually deified the philosopher.[40] He saw philosophy as an exercise of freedom which included the freedom to err. Authority had no place here. Happily there could be no "pope of philosophy."[41] Mendelssohn thought the problem of an infinite world, for example, must be left to revelation.[42] For much the same reason he chose to place his dialogues on immortality (*Phaedon*) in the mouth of a pagan philosopher: this enabled him to avoid revelation altogether. (Socrates had the additional advantage of being a nonscholastic philosopher.)[43]

To ensure the unity of his natural philosophy with Judaism, Mendelssohn not only rooted it in natural religion, criticized Wolff's method, and set limits to philosophy but he also developed several significant points of convergence. For one, he espoused a nomian view of ethics entirely consonant with revelation in general and Judaism in particular. Ethics meant honoring God by following his law: "Observance of duties toward God (is) . . . the only way to make our souls more perfect."[44] In his natural philosophy he of course did not specify the dictates of the Law. He also averred that observance of religion is the best defense against irreligion.

> The transition in matters of religion from doubt to thoughtlessness, or from neglect of public worship to deprecation of all worship, tends to be extremely easy, especially for those spirits who are not under the authority of reason but are ruled by greed, ambition or lust.[45]

He similarly thought that superstition and unbelief were "closely related."[46]

Most important, Mendelssohn introduced a distinction between the practical and the theoretical in philosophy in which he diverged from Wolff and charted the course of his Jewish works. Wolff had identified "practical" with "theoretical" conviction: he thought a priori and a posteriori theoretical arguments that were persuasive engendered conviction and thus fell into the category of effective or "vital knowledge."[47] Mendelssohn dissented. Influenced by English empiricism but even more by his understanding of Judaism, he asserted that mere theoretical argumentation did not necessarily constitute "vital knowledge."

In metaphysics the most demonstrably certain proofs of God's existence were not always the most persuasive. Less certain arguments—for example, the "beauty and order" of the world or physicotheology, or the beauty and order of the laws of motion—were often more effective in guiding people's lives and thus constituted the "vital efficacious knowledge" that yielded conviction.[48]

In ethics the distinction between theoretical and practical knowledge was even greater: here one had to apply judgments to actual situations, yet knowledge of the empirical situation was less certain since it derived from sense impressions or depended on a moral maxim whose application was unclear. Nevertheless, Mendelssohn understood ethics as a "science" that could be learned: through practice and the cultivation of knowledge one could turn virtue into "second nature."[49] In this regard the arts could be of use in providing examples that trained judgment and promoted the "conviction of the heart." Mendelssohn therefore attributed a large role to conscience as the "ability to distinguish good from evil . . . using unclear inferences" (in aesthetics he would accord a corresponding role to taste).[50]

This distinction between the theoretical and the practical accorded with Mendelssohn's version of Wolffianism. In general he stressed the "terrible chasm" in human life between possibility and reality, ideas and applications.[51] He thought the philosopher's task exceeded the mathematician's: whereas the mathematician only needed to demonstrate the connection between concepts, the philosopher not only had to evaluate the internal coherence of concepts but also to assess their truth or falsehood through application to real things. The philosopher had to make "the transition from concepts to reality."[52] In the *Phaedon* Mendelssohn praised Socrates for pursuing those arguments that had practical value, leaving the purely theoretical ones to the sophists.[53] In the same work one of Socrates' disciples (Simmias) asks for arguments that are easily remembered since these have a practical effect.[54] The very subject of the *Phaedon* was eminently practical since it was the keystone of natural religion and of ethics (as the quest for perfection). The immortality of the soul "justifies God; endows virtue with nobility; gives beauty its lustre, desire its charm, sweetens suffering; and makes the vexations of this life worthy in our eyes."[55] In a 1774 sketch of a curriculum for philosophical study Mendelssohn explicitly recommended practical over abstract philosophy.

> Practical philosophy is of far greater importance [than speculative philosophy], in that it is directly linked to the felicity of mankind, and furnishes a

good head as much material for reflection as it does the heart, [and enables the head and heart] to investigate themselves with full rigor and to attain to virtue and true wisdom.[56]

Mendelssohn also stressed the superiority of practice to contemplation:

> The highest stage of wisdom is incontrovertibly doing that which is good. Speculation is a lower stage that leads to the higher. One must achieve the lower in order to reach the higher; but whoever remains on the lower stage only half fulfills the goal of his existence, and must rest content with the fate of displaying the signpost or milestone on the pilgrimage to felicity.[57]

This distinction between practical and theoretical knowledge was to animate Mendelssohn's entire oeuvre. It figured prominently in the controversy with Lavater, informed his aesthetic thinking, inspired his well-known distinction between "enlightenment" and "culture," and was the basis of his preference for "common sense" over "speculative knowledge." It also coincided with his understanding of Judaism; indeed, it may well have resulted from his view of Judaism.

Mendelssohn aimed to produce a reasonable understanding of Judaism by reviving the Andalusian tradition of medieval Jewish practical or pietist rationalism in the cognate disciplines of philosophy and biblical exegesis. He did not aspire to a systematic religious philosophy. He held "Torah and good deeds," not philosophical contemplation, to be a Jew's primary obligation. Revelation set clear limits to theoretical knowledge: man could not attain to cosmic wisdom or divine science since the ultimate truths of God's being and the rationale for the Commandments remained inaccessible to reason. Mendelssohn therefore concentrated on practical knowledge, which in exegesis meant access to the Bible as revelation and commandment through the literal meaning of the text while in philosophy it denoted the means to the logical formulation of key theological issues. Both these disciplines functioned within the boundaries of rabbinic authority.

The distinction between practical and theoretical knowledge informed Mendelssohn's Hebrew works. Mendelssohn eschewed the theoretical, systematic reconciliation of philosophy and Scripture attempted by Maimonides on the one hand and Reinbeck and the theological Wolffians on the other, preferring the practical aids that fostered reasonable belief and understanding. In Judaism such "practical" knowledge has traditionally taken the form of commentary. As one distinguished scholar has put it: in Judaism "not system but commentary is the legitimate form through which truth is approached"; commentary is the "characteristic expression of Jewish thinking about the truth."[58] Rather than systematic exposition, which also would not have been in keeping with his apparent dualism, Mendelssohn chose Hebrew-language commentary as the means to show the congruence of Wolffianism and Judaism: he used Wolffian categories to articulate the revealed religion that complemented and completed the natural one.

CHAPTER TWO

Early Works

Mendelssohn's earliest Hebrew works were commentaries in which he attempted to renew the tradition of philosophy in Hebrew using key terms and ideas of Christian Wolff's philosophy. In his first work, the *Kohelet Musar,* written in the latter half of the 1750s, Mendelssohn used an unconventional form to show the compatibility of Wolffian philosophy and Judaism in a range of texts. Then in a commentary to a work of Maimonides he endeavored to update both the lexicon and substance of medieval Hebrew philosophy. A third work, *The Book of the Soul,* was the exception in being a direct philosophical exposition; it was only published posthumously.

In his first Hebrew work, the *Kohelet Musar* (Preacher of Morals), Mendelssohn chose the contemporary popular medium of a journal. The moral weekly was in fact a monthly that appeared on the same day of the week. It was modeled on the English *Tatler* and *Spectator* (the journals edited by Addison and Steele). As a genre it represented an alternative to scholasticism, metaphysics, and Christian devotional literature. Usually published anonymously, the journal was an intimate forum in which a fictional narrator used letters, essays, conversations, and reports of incidents to discuss ethical, cultural, and practical philosophical issues in an informal manner to shape a natural morality for an educated middle-class audience.[1] With Lessing, Mendelssohn had contributed to such a journal (*Der Chamäleon*) in the mid-1750s, even though the genre was long past its prime. The forms he used in his contributions (such as dialogues and letters) were ones he frequently used in his other German works as well.

The *Kohelet Musar* was the first modern journal in Hebrew.[2] Mendelssohn endeavored to make the journal a vehicle of the Haskalah, shaping a moral outlook for an audience of Talmud students and other adepts at Jewish learning through commentary on Hebrew texts. He pursued this goal by addressing some of the same practical philosophical subjects as in his German works of the period: nature as a source of enjoyment or belief (physicotheology); evil and misfortune in daily life (theodicy); the nature of relationships between man and man and between man and God. In treating these issues Mendelssohn repeatedly employed the same method. He stated the issue using Wolffian categories; gave an example, usually drawn from Jewish texts, to which the categories were applied; quoted passages of rabbinic or Hebrew philosophical literature that confirmed the analysis; and ended with a peroration of Wolffian conclusions to be derived from it. Wolff is never mentioned by name, but Hebrew equivalents are introduced for key terms of his philosophy.

In considering the ethical nature of friendship, for example, Mendelssohn used Wolff's definition of love as taking pleasure in another's increased perfection. His illustration was the friendship of David and Jonathan in the Bible. He pointed out that the rabbinic Sages had seen this friendship as an "unconditional love" (Mishnah Avot 5:17). Mendelssohn asserted that while in human love pleasure arises from the other's achievement of perfection, in the love of God, since he is the embodiment of all perfection, pleasure arises out of obedience to his law.

> Know that love of His holy name consists in pleasure in the knowledge of His perfection. From it will be born the desire to heed His voice and to obey His commandments. This is service [*avodah*] from love. . . . Pleasure in God and love of Him are one and the same.[3]

Mendelssohn then cited a passage from the Babylonian Talmud illustrating this point.[4]

This example demonstrates how Mendelssohn's method produced a seamless transition from natural philosophy to Judaism. In this case the ethical nomianism of his natural philosophy became observance of the Commandments. The example further demonstrates how Mendelssohn transformed the genre to suit his own purposes: whereas the German moral weekly purveyed natural philosophy, Mendelssohn used this forum to offer a revealed, if entirely reasonable, Judaism.[5]

Another subject Mendelssohn addressed was the ideal personality. These sorts of discussions pervaded the German moral weeklies since they were crucial for defining virtue and morality.[6] Mendelssohn posed the issue in terms of the individual's relationship to God and his fellowman. In one instance he contrasted the fool who trusts in God for the sake of material gain—only to think God has abandoned him when his fortunes decline—with the wise man who trusts in God through all events.[7] This comparison affirmed the Wolffian notion of theodicy, and Mendelssohn cited a number of rabbinic sources that concurred.[8] In another essay Mendelssohn contrasted four social types. The hypocritical courtier enjoys court patronage and ill-gotten wealth, exploits the poor, lives ostentatiously, and affects a pious demeanor. The opposite type is the wealthy man who squanders his fortune ministering to the poor and then becomes an object of mockery. The third is the mere unfortunate who loses his possessions through accident and deceit. In contrast to all three, the ideal is the "man of faith" who combines pious study, an honest occupation, family life and trust in God: "The man of faith is blessed; he finds favor in God's sight."[9] The Wolffian idea here is the necessity of society for the individual's pursuit of perfection. Since isolation obstructs this quest, the "isolated man" is by definition wicked. Every individual must take his place in society by finding employment, an idea Mendelssohn supported by citing the medieval philosopher Judah Halevi.

Mendelssohn's discussion of the "man of faith" is noteworthy in two respects. "Man of faith" is largely a new name for the venerable ideal of the "pious scholar" (talmid hakham). The qualities Mendelssohn enumerated for the "man of faith" would also make an exemplary "pious scholar," except that Mendelssohn construed the ideal broadly to include the social category of gainful employment. Moreover, he significantly defined gainful employment as commerce. This view comes as no surprise given his own occupation and those of most Berlin Jews at the time. It does contrast sharply, however, with the advocacy of artisanry and farming one normally associates with the Haskalah. Mendelssohn's unabashed embrace of commerce highlights the differences of opinion within the Haskalah as well as the development of its ideas over time.[10]

Mendelssohn also argued for the importance of the study of the Hebrew language and the Bible. He took issue with the mistaken interpretation of a passage in the medieval exegete Rashi (on a passage of the Talmud: Berkahot 25b) which was often cited to justify the neglect of Bible study. According to Mendelssohn, Rashi endorsed Bible study but not to the exclusion of the rabbinic tradition. Rather, Mendelssohn deemed it imperative that the Bible and the Hebrew language be studied.[11] Hebrew is the primordial and preeminent language: only in it do the names perfectly match their objects. Mendelssohn quoted Maimonides and Judah Halevi in praise of Hebrew, arguing that to neglect the language is a disgrace—even the Jews sold into slavery in Egypt did not forget Hebrew. He pointed to the attention other nations were now lavishing on their vernacular and concluded that Hebrew is a living medium suitable for all occasions and purposes.[12] In the final essay Mendelssohn in fact translated into Hebrew passages from a well-known contemporary poem, Edward Young's "Night Thoughts," in order to demonstrate Hebrew's incomparable qualities as a language of poetry.[13] Here he attempted to renew Hebrew as a medium for poetry, just as in earlier sections he tried to renew it as a medium for philosophy.

The *Kohelet Musar* was patently a commentary, if of an unconventional sort: it was not confined to one text or one subject but commented on many texts, from many periods, on many issues. It was an effort to realize the early Haskalah's aim of renewing Judaism by using its textual heritage to address central issues in a reasoned and reasonable manner. Mendelssohn's first Hebrew biographer suggested that the journal presented an alternative to Talmudic dialectics (*pilpul*).[14] This assertion is true in the same broad sense that we can say the German moral weekly supplanted scholasticism and devotional literature. Mendelssohn attempted to activate the textual heritage, applying texts in a manner entirely foreign to the world of Talmudic dialectics to issues he thought significant to any educated Jew.

Besides using his texts in a novel way, Mendelssohn also chose them selectively. In addition to the Bible and rabbinic literature (Talmud, midrash), he made constant use of the medieval Sephardic school. Maimonides provided support for the Wolffian notion of theodicy; Judah Halevi was invoked for the perfection of Hebrew but also for the need to work as well as study and pray; and Ibn Tibbon supplied examples of translation.[15] The Sephardic writers provided a model for a reasonable understanding of Judaism, thus becoming the main stratum of Hebraica after rabbinic literature. Here were the rudiments of a maskilic view of the textual tradition that owed much to the Andalusian tradition.

Mendelssohn's second Hebrew work was a commentary (1760–1761) on Maimonides' *Logical Terms*. Maimonides had written this succinct account of logical terminology in the twelfth century for a layman. The book was at once an introduction to logic and a philosophical primer.[16]

Mendelssohn republished it with an introduction and a commentary. His aim was to revive the philosophical tradition among those versed in traditional texts. In other words, he addressed the same audience in *Logical Terms* as in the *Kohelet Musar*. In the introduction he defended logic as an entirely pious pursuit necessary to correct belief. Without logic one can neither fathom God's creation nor distinguish right from wrong.[17] Mendelssohn argued that to think without an awareness of logic is equivalent to using language without knowing grammar: one uses language willy-nilly, but how much the better if one understands its rules.[18] Yet Mendelssohn anticipated the charge that logic is a Greek invention foreign to Judaism. The sagacity of presenting a treatise by Maimonides is thus apparent. Maimonides' piety cannot be questioned since he had neutralized the impact of Greek wisdom: "He swallowed the seed but spat out the shell."[19]

While Mendelssohn here set the same limits to philosophy as in his German treatises, he now discussed the revealed wisdom that surpassed and complemented philosophy. He asserted that without Torah and tradition we are "like a blind man in the dark."[20] The true path to knowledge is the combination of Torah and logic.[21] However far man's understanding can go in comprehending God and divine truth, it is only possible through the application of God-given reason to Torah and tradition. Only the prophet who has direct revelation can dispense with logic—an idea fundamental to Judah Halevi.[22] Mendelssohn therefore recommends that students study logic an hour or so per week in support of their traditional textual studies, citing earlier exegetes who did so.[23] Mendelssohn regarded logic as an instrument and not as an end in itself.

Maimonides' succinct exposition served Mendelssohn's purposes, albeit with one important exception. Maimonides' method and philosophy were distinctly medieval. His work might lead the uninitiated student backward to medieval Jewish philosophy, but it could not lead him forward to eighteenth-century philosophy. Mendelssohn's commentary was intended to be the bridge. At the end of each of the fourteen chapters of his treatise, Maimonides provided a list of the terms he had introduced. Mendelssohn used these as a philosophical lexicon: next to each Hebrew term he gave the equivalent in German and in Latin (though in Hebrew characters). He thereby attempted to renew philosophical discourse in Hebrew in a systematic manner—the translation of key Wolffian terms in the *Kohelet Musar* was by comparison episodic—performing the same function for Hebrew that Wolff had for German some four decades earlier. In his early German philosophical treatises Wolff had invented German equivalents for accepted Latin terms. At the end of those weighty tomes he included a glossary which gave the German terms and their Latin equivalents.[24]

Mendelssohn did not rest content with creating an up-to-date philosophical vocabulary. He also introduced the substance of eighteenth-century philosophy. Wherever Maimonides had used Aristotelian or Platonic notions (for example, that God had created form for an existing primordial matter), Mendelssohn corrected the text with the eighteenth-century Leibnizian-Wolffian view (God created both matter and form), which, unlike the Aristotelian view, was not in tension with fundamental Jewish belief.[25] The distaste for scholastic philosophy apparent in Mendelssohn's German writings is present here as well: he is especially critical of those medieval philosophers who endlessly commented on the master without adding anything of their own.[26] In addition, Mendelssohn seized every opportunity to introduce Wolffian categories. At one point in his treatise Maimonides mentioned the idea of external causality. Mendelssohn pounced on this concept, employing the same method as in the *Kohelet Musar.* He expounded the Wolffian conception of theodicy, that is, though things might look accidental to man, to God they are all necessary; he then quoted a rabbinic source and Maimonides' own *Guide of the Perplexed* that there is no arbitrary evil. He then concluded with a peroration of Wolffian concepts.[27]

Mendelssohn's commentary deserves consideration from a number of perspectives. The text was in keeping with Mendelssohn's emphasis on practical knowledge. As the foundation of philosophy, logic was common to both the speculative and the pietist traditions of medieval Jewish rationalism. This was a Maimonidean text Mendelssohn could use without hesitation.

The republication of this text was characteristic of much of the early Haskalah in its effort to revive the knowledge of philosophical logic in particular and the medieval Hebrew philosophical tradition in general. Israel Samoscz had published a similar commentary, entitled *Ruah Hein,* on the philosophical and foreign terms in Maimonides' *Guide of the Perplexed.* He asserted that he wanted to share the knowledge derived from other authors he had found helpful in trying to pry open the *Guide*'s "locked gates."[28] He later wrote commentaries on two other central philosophical works of the medieval period, Judah Halevi's *Kuzari* and Bahya ibn Pakuda's *Duties of the Heart.* Mendelssohn's commentary would have been inconceivable without Samoscz's example and tutelage.[29]

Mendelssohn's commentary also fit his theological Wolffianism: while defending philosophy from the point of view of religion, he also limited philosophy's purview. Reinbeck had done much the same, for example, in the second half of his *Considerations on the Augsburg Confession.* In response to criticism of the unmistakable Wolffianism of the first volume, Reinbeck had offered a sustained vindication of philosophy's service to theology in the second. He argued that philosophy, as the "science of the possible," is an indispensable aid in achieving correct belief.[30] It first teaches the use of reason to scrutinize the truths of nature. It then leads to the truths of Scripture, helping us to understand the objects behind the words, and thus enables us to formulate distinctions and categories.[31] Physics and mathematics are similarly essential to comprehending the central scriptural passages that treat nature.[32] Finally, philosophy shows that the truths of nature and the truths of Scripture are in absolute agreement.[33]

While emphasizing the utility of philosophy, Reinbeck set it clear limits (as Mendelssohn would). Philosophy has distinct boundaries in regard to natural matters—all the more so in divine ones. Philosophy not only presupposes and, through its investigations, confirms revelation but also accepts miracles and respects mysteries.[34] Reinbeck made the argument common to the theological Wolffians that ultimate theological issues were not contrary to reason (*contra rationem*) but beyond it (*supra rationem*). Reinbeck further argued for the use of Wolffianism from the pulpit. While scholastic subtlety and natural science were not appropriate, philosophy was, since it provided concepts, revealed causes, and imparted the understanding of nature ("admiration and reverence for God's power, goodness and wisdom") which restored skeptics and doubters to belief.[35]

Despite the general harmony between Mendelssohn's commentary and Reinbeck's introduction, there is one discordant note. Reinbeck dealt exclusively with Wolffian philosophy. Mendelssohn introduced that philosophy by commenting on a medieval text. In this regard Mendelssohn parted ways with the Protestant theologians who dismissed medieval philosophy without hestitation (as did the Protestant Enlightenment in general). Yet Mendelssohn did not thereby part ways with the religious Enlightenment. Catholics in the Holy Roman Empire also turned to medieval philosophy. In search of an alternative to baroque scholasticism, for example that of Francisco Suarez (1548–1617), Reform Catholics returned to Aquinas at the same time that they turned to Wolff. The Haskalah and Reform Catholicism thus had a fundamental affinity, and it extended beyond this one instance to other areas, such as the study of neglected texts like the Bible. Recognizing this affinity enables us to see that aspects of Mendelssohn's thought (or of the Haskalah for that matter) which have hitherto been deemed entirely distinctive were in fact characteristic of the religious Enlightenment.[36]

Together with his German philosophical works, the *Kohelet Musar* and *Logical Terms* show the consistency of Mendelssohn's position as an Enlightener, a *maskil,* and a theological Wolffian. The two works further illustrate that commentary was the medium of his Jewish thought. In this regard another of Mendelssohn's Hebrew works of the 1760s, *The Book of the Soul* (Sefer HaNefesh), is the exception that proves the rule. Composed of two systematic expositions, Mendelssohn withheld it from publication. David Friedländer, his self-styled "friend and disciple," published it a year after Mendelssohn's death (1787).

In the first composition, "The Soul," Mendelssohn made good his original plan of writing a treatise in Hebrew on the immortality of the soul.[37] He dispensed with the *Phaedon*'s dialogue form and pagan foil ("What have we, the followers of the true religion, to do with the sons of Socrates") to recast its first two arguments into a series of theses and the last into a brief essay. First, the soul must be a simple, incorporeal substance to be capable of perception (corporeal or complex entities are only the objects of perception). Second, such incorporeal substances are eternal: they exist and expire supernaturally, "by means of a miracle" (whereas corporeal bodies are subject to natural causation, that is, they deteriorate over time).[38] Since all God's acts are good and the destruction of a soul is evil, it is therefore impossible that God destroys souls. Finally, the soul retains the "perfections and abilities" it acquired during the body's life after the body's death. Because the pursuit of perfection is man's vocation, morality would be undermined were God to destroy its fruits.

The second composition, "Discourse on the Soul's Connection with the Body," was related to the first in addressing an aspect of the soul which had implications for morality: Did the Leibnizian doctrine of the preestablished harmony (between bodies and souls) preclude free will? Mendelssohn gave a detailed defense of the Leibnizian view. Perceptions arise from the soul's own power or from prior representations that are in harmony with the motion of bodies. Neither the preestablished harmony nor its corollary, predeterminism, contravened free will, since both allowed the individual to choose to pursue his perfection. Moreover, divine retribution was also in keeping, as God punished only to educate the sinner ("there is no punishment except for the sake of the sinner, that he may desist") by removing the source of his sin ("the source of sin is the ignorance of good and evil").[39]

The topics of these two compositions were perfectly suited to convey the convergence of Wolffian philosophy and Judaism. On the one hand, the subjects were key elements in the "rational psychology" of medieval Hebrew philosophy. Mendelssohn pointed out that the idea of immortality was a "basic tenet" of Judaism.[40] Discussions of the relations of body and soul were commonplace in medieval Jewish philosophy; in his introduction to the posthumous publication Friedländer pointed to those in Maimonides, Gersonides, Yitzchak Arama, and Saadya.[41] On the other hand, the subjects were also formative for Leibnizian-Wolffian philosophy and theological Wolffianism. Mendelssohn used his discussion of the immortality of the soul to assert the idea of theodicy (we fail to comprehend the goodness of God's acts because of our lack of understanding), which he confirmed with a quotation from Maimonides.[42] The same discussion, that souls are beyond natural causes, gave him an opportunity to defend the possibility of miracles, which the theological Wolffians had understood as acts beyond reason (*supra rationem*). The argument that God does not destroy the "perfections and abilities" a soul has acquired served as a platform to broadcast God's morality.

> Only in this manner are God's ways in order. Without it, God forbid, the same lot would befall the good man and the evil, he who serves God and he who does not. The wicked would fare as the righteous. Heaven forfend that the judge of all the earth would not dispense justice.[43]

And the issue of the preestablished harmony allowed Mendelssohn to introduce the basic laws of Newtonian physics.[44]

Despite substantial continuity with his earlier works, *The Book of the Soul* did differ: it was a freestanding philosophical work whereas the *Kohelet Musar* and *Logical Terms* were commentaries. Mendelssohn here continued his effort to renew Hebrew as a philosophical idiom. In "The Soul" he coined Hebrew equivalents for a number of Wolffian terms and in the "Discourse" he continued the practice of giving Latin or German equivalents for his new coinages. Yet he also went beyond this. He spent the first half of the "Discourse" defining the key terms of Leibnizian philosophy which were indispensable to his argument about the preestablished harmony. The result is that the "Discourse" is something of a primer in Hebrew of Wolffian philosophy. It presumed an audience willing to study this philosophy directly. This unmediated presentation obviously had to do with the essay's origins. Mendelssohn wrote the "Discourse" as a letter to Hartog Leo, a *maskil* with whom he corresponded on issues of philosophy, Jewish law, and biblical exegesis.[45] The result, as Friedländer noted in his introduction, was that the work was not suitable for the uninitiated.[46] While "The Soul" presumed less of readers than the "Discourse," it was also an independent exposition of Wolffian philosophy. However appropriate Mendelssohn thought the contents were for his fellow Jews, the form of the works assumed an audience for philosophy in Hebrew which simply did not exist in the 1760s. Whatever Mendelssohn's reasons for withholding *The Book of the Soul* from publication, then, the fact that he did so fully accorded with the pattern of his published work in Hebrew.

The content of these early works is familiar. The themes were the stock-in-trade of the Andalusian tradition and Jewish rationalist thought from the tenth through the seventeenth centuries. The only new component was Mendelssohn's Wolffian articulation and, in some cases, the replacement of medieval with eighteenth-century philosophical notions. The lack of any original content is significant, for it underscores the essential conservatism of Mendelssohn's ends, which assumed an essential harmony between the Andalusian tradition and Wolffian philosophy.

CHAPTER THREE

"A Golden Bridge"

The philosophical phase of Mendelssohn's career concluded with the Lavater affair in 1769–1770. By the end of the 1760s Mendelssohn had espoused a philosophical position that he would retain without substantial alteration until the end of his life.[1] In his Hebrew works he had made a case for the essential agreement of that philosophy with Judaism. Nevertheless, he sustained a public dualism by publishing philosophy exclusively in German and commentaries on Jewish subjects in Hebrew. The Lavater affair challenged Mendelssohn to defend this position as well as his fundamental ideas. The way in which Mendelssohn responded showed that his dualism was induced by external constraints rather than the internal needs of his philosophy and that he would divulge his views on Judaism (and perforce Christianity) only under duress. Though Mendelssohn acquitted himself well, it was at the cost of inordinate strain.

Johann Caspar Lavater (1741–1801) was a Swiss Protestant pastor whose chiliasm set him at odds with the theological Enlightenment and led him to the belief that Mendelssohn's conversion would trigger the messianic process.[2] On the strength of conversations (1763–1764) in which Mendelssohn expressed a "philosophical respect" for Jesus and a later wishful report that the "philosophical Jews" of Berlin were deists ripe for conversion to unitarian Christianity, Lavater precipitately offered Mendelssohn a "golden bridge" to Christianity.[3] The "golden bridge" took the form of a dedication to a partial translation of a French-language apology for Christianity. Charles Bonnet's *Palingenesie* had taken issue with Mendelssohn's *Phaedon* and the Enlightenment by arguing that only revelation could provide certain knowledge of the soul's immortality.[4] Lavater invited Mendelssohn to repudiate Bonnet publicly or to "do what Socrates would have done, had he read this work and found it irrefutable," namely, convert.[5] Lavater thus posed a public challenge to Mendelssohn as a philosopher and as a Jew.

Lavater's dedication put Mendelssohn in a quandary. Should he articulate his hitherto unspoken assumptions and abandon his public dualism? Should he defend his Judaism and confute Bonnet's Christianity? To counterattack risked overstepping the bounds of Enlightenment toleration, while to refrain from battle risked giving the impression that he was unable to defend himself. Mendelssohn characteristically took a middle way. He parried the attack in public, drawing on the central categories of his thought to defend toleration. In private notes and correspondence, he conducted a vigorous counterattack, using those same categories to vindicate Judaism and criticize Christianity. We will confine ourselves here to the main points of his public pronouncements, since his private ones became public in more developed form a decade or so later when he faced a second, more serious challenge.

Lavater had explicitly addressed Mendelssohn as a philosopher.[6] Mendelssohn responded as one, attempting to defend his version of Wolffianism as a tolerant philosophy grounded in universal ideas of natural religion and natural law. He argued that issues of revelation had no place in philosophy's domain. Mendelssohn acknowledged that from the outset his own philosophical studies had aimed to prepare him to scrutinize thoroughly his religious beliefs. He thus asserted the sincerity of his religious convictions. At the same time he boldly announced that he was under no obligation to account for them publicly. Instead, he had chosen in his works "to avoid all religious controversies, and in public writing to discuss only those truths of equal importance to all religions."[7]

Mendelssohn obviously followed Wolff in regarding only natural religion as an apposite subject for philosophy. He justified that view by arguing—as he had done so often before—that natural religion was the indispensable means to promote man's vocation, the quest for virtue that leads to eternal felicity. He had chosen this path in his own life: "I hoped to refute the contempt in which the Jews are held not through polemics but through virtue."[8] He unequivocally recommended it to others: "He who in this life leads men to virtue cannot be damned in the next."[9] Mendelssohn made this last statement about Solon and Confucius. He had no doubt that they had earned eternal felicity. He could not admit Lavater's claim, or for that matter any other, that one religion had a monopoly over salvation. He thus affirmed the universality of natural religion against the exclusivity of Lavater's Christianity.[10]

Mendelssohn did not stop there. He argued for philosophical as well as religious toleration. He recapitulated his earlier attacks on the presumption of any philosophy to absolute truth (recall his statement that there was no "pope of philosophy"). The philosopher must do his best to set aside his prejudices and to search assiduously for the truth, yet he must also be prepared to admit the legitimacy of other points of view: "[The philosopher] must never lose sight of the fact that this is only his conviction, and that other reasonable beings who begin from another point of departure, and follow a different guide, could reach entirely contradictory opinions."[11]

Mendelssohn undergirded this defense of religious and philosophical toleration with his distinction between practical and theoretical knowledge. Though the philosopher had an unavoidable obligation while seeking the truth to correct errors, there were occasions when he should desist from doing so, at least publicly. Those erroneous ideas that were merely theoretical and "were too far removed from practical life to be directly deleterious" could be ignored.[12] This was especially the case if these errors produced virtue, and Mendelssohn had no doubt that this could be so (he obviously had Christianity in mind). If the errors subverted natural religion or undermined natural law, however, they could not be ignored under any circumstances, since natural religion and natural law constituted the universal basis of morality, society, and ultimate felicity.[13]

Mendelssohn's defense of toleration required one more element: he had to show that Judaism was also tolerant. In consequence, for the first time in a German-language work he pointed to the harmony between his philosophy and Judaism. He asserted that Judaism possessed no conversionary impulse. The law of Moses was binding only for those born to it. For all others the Law was a positive obstacle: the rabbis discouraged prospective converts by requiring that they be made aware of the heavy burden of the Law. Judaism taught instead that the rest of mankind was enjoined to "abide by the law of nature and the religion of the patriarchs."[14] Mendelssohn thus identified natural law with the seven laws of Noah, going beyond the arguments of his Hebrew works and creating the foundation for the view he would elaborate in detail in the 1780s that Judaism was in perfect harmony with natural religion and reason.[15] All those who followed these injunctions, since they were a guarantee of virtue and morality, were entitled to a place in the world to come. Mendelssohn stressed that Judaism had a special category for those who gain eternal reward through moral achievements, "the righteous of the nations." Judaism laid no claim to a monopoly over salvation but rather recognized numerous paths to it.

Mendelssohn answered Lavater's challenge with a multifaceted defense of toleration. His deftly restrained replies won accolades from many. As his friend and publisher Nicolai pointedly put it in a letter to Lavater: "You wished that he not remain a Jew; he had no objection to your remaining a Christian."[16] Yet Mendelssohn's replies were not decisive in Lavater's retreat. Lavater had mistaken the temper of the times. Mendelssohn was not his only victim. In 1764–1765 he had toyed with the idea of trying to convert Rousseau (a Catholic), and he did in fact try to convert Goethe and the poet Ramler (both Protestants). His importunate chiliasm posed a challenge to the Enlightenment in general and the theological Enlightenment in particular. This was his undoing. Lavater had expected the enlightened world to applaud him. Instead, he encountered the immediate and resolute disapproval of Bonnet and leading theologians and the concerted opposition of an influential group of secular and religious Enlighteners.[17] The Enlightenment rallied against him and he reluctantly retracted. Lavater conceded not to Mendelssohn then but to the Enlighteners who had closed ranks around him. Yet Lavater did not renounce his chiliastic dreams. He continued to raise objections to Mendelssohn's arguments, and to the end he remained hopeful that Mendelssohn would be brought to the baptismal font.[18] The Enlighteners' disapproval and active opposition merely made Lavater admit the mistake of a public challenge. He felt he had no choice but to withdraw it.[19]

Just as it would be misleading to attribute Lavater's retreat to Mendelssohn's reply, so it would be misleading to ascribe Mendelssohn's dualism to his philosophical ideas. His dualism was the offspring of his parlous position as a Jew. For centuries European Jews had maintained a clear division of language and style between apologetic works for non-Jews and those for fellow Jews. This was the cultural corollary of the autonomous community's dualist structure, whereby Jews retained control of their religious and civil life (through their courts, schools, synagogues, and welfare institutions) in exchange for the remission of taxes and political obedience.[20] In 1769–1770 Mendelssohn had no compelling reasons to risk abandoning that tradition. He knew full well that the influential Enlighteners who had closed ranks to oppose an impetuous chiliast because he threatened the Enlightenment itself could not be expected to do the same in a public discussion of revealed religion which would pit Judaism against Christianity.

As the "Juif à Berlin," "Jud Moses," "un Juif Philosophe" or the "circumcised" philosopher, Mendelssohn was an outsider, and he possessed an outsider's heightened sensitivities. These alerted him to the limits of the toleration he championed; despite the Enlightenment's faith in the reading "public" as an alembic of truth, not all subjects were admissible. Mendelssohn was convinced, for example, that the issues he and Lavater discussed were not sufficiently understood to get a fair hearing.[21] He also had to take account of his civil status. He had taken the precaution, for example, of seeking the Berlin consistory's permission before replying to Lavater, and in replying to him he had rued the fate of his brethren: "The civic status assigned to my coreligionists is so far from being conducive to the free development of intellectual capacities that it hardly increases one's happiness to recognize the true meaning of the rights of man."[22] Jews had to be grateful to those states that admitted them under "bearable conditions." To repay that debt by attacking "the religion of the majority" would be tantamount to an assault on "one's guardian at that point where the most virtuous men are the most sensitive" as well as an attack on the state itself.[23]

Mendelssohn made it clear then that for all the Enlightenment's vaunted advocacy of toleration, which was an incontrovertible achievement, the Jews remained degraded subjects and Judaism an inferior religion, especially in Prussia. That Mendelssohn maintained his dualism despite the harmony of his philosophy and religion showed the extent to which that toleration was imperfect.

Mendelssohn had chosen merely to parry Lavater's thrust, yet he still was compelled to divulge some of his inmost thoughts in a controversy that patently distressed him.[24] The general strain of the affair aggravated his physical and psychological condition. A nervous debility (linked to his deformity) that prevented abstract thinking had begun to affect him before the affair. It now grew worse. Mendelssohn ceased to write sustained philosophical works. He of course continued to publish essays and reviews and to discuss philosophical issues with his friends and acquaintances, yet only in the last years of his life would he again write a full-scale philosophical disquisition. Mendelssohn was not the sole object of Lavater's chiliasm, but he was the most vulnerable. While Goethe vigorously rebuffed Lavater's proselytizing, the two remained friends.[25]

Mendelssohn suffered long-term consequences. When asked what he did during his long hours of enforced idleness, he replied that he "counted the roof tiles" on his neighbor's house.

Mendelssohn subsequently redirected his energies. Shortly before the appearance of Lavater's challenge he had written a commentary on the Book of Ecclesiastes. He now wholeheartedly embraced the enterprise of biblical translation and commentary.

PART TWO

Exegesis

Mendelssohn had expressed his desire to revive the tradition of Jewish biblical exegesis in his first Hebrew work.[1] He had good reason. From as early as the sixteenth century the Bible had disappeared as an independent subject from the curriculum of baroque Judaism: the study of Talmud held pride of place, with Kabbalah next. When the Bible was studied there was such an overwhelming preference for homily that little or no attempt was made to distinguish it from the literal meaning of the Bible based on grammar and syntax. Not all were satisfied with this situation. Leading scholars from the time of Judah Loew of Prague (1525–1609) lamented Ashkenazic Jews' failure to study the Hebrew language and Bible and they suggested changes to the curriculum of the schools, often pointing appreciatively to their Sephardic brethren who systematically taught these subjects.[2]

It was to be Mendelssohn's enduring achievement of the 1770s and early 1780s to make the Bible central to the Haskalah. Mendelssohn understood the Bible as the foundation of Judaism because it was the primary source of practical knowledge. Scripture therefore merited intensive study in its own right, and his commentaries were designed to facilitate such study. Mendelssohn's efforts to revive biblical exegesis and Hebrew philosophy were inextricably connected. The issues that concerned him in his Hebrew philosophy reappeared in his exegesis; indeed, in his exegesis he made use of his early philosophical efforts.

CHAPTER FOUR

Ecclesiastes

Mendelssohn inaugurated his exegetical enterprise with a commentary on Ecclesiastes. The work antedated the Lavater affair, having been written sometime in 1768 and published in late 1769 or early 1770. It originated in the period when the *Phaedon*'s extraordinary success encouraged him to bring the book's ideas to a Jewish audience.[1] Written prior to the *Book of the Soul,* which remained unpublished during Mendelssohn's lifetime, the Ecclesiastes commentary belonged in form and content with his earlier Hebrew commentaries, the *Kohelet Musar* and the *Logical Terms.* It explored two central ideas of natural religion, immortality of the soul and providence, in a popular form, albeit using Wolffian categories. Like the earlier commentaries, this one passed effortlessly from natural religion to Judaism. Yet it was also a new sort of commentary in its effort to revive the tradition of biblical exegesis.

The continuity with Mendelssohn's earlier philosophical works in Hebrew is apparent in the titles: the Hebrew for Ecclesiastes is *Kohelet,* Mendelssohn's first Hebrew work was entitled *Kohelet Musar.* Mendelssohn defined Kohelet as the "assembler" or "preacher" who "collected wisdom, ethical sayings, and much eloquence."[2] As in the *Kohelet Musar,* Mendelssohn focused on practical knowledge (wisdom and ethics), and his choice of Ecclesiastes was thus eminently suitable. Ecclesiastes belongs to the "wisdom literature," those books of the Bible, including Job, Proverbs, and by association Psalms, which were composed in the postexilic period (5th–2d century B.C.E.) and have a broadly human and individual outlook in contrast to the national and collective one of the

Pentateuch and prophets.[3] These books had attracted the attention of the medieval rationalists because they provided a pious medium for the discussion of philosophical issues.

Mendelssohn used his commentary to reiterate his preference for practical over theoretical knowledge, yet he also argued that worldly wisdom is insufficient if not linked to the superior wisdom of natural and revealed religion. This argument echoed his commentary on Maimonides' *Logical Terms,* where he insisted that to have logic without Torah and tradition is to be "like a blind man in the dark."[4] To the verse "Of making many books there is no end, and much study is a weariness of the flesh," he commented: "For action rather than commentary, study, or reading is the essence. Action is the goal, foundation, and essence of all."[5] He emphasized the gulf between theory and practice—"there is a great difference between the precepts of wisdom and the practice of the wise"—and the inability of worldly wisdom to raise its possessors above the rest of humanity—"because of his humanity, even the wise man cannot be freed of defect."[6] Similarly, worldly wisdom alone is incapable of engendering either true happiness or success.[7]

Superior wisdom was to be found in the "fundamental tenets of the true religion," that is, the ideas of providence and immortality integral to natural religion and Judaism.[8] Mendelssohn passionately claimed that the events of this world are illusory.

> If I wish to understand something of the ways of providence, it is necessary to become acquainted with all of God's works, with what was and what will be, in this world and the world to come. For no one can grasp any aspect of the way of superior [i.e., divine] wisdom by considering only the actions taken in this world. This would be like a dream without an interpretation, a question without an answer. One will not attain a true explanation of events and the [divine] decree that informs them, if one does not look beyond to include what occurs in the world to come.[9]

The recognition of providence and immortality affords escape from this seemingly inscrutable world, from the "dream without an interpretation." Were there no world to come, the God who sits in constant judgment would have created intelligent beings only to condemn them to witnessing insufferable injustice without hope of redress. Because belief in immortality ultimately provides that redress, it is the foundation of morality, the guarantee of justice, the key to understanding, and the "source of life."[10] Adopting the technical language of the *Phaedon,* Mendelssohn asserted that the soul is a simple, imperishable substance that sets man apart from beasts; thus the loss of consciousness is the worst fate a rational being can suffer.[11] Providence and immortality constitute "genuine superior truth" and enable man to pursue his God-given vocation, the quest for perfection.[12] Although this world and the next are governed by a thoroughly just divine decree, Mendelssohn denied, as he had in the discussion of the preestablished harmony in his German works, that this governance entails a determinism that precludes freedom.[13]

The search for this "superior" truth itself constitutes "superior conduct." It is an effective, though by no means infallible, antidote to sin, since sin has a cognitive component. While ignorance is not in itself evil, when combined with the passions it generates evil.[14] In contrast, superior knowledge engenders an acknowledgment of God's abiding justice and thus, through an acceptance of fate, metaphysical composure. That composure, in turn, allows its possessor to adopt the golden mean between sybaritism and asceticism. The golden mean would ideally be combined with the effort to develop all faculties, rather than cultivating one at the expense of another. The pursuit of wealth is acceptable, for example, if combined with "the study of Torah and good deeds."[15] Religion should likewise encompass all faculties and emotions.

> In sum, our Torah is divided between piety on the one side and love and joy on the other. In each one we approach nearer to God. Submission and fasting on fast days are no closer to God than joy on Sabbath and festivities so long as one's joy is motivated by devotion and sincerity. . . . The most important point is that one's goal be the sanctification of God's name.[16]

This passage on the ideal personality epitomizes Mendelssohn's exegesis. It shifts from natural to revealed religion without comment or difficulty. It also contains many of the elements he attempted to harmonize. He quotes from Judah Halevi's *Kuzari* to illustrate the ideal of the golden mean, and his discussion of the ideal personality recalls the *Kohelet Musar*.[17] The rejection of asceticism in favor of temperate enjoyment of the world was a stock-in-trade argument of the German Enlightenment. Mendelssohn had explicitly rejected asceticism in his German philosophical works as inimical to that development of the faculties which leads to felicity.[18]

These arguments that were the link to Mendelssohn's earlier commentaries were one side of the *Ecclesiastes*. The other side was his concern with biblical exegesis itself. Mendelssohn tried to revive the medieval Jewish exegetical tradition that focused on the text's literal meaning. In so doing he had to surmount an obstacle for which there had been no equivalent in his renewal of Jewish philosophy. Medieval Jewish exegesis posited four simultaneous modes of interpreting any biblical text (literal, homiletical, allegorical, esoteric). Since the seventeenth-century scholars like Spinoza, Capellus, Morinus, and Richard Simon had developed a critical approach to the Bible; they contested many traditional theological interpretations, including the rabbinic ones, which some of them derided as little more than homily or fantasy.[19] Because of these attitudes, which the Enlightenment had absorbed in the course of the eighteenth century, Mendelssohn had to take a position on the very nature of Jewish exegesis before he could urge its revival or provide an example. Mendelssohn consequently introduced his commentary with a "natural" defense of all Jewish interpretation in keeping with both his natural philosophy and his Jewish faith. This defense showed him to be in principled opposition to the mainstream Enlightenment view of the Bible as that view developed in the second half of the eighteenth century. His opposition, which is manifest in the commentary on Ecclesiastes but finds full articulation in his work on the Pentateuch, is apparent in his attitude toward rabbinic exegesis, the Masoretic text, and historical-philological criticism.

Mendelssohn provided a defense of Jewish exegesis on the basis of language.[20] He argued that the multiple meanings presumed by medieval exegesis are inherent in the very use of language, and he employed Maimonidean categories of "primary" and "secondary" intention to explain how these multiple meanings are possible.[21] The primary intention arises from the "context and connectedness of discussion." The speaker and listener are concerned with the sense the words convey rather than with the words themselves. Mendelssohn supported this view by citing a well-known passage in the medieval exegete Ibn Ezra (Exodus 20). Ibn Ezra resolved what he regarded as the most difficult of all exegetical problems, the variations in the wording of the two versions of the Decalogue, by asserting that "the meanings are inviolable, the words are not."[22] Mendelssohn thought that "natural speakers" in particular use language to impart a "primary intention," though he acknowledged that "inspired" speakers and prophets do as well.[23]

The secondary intention, in contrast, does not emerge from the context of discussion—in fact, the two must not agree—but from the "close scrutiny of each and every word, each and every letter, and each and every jot."[24] The natural speaker will use "wit and intelligence" to hint at a meaning he does not desire to state explicitly. Mendelssohn cites the example of Judah's reply to Joseph (Genesis 44:18). After the silver cup had been found that Joseph had had his servants plant among Judah's possessions, Judah appealed to Joseph, concluding with the phrase, "for you are like Pharaoh." Mendelssohn quotes the medieval exegete Rashi, who pointed out that the literal meaning is that Joseph is as important as Pharaoh, whereas the "homiletical" meaning is that he will suffer as Pharaoh had suffered (according to rabbinic tradition, Pharaoh had been afflicted with leprosy for trying to take Sarah from Abraham). The "homily" here is the secondary intention and the proof for its existence is counterfactual: Judah could easily have used other words for the primary intention which would not have conveyed the secondary one. This is an example of a natural speaker using a secondary intention. Mendelssohn thinks that inspired speakers and prophets, because they choose each word with a "specific intention," are prone to such secondary intentions.[25] While Mendelssohn focused on the first two levels of rabbinic interpretation, he also defended the last two, if briefly. The third level arises from acronyms, acrostics, and numerology; the fourth from those meanings concerning "wondrous matters" which are deemed "fit to be hidden and disguised from the masses and only to be revealed to chosen individuals."[26]

Mendelssohn's natural defense of rabbinic exegesis was of a piece with his general thinking. He averred that multiple meanings are entirely in keeping with reason.

> There are four methods of interpreting our holy Torah—the literal, homiletical, allegorical, and esoteric—as is well known. All of them are the words of the living God and are in agreement. This does not contradict the laws of reason or inference, nor is it alien and disturbing to human reason.[27]

This is the case because the "superior wisdom" according to which God had created the world dictated that "one act served many ends." Mendelssohn argued by analogy with the physical world. Just as the limbs of the body and the elements serve more than one purpose (the nose "breathes," "smells," and "discharges fluids" as well as being "an ornament to the face"; the air is used for breathing and transmitting noise as well as for the wind, rain, and dew), so words can bear multiple intentions. Mendelssohn corroborates this natural argument with quotations from rabbinic literature ("one verse is subject to many interpretations") and mystical literature ("as for this verse, it has many meanings, and so it is with all the words of the Law, there are many meanings in each of them and all are right and good").[28]

Mendelssohn supported his natural defense of rabbinic interpretation with an argument by analogy with creation. This sort of argument "from design" could easily have been drawn from any number of medieval rationalists—Ibn Ezra used it in his introduction to the Bible, for example—yet it was also a version of the "physicotheology" endemic to the German Enlightenment.[29] It was thoroughly characteristic of Mendelssohn to use an argument from the heart of the Enlightenment, but it was especially poignant when he did so to defend rabbinic exegesis against its Enlightenment critics. When combined with quotations from rabbinic and mystical literature, the argument recalled the *Kohelet Musar* in its method of demonstrating the convergence of Enlightenment and Jewish thought. The argument also anticipated his introduction to the Pentateuch: whereas here in *Ecclesiastes* he offered a natural defense of the multiple levels of rabbinic interpretation, there he would offer a natural defense of the biblical text and the authority of the Masoretic tradition.

While Mendelssohn defended all levels of rabbinic exegesis, his principal interest was literal interpretation. He maintained that all forms of rabbinic exegesis agreed with the literal meaning and that the rabbis never neglected it. "There is no doubt that in every instance where our Sages of blessed memory interpreted according to their lights, they did not disregard the literal meaning and did not abandon the primary intention."[30] Nevertheless, he justified his own exegetical undertaking by asserting that in the case of Ecclesiastes "all of the commentators who have preceded me have not fulfilled the obligation of establishing the literal meaning."[31] What Mendelssohn had in mind was that the rabbis and exegetes had paid attention to individual words, yet they had not sufficiently studied the continuous text as units of meaning, with the result that the import of Ecclesiastes remained in dispute.[32] (Here Mendelssohn implied that the inherited notion of literal meaning was inadequate. In his Pentateuch commentary he would redefine it.)

Mendelssohn thus addressed the controversial status of Ecclesiastes. The Mishnah recorded the classic dispute between the houses of Hillel and Shamai over its inclusion in the canon. Although the Hillelites prevailed, largely as a result of Solomon's authority, the arguments against the book's sacred character continued to circulate in rabbinic literature: it was alleged to contain contradictions, to be composed of mere sayings, and to include opinions that bred skepticism or, still worse, heresy.[33]

Mendelssohn set out to demonstrate that all such doubts could be allayed by reading Ecclesiastes as a form of philosophical dialogue in which the contradictory, skeptical, or heretical options were to be attributed to notional interlocutors. Solomon could thus be seen to quote current opinions or worldly wisdom in order to assess them. With this method Mendelssohn systematized the insights of earlier rationalist exegetes. Saadya Gaon had pointed to one passage in Ecclesiastes and Ibn Ezra to a number in which they thought Solomon presented other people's opinions. Maimonides had employed the method systematically for another book of wisdom literature by treating Job as a philosophical parable.[34] Mendelssohn thought that if Ecclesiastes were read as an early philosophical dialogue—the very form in which Mendelssohn himself excelled—the passages that bothered the rabbis or Ibn Ezra could be harmonized with the view that "all of his [Solomon's] words were inspired."[35] This argument is also noteworthy for its attention to the "oral" quality of the text, the dialogue, as such an argument for the "oral" character of the Bible was to be formative for Mendelssohn's understanding of the Pentateuch.

Ecclesiastes 9:4 had caused at least one rabbi consternation ("For he who is reckoned among the living has something to look forward to— even a live dog is better than a dead lion") because he understood it to show that Solomon denied immortality in asserting that the humblest animal, by virtue of being alive, is superior to the most noble because he is dead. Mendelssohn sees this verse instead as belonging to an extended passage (8:10–9:12) in which Solomon expounded the beliefs of those who try to understand God's justice and man's fate solely on the basis of events in this world. The folly of this view is evident in the behavior of those who espouse it: because the world is rendered inscrutable, like "a dream without an interpretation," they vacillate between despair and sybaritism, leading miserably misguided and immoral lives.[36]

This example shows that Mendelssohn felt it necessary to introduce divisions that did not follow the traditional chapters and verses. He defended this practice by arguing that the traditional divisions were intended "for the convenience of the reader" attempting to find a particular passage but did not bear on the meaning. He had been tempted to renumber the chapters and verses but refrained from doing so after consulting the Talmud. Instead, he provided the reader with a scheme of his own divisions that forms the basis for this commentary.[37]

Mendelssohn also addressed eight contradictions that Ibn Ezra had identified, resolving these through various methods of literal interpretation: some he ascribed to Solomon's notional interlocutors, others he explained through reference to the context in which they appeared or in light of the leading ideas of the work.[38] Mendelssohn's solutions make clear that however ingenious his means, his commentary aimed to deal with the accepted concerns of Jewish exegesis. He acknowledged this himself in observing that much of what he had to say was derived from previous exegetes, especially Ibn Ezra and Rashi, and that where he found himself in agreement with their interpretations, as he did in many instances, he simply recapitulated them without alteration.[39]

Mendelssohn's preoccupation with accepted Jewish exegetical concerns went hand in hand with his effort to demonstrate the harmony of Judaism and the Enlightenment. He announced that he felt no compunction in using non-Jewish exegesis.

> Since our Sages admonished us to accept the truth whatever the source, I have also searched among the works of the gentile exegetes, and if I found them to have expressed a particular truth, I have exalted it to the Lord and it became holy.[40]

Mendelssohn felt truth was essentially neutral and universal; whatever its origins, it could be sacralized. He thus revealed his unshakable confidence in his ability to harness the best of contemporary culture for pious ends. In this effort Mendelssohn thought he had good precedent. Maimonides had made similar claims, and in his own commentary on the *Logical Terms* Mendelssohn asserted that Maimonides had so purified logic of its Greek provenance that it could be used for sacred study.[41]

In recording his debt to his predecessors, Mendelssohn also mentioned the exegete he had consulted on grammatical issues.[42] He thus pointed to still another aspect of his commentary. Mendelssohn had divided his commentary in two: one on the meaning of the text, another on the words. The latter was often ancillary to the former, helping to illuminate problems of meaning through technical grammatical discussions. Mendelssohn in fact yoked grammar to philosophy in a notable manner, using either the sublinear vowels or the Masoretic accent marks to support his highly philosophical interpretations.[43] This use of the Masoretic marks raises a significant issue.

An authoritative text of the Bible was essential for Jewish law. The system of accent marks the Masoretes ("transmitters") had introduced by the eighth century C.E. established precisely how the sacred text was to be read, thus fixing it for purposes of study and worship. In their zeal to attain the true meaning of the Bible, the European scholars of the seventeenth and eighteenth centuries who challenged rabbinic exegesis also challenged the Masoretic text. The discovery of the Samaritan Bible (first published 1616) and the collation of variant manuscript readings in the Kennicott Bible (1776) fueled this challenge to the Masoretic text's authenticity.[44] Mendelssohn was well aware of these trends; he had even reviewed important recent works of biblical scholarship.[45] While he did not explicitly discuss such issues in the Ecclesiastes commentary (he would do so in his introduction to the Pentateuch), he did rely on the Masoretic accents in trying to determine the text and its meaning.[46]

Mendelssohn's respect for the authority of the Masoretic text testifies to the conservative nature of his exegesis. His attitude toward Solomon's inspiration reinforces this impression. He accepted that Solomon was the author of Ecclesiastes and not only maintained that his every word was "inspired" but argued the same for a specific point of scientific knowledge. Mendelssohn understood one metaphor ("Before the silver cord snaps and the golden bowl crashes, the jar is shattered at the spring and the jug is smashed at the cistern"—12:6) to refer to human anatomy and specifically to describe the circulation of the blood. Mendelssohn in fact thought that Solomon had characterized the circulation of the blood in accord with Harvey's theory (1628) and that Solomon's understanding was the result of superlative intelligence or divine inspiration.

> It is apparent from this that the circulation of the blood or the circulation of the spiritual humors from the brain to the sinews that I have recalled was known to King Solomon, may he rest in peace. Whether he knew it by the powers of his great intelligence, or it was made known to him by divine inspiration, the fact is that this theory was hidden to the sages of all the ancient nations and was not made known until a century ago by experiments.[47]

This sort of argument had a distinguished pedigree. Judah Halevi had asserted, for example, that Solomon was the source of all the sciences and that his knowledge was first transmitted to the nations of Asia Minor and then to the Greeks and Romans.[48] Whatever its merit, this argument legitimized the study of science by giving it the imprimatur of tradition. That Mendelssohn made this sort of claim in regard to Harvey's theory was entirely in keeping with his intellectual lineage, the Haskalah included. The quest for scientific knowledge played an influential role in stimulating the Haskalah, and its earliest adherents used this traditional argument.[49] For the importance of science in Mendelssohn's milieu one need only recall the medical students Gumpertz and Kisch, the focus of Israel Samoscz's first book on the exegetical uses of science (1741), and the formative role of Newton and mathematics in Christian Wolff's philosophy.

A final noteworthy aspect of the commentary on Ecclesiastes is that in the revival of exegesis, just as in the revival of philosophy, precise language had an important place, which for Mendelssohn meant the use of German as well as of Hebrew. Unlike philosophy, exegesis did not entail the coining of technical terms, yet because of the philosophical content of Mendelssohn's commentary exegesis did involve the clear articulation of abstract notions in Hebrew. Mendelssohn used German translations (in Hebrew characters, clearly marked by parentheses) to illuminate these formulations, giving equivalents for individual words, but even more striking, for phrases, full sentences, or even groups of sentences.[50] As with his argument for Solomon's use of science, this practice also had a distinguished pedigree. The medieval exegete Rashi had used French to clarify matters in his own commentary, with the result that his glosses are an important source of medieval French.[51] The important difference is that Rashi used the vernacular primarily for words in the biblical text itself, whereas Mendelssohn used it primarily for abstractions in his commentary. Here again one sees the continuity between Mendelssohn's philosophical and exegetical endeavors.

That Mendelssohn's commentary placed him at the forefront of the Haskalah's efforts to revive biblical exegesis can be shown by comparison with two contemporary works. In 1760 Judah Leib Minden published a simplified dictionary of biblical Hebrew (*A Dictionary on God's Behalf*). Based on a medieval dictionary, the work defined every word in the Bible in Hebrew with a German translation (in Hebrew letters) and citations of biblical passages. Minden saw the work as a manual for teachers and students. He complained that the Bible was not properly taught because teachers lacked an adequate understanding of Hebrew as well as of the language into which they were translating and that the extant translations had glaring mistakes. His book would aid teachers by making available in simple form the roots of all words. Minden anticipated the charge that he paid attention only to the literal meaning and ignored the others: he asserted that it is imperative to understand the literal meaning before proceeding to the "other trees of the orchard." Minden lamented that the study of the Bible had suffered because of the study of Talmud. His work carried an approbation from the rabbi of

Berlin who praised its "great utility" insofar as it would "remove stones" from the path of the Torah. Minden essentially aimed to provide for exegesis what Mendelssohn had for philosophy; and like Mendelssohn's *Logical Terms*, Minden's work was also an updated medieval text.[52]

A few years later, in 1765–1766, Naphtali Herz Wessely, who was later to collaborate with Mendelssohn on the commentary to the Pentateuch, published a two-volume study of selected synonyms in the Bible in which, like Mendelssohn, he defended rabbinic interpretation. Wessely asserted that the rabbis always interpreted in accord with the literal meaning and that all their interpretations were grounded in the text and based on an expert command of the language.[53] Nonetheless, he felt it his duty to explore further the literal meaning. Because every word of the Bible was intentional and inspired and because words were employed with absolute consistency throughout all of the books of the Bible, mapping the rules that governed the use of synonyms (for example, those for "knowledge" and "wisdom") would reveal the meaning of entire passages.[54]

In the concluding sentences of his introduction, Mendelssohn announced that should his commentary be well received and should God favor such an undertaking, he would attempt to write similar commentaries on the Books of Job, Proverbs, and Psalms.[55] This plan to comment on the remaining books of Wisdom literature was never realized. That the commentary on Ecclesiastes went largely unnoticed by the Jewish audience to which it was addressed was not especially significant: of Mendelssohn's early Hebrew works, only the *Logical Terms* seems to have attracted much attention, being republished twice during his lifetime.[56] That German Bible scholars noted the commentary as a rare defense of rabbinic literature and that it was quickly translated into German and published (1771) also did not contribute to Mendelssohn's thinking about a change in audience.[57] Rather, the decisive factor was the Lavater affair. That challenge to the ideas of natural religion and toleration made Mendelssohn turn temporarily to a general audience and from commentary to translation.

CHAPTER FIVE

Psalms

Mendelssohn spent some thirteen years on his translation of Psalms (ca. 1770–1783). His original intention was to produce a nonpartisan German translation that, as a document of natural religion, would be a common source of practical knowledge for Christians and Jews. This original intention was augmented over the years, but we shall limit the account here to it. Later motives belong to the political configuration of the 1780s and will be discussed in chapter eight.

Mendelssohn had begun to voice distinct ideas about the nature of biblical poetry a dozen or so years before the Lavater affair. In a 1757 review he asserted that to understand Hebrew poetry one "must combine with a knowledge of the language a sure philosophical taste," and he praised the English scholar Robert Lowth, author of *The Sacred Poetry of the Hebrews* (1753), for studying the aesthetic aspects of biblical poetry. Lowth displayed "more taste and knowledge of beauty than pedantic erudition," and Mendelssohn recounted at length (some forty pages) how Lowth construed biblical poetry as quintessentially "sublime."[1]

The Lavater affair prompted Mendelssohn to act on his own strictures and to develop a nonpartisan exegesis that would be an antidote to prejudice. Lavater's retreat marked a triumph for toleration. Mendelssohn sought a means to strengthen the convictions that had secured it. That he chose Psalms as a means to address this problem testifies to the hold the Psalms had on him: he had found them a source of solace and belief.

We all sing to ourselves, the wise man does it as well as the fool. Have you ever read the Psalms from this point of view? It strikes me that many of the Psalms have the qualities that make it possible for them to be sung by the most enlightened person with true edification. . . . At least this is certain: the Psalms have sweetened many bitter hours for me, and I sing and pray them whenever I feel a need to sing and pray.[2]

Noting some passages in Prophets which had been the subject of competing Jewish and Christian messianic interpretations, Mendelssohn asserted in his private writings during the Lavater affair that he was neither made for exegesis nor, thankfully, dependent for his faith on it.

Exegesis is an admirable discipline. It demands as much wide reading, as much healthy common sense, as much knowledge of man in his particular circumstances, as much good taste and shrewd judgment as any form of study. But my head is not made for this sort of undertaking, and I have never been especially drawn to it. I thank my Creator daily that He did not make my felicity dependent on exegetical investigations. I would be the most miserable creature on the earth if my religion bound me to this laborious exercise.[3]

In subsequent correspondence Mendelssohn explained his desire for an exegesis devoted to "edification." In reading the Psalms he wished to avoid all theological presuppositions and he pointed especially to the "prophetic and mystical" interpretations that had lured exegetes into putting faith before the plain meaning of the text.[4] He thought that the appropriate way to read the text was as a "philosopher and critic" and that such a reading would afford a "reasonable edification."[5]

Mendelssohn had previously used this term "edification," central to the religious Enlightenment, in an early philosophical work when a fictional interlocutor asserted that philosophy had restored his faith.[6] That he used it in regard to Psalms—and modified by the adjective "reasonable"—emphasized his desire for an exegesis that would promote universal religiosity through attention to the work's ideas (exegete as "philosopher") and its aesthetic qualities (exegete as "critic"). Mendelssohn thought Psalms eminently suitable for this task of edifying readers of all faiths because (following Lowth) he considered this book a model of the "sublime." Because Mendelssohn saw his translation of Psalms in terms of the aesthetic category of the "sublime" as well as the spiritual category of "edification," a brief account of his aesthetic ideas is in order.

In the first half of the eighteenth century German became a language of philosophy; in the second half of the century it became a language of literature. A literary culture blossomed of which Lessing, Schiller, and

Goethe were only the most familiar names. One essential part of that culture was an awakening of aesthetics from midcentury. This awakening occurred in the media of philosophy and criticism. As a philosophical discipline aesthetics developed out of Wolff's philosophy, while criticism evolved in the journals of the Enlightenment.[7] Mendelssohn had a hand in both. A consummate essayist, Mendelssohn was a regular reviewer of contemporary belles lettres, in German, French, and English, and aesthetic theory in the major journals of the Berlin Enlightenment (his friend Nicolai published many of these journals).[8] When Frederick II of Prussia published a volume of poetry in French in 1760, for example, Mendelssohn was assigned the review and discreetly chided the monarch for neglecting German. For philosophical aesthetics, Mendelssohn was the exemplary *animateur des idées*: he broached crucial ideas that others then developed systematically. He influenced many of the major strands of aesthetic thinking in Germany—from Lessing's notions of drama and the relationship between poetry and the plastic arts (*Laokoon*, 1766), to Schiller's ideas on the role of art in human development (*On the Aesthetic Education of Man*), to Kant's conceptions of the disinterestedness of beauty and the existence of a third faculty for aesthetic judgment.[9]

Wolff's philosophy was the point of departure for philosophical aesthetics because of its ambiguity. Wolff had brought aesthetics under the aegis of philosophy by including beauty in his secularized notion of perfection and he had broken with the Renaissance tradition of seeing art as a pleasing but inferior form of truth (a "sugar-coated pill") by assigning it the distinct task of giving pleasure. Yet he had treated aesthetic issues only en passant; he had made beauty the sole aesthetic category and subsumed it to the faculty of desire, and he had not developed the relationship of beauty to other areas of philosophy.[10] From midcentury Wolffian philosophers began to alter the legacy by treating aesthetics as an independent branch of philosophy (the term "aesthetics" came into use after 1750) and enhancing the status of the sensual cognition it afforded.

Mendelssohn contributed to these developments, helping to liberate aesthetics from metaphysics through a psychological turn: "Every rule of beauty is simultaneously a discovery in psychology."[11] He argued that beauty derives not from the perfection of the object being represented but from the harmony of all parts of the representation itself (in his parlance, "a perfect sensuous representation").[12] Art was thus created not by imitating nature but by the artist elevating himself above nature—

either by imitating an abstract beauty or, failing that, imitating the Greeks—so as to introduce a beauty that does not inhere in nature itself.[13]

One result of this psychological reinterpretation was that Mendelssohn could account for a variety of aesthetic experiences depending on the nature of the object represented, such as the ugly, the comic, or the tragic. Another result was that art acquired its own laws. The suicide that in life is morally reprehensible on the stage is aesthetically commendable: "The stage has its own morality."[14] Similarly, the "genius" who is a "second creator" in producing beauty is not a craftsman enslaved to fixed norms but naturally puts those norms in the service of his art.[15]

Mendelssohn's psychological reinterpretation also had the important result of making aesthetics practical rather than theoretical knowledge: the limits Mendelssohn set to abstract reason in the philosophical works obtained here as well. Human reason is incapable of grasping the full perfection of God's creation. Because artistic beauty is transmitted by the senses, it makes available an "intuitive knowledge" of perfection.[16] That intuitive knowledge, which is quintessentially human because beauty is both created and perceived by humans, is also "vital" knowledge: it has a distinct role in moral as well as general human development. Beauty only vouchsafes true pleasure when the soul is placed in a condition to improve itelf.[17] Art aids our education to morality by providing "fiery and sensual perception."[18] Art is a more efficacious guide to morality than reason: whereas reason "points the path to felicity," art "bestrews [the path] with flowers."[19] More important, art plays a significant role in the harmonious development of all faculties, which is the goal and ground of felicity. Man is distinguished from other entities through the possession of both reason and the senses; God has only reason, animals have only senses. Art is the highest means to cultivate the senses, pointing at once to man's inherent limitations as well as to his unique endowments.[20]

Mendelssohn regarded the sublime as a particular possession of art and the highest form of beauty. He realized that in common parlance the "sublime" meant any object immeasurable in strength, size, or virtue. God, for example, was usually held to be the "most sublime being." Mendelssohn insisted instead that the sublime was not natural but artistic, existing only as a human creation. Art enables us to perceive the immeasurable by presenting it within boundaries and at a distance. He defined the sublime, therefore, as "the perfect sensuous presentation of the

immeasurable . . . whose greatness . . . reaches a certain degree of perfection."[21] Its effect on the beholder is an admiration so potent as to
exclude any other emotion or concept: "Like the sun, it illuminates
alone, its radiance eclipsing all lesser lights."[22] The sublime can be of
two types. Either the content may be truly sublime—appropriate subjects being "God, the world, eternity"—or similar ideas—in which case
the mode of expression must be inferior to the topic, that is, either un-
adorned or "naive." Or else the sublime may reside in the artist's treatment, in which case our admiration is aroused by the artist's "genius."[23]

Mendelssohn offered his definition of the sublime in a general essay
of 1758 ("On the Sublime and the Naive in the Beaux Arts"). He cited
many examples from ancient and modern literature—Seneca and Shake-
speare, Horace and Corneille, Cicero and (Johann Elias) Schlegel—
among which the Bible, and especially Psalms, figured prominently. He
used three passages from the Bible, for example, to illustrate the sublime
of content: one from the Pentateuch (Genesis 1:3: "Let there be light")
and two from Psalms (46:2–3; 19:6) to illustrate the sublime of treatment. In all cases Mendelssohn noted the concision of the Hebrew language as a central feature of the passage's sublime nature.[24] For many of
the same reasons Mendelssohn cited certain psalms as exemplary instances of the lyric in a general essay on that topic.[25] In sum, Mendelssohn regarded some of the psalms as exemplary instances of the artistic sublime which could play so significant a role in moral and general
development.

Why did Mendelssohn translate Psalms? He regarded his project as
a contribution to practical knowledge for a general audience—Psalms
as a source of natural religion—just as his commentary on Ecclesiastes
contributed to practical knowledge for a Jewish audience. For Mendelssohn aesthetics and theology were not only naturally linked but indis-
solubly wedded. The fundamental beliefs in God, providence, and immortality which guided behavior were also the basis of the sublime. He
had broached this issue earlier. In his review of Lowth's study of biblical poetry, he had asserted that "the divine poets among the ancient Hebrews" composed according to the "rules of art" so that they were able
to "arouse the sublimest sensations in us" and thus knew "how to make
their way directly to our hearts."[26] In his commentary on Ecclesiastes
he briefly commented on how poetry functions—through the concrete
(6:3) and through metaphors (12:6)—and he made the significant argument that poetry serves practical knowledge: "Words of truth were
written in sweet and honest poetry in order that they penetrate the heart

of the nation. Indeed, they made a considerable impression."[27] As a notable example of the poetic sublime, Psalms could serve the general end of "edification." The connection between the sublime and edification, albeit implicit, is unmistakable. The sublime's aesthetic impact is admiration; its spiritual impact is edification. The topics that make Psalms sublime (for example, "God, world, eternity") also make it a virtual compendium of natural religion. Once available in a nonpartisan German version, Psalms would be a primer of religiosity that would contribute to general human development.

To achieve this goal Mendelssohn's translation had to restore the lyrical form of biblical poetry.[28] Mendelssohn thought the Bible represented one of the great traditions of lyric alongside the classic and Nordic.[29] Only when the translation revealed those original aesthetic qualities would edification be attainable. This meant not only a translation free of theology but also one that was primarily literary rather than scientific: Mendelssohn translated as a "philosopher" and as a "critic."[30] Initially intending to publish his translation as a "sample of Hebrew lyric" in the 1771 edition of his *Philosophical Works,* he tried to render into German the "spirit of the original text," its "true sense."[31] He thus avoided literal translation and also took the liberty of translating terms according to sense and rhythm rather than technical consistency.[32]

The idea of restoring Hebrew lyric was in the air in the late eighteenth century: five German translations of the Psalms appeared within the space of a few decades.[33] While Mendelssohn consulted these translations, the single most important influence was Luther, which Mendelssohn freely admitted: those passages he thought Luther had translated accurately and elegantly he retained.[34] In fact, in the decade or more that Mendelssohn worked on his translation, he progressively tried to distance himself from Luther's overweening influence, particularly in the last stages as he prepared the text for publication.[35] For all of Luther's influence, Mendelssohn remained here, as in the Ecclesiastes commentary, true to the Jewish text as established by the Masoretes, despite his awareness of some corruptions.[36]

Mendelssohn's hopes for his translation were, alas, unfulfilled. Because two composers subsequently used his renditions in setting Psalms to music (Schubert, psalms no. 22 and 91; Ludwig Spohr, psalms no. 8, 23, and 130), there has been a general impression that the translation was popular and influential. Nothing could be further from the truth.[37] Already in 1786 David Friedländer noted lugubriously that the work had failed to create the "sensation" it should have.[38] In many ways it was a work without an audience. Presenting Psalms as a literary document of general religious sentiment placed Mendelssohn in the best humanist company: in the seventeenth century the Dutch scholar Hugo Grotius, for example, had treated the psalms as expressions of individual piety free of divine inspiration.[39] Most of Mendelssohn's Christian contemporaries were not interested in a translation cut from that humanist cloth. Leading Bible scholars regarded a nonchristological version of Psalms as inadmissible. The Göttingen orientalist J. D. Michaelis, who crossed paths and swords with Mendelssohn on numerous occasions, began his scholarly career with a vindication of the christological exegesis of Psalms and maintained that view.[40] At the other extreme, Eichhorn had argued that Psalms must be read without any attention to "edification."[41] At least one reviewer complained that the work was as much a commentary as a translation and that Mendelssohn's interpretation was no more legitimate than the theological ones he had eschewed.[42] There were also aesthetic objections. One was that the translation was too lyrical and insufficiently scientific for theologians yet not lyrical enough for poets and writers.[43] Another was that most Germans were so accustomed to Luther's Bible that any other version was jarring. One reviewer even contended that Mendelssohn had failed in his express intention of rendering "Hebrew or Davidic originality."[44]

Among Jews the translation achieved success once it had been recast as a traditional text. A five-volume version appeared between 1785 and 1790 containing the Hebrew text, Mendelssohn's translation printed in Hebrew letters, the commentary of a sixteenth-century Italian Jewish scholar, Obadiah Seforno, a lengthy introduction by the editor Joel Brill, and a glossary of High German words. Not only was the first edition heavily presubscribed, with the subscribers ranging geographically from Amsterdam in the west to Warsaw in the east, from Copenhagen in the north to Hundersdorf (Hungary) in the south, but the version was reprinted at least ten times in the next century.[45] Here is additional confirmation that the appropriate medium for Mendelssohn's work for a Jewish audience was commentary.

CHAPTER SIX

The Pentateuch

During the thirteen years that Mendelssohn labored over his translation of Psalms, he also turned to the Pentateuch. This work crowned his exegetical efforts. He had commented on and provided an introduction to Ecclesiastes; he had translated the Psalms. He now translated the Pentateuch, commented on portions of it (Genesis 1–5; Exodus), edited commentaries he commissioned for the remainder, and provided an extensive introduction. This work consummated his efforts to reactivate the Andalusian tradition of Jewish exegesis and philosophy. He now made full use of that pietist tradition, the result being a striking application of a usable Jewish rationalism fully in accord with, indeed deliberately in defense of, rabbinic authority.

Although this work is generally referred to as the *Biur* (Hebrew for "commentary"), that name designates the commentary alone. The entire work, drawing on the liturgy for the reading of the Bible, was entitled the *Book of the Paths of Peace*; the introduction was called "Light for the Path."[1] Since this work was multifarious, the relationship between its parts should be clarified at the outset.

The translation was paramount. By Mendelssohn's own account, he undertook the project for the instruction of his sons.[2] Yet he quickly realized the work's general pedagogical utility: the reasons that recommended a new translation for his own children also recommended it for others. The two kinds of extant translations were thoroughly unacceptable for Jews. The word-by-word Yiddish translations that dated from the late seventeenth century lacked an adequate command of Hebrew and failed to convey the literal sense of the text. In addition, Mendelssohn felt that Yiddish was unequal to the task of rendering the Bible because of its grammatical imprecision: he regarded Yiddish as a colloquial language suited to conversation and correspondence and he happily employed it in that manner.[3] The available German translations, whether Luther's or those of more recent origin, were pernicious for Jewish youth because they conveyed erroneous christological interpretations. Worse still, by not adhering to the Masoretic text they imparted the idea that the Bible was not divinely revealed and immutable but was a human document subject to corruption and correction.[4]

Mendelssohn's translation aimed to convey the literal meaning of the text through a fluent German translation. To achieve this result, Mendelssohn drew on the full range of his German, from prose to poetry, from simple diction and syntax to complex and even archaic language and constructions.

The commentary was designed to support the translation. Mendelssohn initially entrusted the task to his children's Hebrew tutor, the accomplished Hebraist Solomon Dubno, who had encouraged Mendelssohn to make public the translation designed for private use.[5] Dubno's charge was to explain why Mendelssohn had chosen to translate passages in a particular way, whether for reasons of grammar, accent, or vocalization, and to show how the choice accorded with the opinions of the leading medieval exegetes, such as Ibn Ezra, Rashi, Ramban, Kimhi, and Rashbam. The commentary was thus to provide a usable digest of the medieval literalist tradition. Dubno was also to write accompanying notes on the Masoretic text (the "Tikkun Soferim").[6]

It soon became obvious that Dubno could not manage these tasks on his own. Mendelssohn took responsibility for certain portions of the commentary (Genesis 1–5, Exodus), making the commentary a joint undertaking. Yet even this assistance was insufficient. Dubno abandoned the project in the middle, others had to be recruited, and finally the commentary became a collective effort. The contrast with Mendelssohn's earlier exegesis is thus marked. In the Ecclesiastes commentary Mendelssohn had corresponded with one maskilic friend, Hartog Leo, who offered comments that Mendelssohn then incorporated into the published commentary (although clearly delineated by parentheses from his own comments). Here a group of *maskilim* participated. Naphtali Herz Wessely provided the commentary to Leviticus while two younger (and less able) *maskilim,* Herz Homberg and Aaron Jaroslav, worked on Numbers and Deuteronomy. While Mendelssohn remained the chief editor and driving force, the participation of four others attested to a shift in the nature of the Haskalah.

When Mendelssohn came to Berlin in the 1740s a number of like-minded Jews (Samoscz, Gumpertz, Kisch) had aided him in his intellectual efforts. In the 1770s he again found a group of kindred spirits, yet the faces were new. In the 1770s Berlin had become a magnet for would-be *maskilim*: Frederick the Great and Mendelssohn symbolized the dual status of the city as the center of Enlightenment and Haskalah. Located at the crossroads of eastern and central Europe, Berlin also offered these men—usually impecunious and often émigrés from eastern Europe—the possibility of pursuing their dreams. Berlin Jewry was sufficiently large and prosperous, especially after its dramatic leap in wealth during the Seven Years' War (1756–1763), to hire as tutors and clerks men versed in Hebrew and vernacular languages. Many wealthy Jews were in fact eager to act as sponsors, since they saw the Haskalah as a means to reconcile their Judaism with the cultural trappings they had acquired.[7]

The introduction, "Light for the Path," was also designed to support the translation. Mendelssohn initially entrusted the task to Dubno, who apparently abandoned the entire project when Mendelssohn decided that the introduction he presented was inappropriate and refused to print it. This incident has received considerable attention and some commentators have questioned Mendelssohn's behavior.[8] Whatever one's view of the matter, the irreducible fact is that Mendelssohn produced a very different sort of introduction than Dubno. As far as can be ascertained from the few pages that survive, Dubno's introduction focused narrowly on the nature of the Hebrew language and its grammar.[9] In contrast, Mendelssohn provided a general introduction to the Bible for the Jewish reader.

While the translation, introduction, and commentary are each of independent interest, the *Book of the Paths of Peace* in fact functioned as a unit. We will therefore treat it as such, examining three central themes: the Bible as a source of practical knowledge, literal meaning as the focus of exegesis, and the use of history.

PRACTICAL KNOWLEDGE

Mendelssohn regarded the Pentateuch as the primary source of practical knowledge for the Jews since it teaches truth by prescribing behavior through law. He had articulated the essence of this argument in his private writings during the Lavater affair; it now informed his commentary on the first lection (parashah) of Genesis and the entire Book of Exodus.[10] By treating such themes as the role of trust and faith in the formation of Israel's belief, the nature of the Commandments, the limits to theoretical reason, and the relation of reason to good and evil, Mendelssohn's commentary revealed the continuity between his general philosophy and his Judaism.

That practical knowledge is man's true province and the Bible its pre-eminent source emerges from Mendelssohn's understanding of the role of trust and faith in Genesis and Exodus. Mendelssohn gave key terms a practical definition. He explicated God's "testing" of Abraham (Genesis 22:1), for example, as illustrating the need for convictions to be translated into actions. He asserted that the Hebrew verb in the passage implied that God "had given a time and a place to exercise his [Abraham's] heart in the ways of reverence and the service of the Lord."[11] Not only is abstract knowledge insufficient, practical knowledge must be exercised.

> The intention [of the tester] is to reinforce and exercise the heart of the testee to the utmost, so that [these ideas] will become the possession and fiber of his soul. For realization is not attainable with the knowledge and understanding of proper morals alone. Rather [it requires] in addition perseverance in the actions that flow from them and habituation to those actions so that they are impressed upon the heart. Thus will he be resolved always to be ready and willing to follow their dictates and perform the acts they require joyfully and without sloth or negligence.[12]

In his German works Mendelssohn repeatedly argued that virtue must be made into a "second nature" by the constant exercise of moral judgment.[13] He understands the story of Abraham in that very light.

Mendelssohn used the phrase "path of truth," from the story of Rebecca and Isaac (Genesis 24:48), to define the concepts of "truth" and "faith" in a practical manner. "Everything that is in the soul just as it is in the world outside the soul is true."[14] Mendelssohn did not invoke the abstract Wolffian principle of noncontradiction to define truth. Instead, he preferred a practical definition based on the identity between the soul's contents and the external world, and he then used that practical understanding to define faith and faithfulness. "Everything whose outside is identical with its inside will not deceive; it is proper to trust in it and to depend upon it, and for this reason it is called faithful." Or again: "The idea is in the soul, whereas language and action are outside the soul. The man whose lips, heart and actions are all equal is called a man of faith."

These definitions underpin Mendelssohn's understanding of Exodus as the story first of Moses' and then the people Israel's growing trust in God and their readiness to act on their faith in him. Truth, trust, and faith are not abstract concepts but forms of practical knowledge that lead to action.

An important event in Moses' relationship to God is the encounter at the burning bush (Exodus 3). Mendelssohn understood that relationship to be founded not on a miracle, however awesome, but on a series of promises that constituted a "convenant." He insisted that the "sign" of Moses' mission is God's two promises to Moses. First, God promised that Moses would succeed in his confrontation with Pharaoh. Here the burning bush serves as witness: "Just as you saw that the bush did my bidding and was not consumed, so you will undertake my mission and will suffer no injury."[15] Second, God promised that

> on this very mountain where he saw the great and awesome sight [of the burning bush], [the people of Israel] will worship God, Moses will offer sacrifices, Israel will receive the Torah, and Moses will make a convenant with them to be a chosen people to God, and He will be their God.[16]

The true message of God's miraculous liberation of Israel from Egypt is the trust it inspires. When Moses' trust begins to wane (Exodus 5:22–23), God assures him that he (God) remains "faithful," promising that Pharaoh, "will send them out with a strong hand, yea, with a strong hand will he drive them out of his land."

The transformation of Aaron's rod into a snake is another example. According to the text this is a "wonder" (Exodus 7:8) and Mendelssohn calls attention to the difference between a "wonder" and a "sign." A "sign" serves to "commemorate or proclaim"; a "wonder" serves to "verify." "Sign" is the more general category: "Every wonder is a sign, but not every sign is a wonder." In particular, a wonder "entices the heart to believe": it is a form of evidence that evinces practical knowledge.[17]

This story of the growth of trust and faith reaches a first climax after the parting of the sea when "the people feared the Lord; and they believed in the Lord and his servant Moses" (Exodus 14:31). Mendelssohn commented on the phrase "and they believed": "that He is true and faithful to uphold His word"; and on the phrase "and his servant Moses": "that he is His emissary and will do only what God commands."[18]

"Trust" and "faith" are put to the test by the harsh conditions of desert life: will God provide the immediate needs of food and water? At

God's promise of manna (Exodus 16:4), Mendelssohn used the practical definition of the verb "test" he had introduced on the occasion of the "testing" of Abraham (Genesis 22:1):

> The meaning is that their eyes will be fastened upon me [the Lord] for their daily bread. For this reason they will test themselves and accustom themselves to trust in me. Faith in the Lord will again become the fiber of their souls.[19]

The story of the Golden Calf is the second climax in the narrative of Israel's faith and trust in God. The Israelites who descended into idolatry showed an obvious lack of faith and trust. Once Moses had been recalled from the mountain, the calf destroyed, and the guilty put to the sword, God restored his relationship with Israel by creating a new covenant, which Mendelssohn understood in terms of "trust":

> According to these words I have made a covenant with you . . . and I will write a second set of tablets, and these will be a deed of witness, a [sign of] trust that I will be with you, will forgive you and will transform you into a nation of inheritance, as you prayed before me. I will also do that which you requested: I will perform a miracle before the entire nation, and all who see it will be astounded.[20]

Furthermore, in commenting on God's proclamation of himself when passing before Moses after fashioning the second set of tablets (Exodus 34:6), Mendelssohn added: "Truth is the faith to abide by His word and to reward those who uphold His desire."[21]

This relationship of trust and faith results in Israel's obedience through the Commandments—as already noted in God's second promise to Moses (Exodus 3:12)—and the Commandments, as the conjunction of God's will and Israel's faith, are the preeminent form of practical knowledge. Israel's experience of God's fulfilling his promise to liberate them from Egypt results in their trust and willingness to follow his injunctions. Beginning with the initiation of the calendar, these are forms of practical knowledge rather than abstract truth.[22] The first of the Commandments, the observance of Passover, commemorates not the "gift of blood," the fact that Israel's firstborn were spared, but the realization of trust through the fulfillment of God's promise.[23] The injunction to remember the firstborn with a "mark on your hand and frontlets between your eyes" (Exodus 13:16) Mendelssohn construes (following Nahmanides) as a remembrance of the exodus from Egypt and thus as a refutation of disbelief (either doubt of God's creation or of his providence). The injunction verifies God's creation of the world and his ability to intervene miraculously in it, even though he obviously does not do so in every generation. God revealed his laws in such a way as to ensure belief in them as well as in Moses, his prophet.

> [The nation] will hear with their own ears. Neither solely from the mouth of a herald, nor solely by means of signs and wonders, but rather through the ear's hearing, since I have sent you to them to place my Torah before them. For this reason they will forever trust in you . . . since your embassy to them has been validated by a proof that brooks no objection or doubt, namely, the evidence of the senses known to a large public.[24]

That the Commandments are a form of practical and not theoretical knowledge is unmistakably articulated in Mendelssohn's commentary on the first commandments of the Decalogue (Exodus 20:2). These commandments are not intended to teach the abstract truth of God's existence: they presuppose Israel's belief in his creation and providence. Instead, they aim to teach Israel that it was a "chosen people" who had accepted "the yoke of His Kingdom and His government." God spoke to Israel not as the God of Creation but as the God of the Exodus from Egypt. As a result of the relationship of trust and faith realized in that event, "God gave the Torah, commandments, laws, and injunctions" to Israel "alone."[25]

The distinction between practical and theoretical knowledge here is of cardinal importance since it lays the foundation for universal belief in God. By understanding the Commandments to confirm rather than to confer belief, Mendelssohn posited the universality of theism. The God of Creation—as distinct from the God of the Exodus—spoke a universal language.[26] Israel had no monopoly on or special knowledge of any abstract truth. Other nations believe in God, but even more their forms of worship are valid. Whatever the form of worship—idols, animals, or the stars—the other nations thereby acknowledge a higher being and embrace God's rule: "In the judgment of reason there is no cause to forbid such worship to the sons of Noah."[27] Such worship is forbidden to the sons of Israel since they have accepted the laws of the Torah.[28] For the other nations such worship is a form of subjection to God's will and has practical value, promoting virtue and preventing evil.

Here is a plea for toleration through the sort of argument Mendelssohn had made during the Lavater affair: knowledge that promotes virtue and does not contradict the laws of nature or deny God's being is to be respected.[29] With this argument Mendelssohn had secured the foundation of natural religion even as he delineated Israel's singularity, a task he would continue in his book *Jerusalem*.

Mendelssohn in fact balanced these two elements in his discussion of
Israel's election (Exodus 19:5–6). Relying on the Jewish exegete Obadiah Seforno (1470–1550), who lived during the Italian Renaissance,
Mendelssohn stressed that while all humanity was dear to God, Israel
had a special role.

> For indeed all of the earth is Mine, all of the nations are Mine and the en-
> tire human race is dearer to Me than all of the lower beings, since it alone is
> the ultimate purpose of them all, as [the Rabbis] of blessed memory said:
> "Beloved is humanity which has been created in God's image." The saintly
> of the nations are without doubt cherished by Him. *But*: . . . All of the na-
> tions are like one people, and you are like the priests specially appointed for
> the worship of God, to instruct and teach the entire human race to call upon
> the name of God and to worship Him.[30]

The "but" (German: *aber*) connecting the two clauses (Exodus 19:5 and
19:6) in Mendelssohn's translation shows the indissoluble link yet also
the immutable distinction between the nations and Israel.[31]

The Law was the sign of Israel's election as a priestly people, and
Mendelssohn emphasized that the Law was a form of practical knowledge. On the separation of milk and meat (Exodus 23:19) in his discussion of the dietary laws he commented:

> It is not to be inquired why the Holy One blessed be He forbade us meat
> and milk, since He obligated us to many commandments whose explanation
> He did not reveal. It must suffice for us that we know that they are com-
> manded by Him, may He be blessed. Since we have accepted for ourselves the
> yoke of his kingdom, we are required to perform His will. The purpose [of
> the Commandments] is in their performance, not in the knowledge of their
> explanation.[32]

In taking this position Mendelssohn did not denigrate efforts to discover
the precise significance of the dietary laws, although he did think they
might be counterproductive since, doomed to being inadequate, they
either opened the way to facile refutation by Jews or mockery by gentiles. Rather, Mendelssohn identified with the medieval school of thought
represented by Judah Halevi which understood the Commandments as
essentially heteronomous: they are reasonable from the side of the divine legislator yet impenetrable to those for whom they were legis-
lated.[33] This view also informed Mendelssohn's insistence that the Decalogue did not teach abstract truths otherwise unavailable to mankind
and influenced his arguments that Israel is a "community of believers"
and the Bible its handbook of practical knowledge.[34]

The practical value of the Commandments is further evidenced by

Mendelssohn's understanding of them as an antidote to the temptations and sins that arise from society. A pervasive theme of his commentary is that man is a social being. In commenting on the creation of man (Genesis 1:26), he considered why the Hebrew verb giving man control over lesser creatures was plural.

> Because man is male and female, perhaps there is a hint of the aim that man will be social by nature: he will join with those like him and will live with them in a social collective. Each will help his brother to achieve success. An individual can rule all living things and all of the earth not on his own, but only with the help of the general collective.[35]

That man was by nature social and in need of society was a tenet of Wolff's philosophy which Mendelssohn had already articulated in his early works, including his first Hebrew work, the *Preacher of Morals*.[36] Mendelssohn also developed this theme in his commentary. Man was not only social by nature, requiring society to gain his God-given dominion over other living creatures (Genesis 1:28), but the attainment of the true vocation of mankind, the development of the faculties that lead to felicity, was also dependent on society.

> Man is by nature social and will not achieve success without help from others of his kind; if he remains alone, his mental faculties and attributes will not pass from potentiality to actuality, and he will resemble the animals, and will perhaps not even achieve their merits.[37]

Mendelssohn had also sounded this theme in his earlier Hebrew and German works.[38] In his peroration to the Book of Exodus he articulated its dialectical complement. The very society that is imperative for man's true vocation also gives rise to luxuries and temptations that allow desire to triumph and mislead man into sensual pleasure and dissipation. This process is natural. Society progresses from the necessary (food, clothing, shelter) to the useful arts (road building, metalwork, writing) and finally to the ornamental, decorative ones (embroidery, painting, goldwork). All of these contribute to the health of the nation so long as moderation prevails. Once such moderation is lost and the desire for luxury runs rampant, domestic tranquillity is at risk as envy and competition push society to the brink of civil war.[39] God provided Israel with an antidote to this danger in the form of the Commandments. The fact that the Jews must dedicate to God the first fruits of all their arts that contribute to "the maintenance of the state and society" means that they "will remember God in all their acts" and "will not pursue luxury and vanity." When Israel followed the Commandments it prospered: it was, for example, ordered to build the Temple. When it later failed to follow the Law, then "the love of pleasure and glory grew among the king and the nation and overflowed into luxury, then what happened to them happened as is well known from the books of our prophets." The Commandments are Israel's special gift, its bulwark against the evils that can potentially emerge from the society that is necessary to man's true vocation. "Blessed is His great name who distinguished us from the nations by giving us His Torah of truth, good laws, and righteous judgments so that His love and reverence will be with us for all times."[40]

The corollary to Mendelssohn's emphasis on practical knowledge is the limitation to theoretical knowledge—an idea that already played a role in his early philosophical works.[41] This idea now took the form of a discernible opposition to Aristotelian naturalism. The introduction of Aristotelianism into Judaism in the Middle Ages had exacerbated the tension between philosophy and revelation: its naturalism cast doubt on divine omnipotence (preexistent matter vs. *creatio ex nihilo*), and its belief in the contemplative ideal (the preeminence of theoretical knowledge through a comprehensive science of the divine) challenged the status of ritual and commandment. Mendelssohn's consistent opposition to these Aristotelian elements often put him at odds with Maimonides. This opposition is evident in respect to two issues: the nature of Creation and the relation of reason to good and evil.

Commenting on Creation (Genesis 1:2), Mendelssohn stressed the act as *creatio ex nihilo,* by which God called forth existence out of nothingness. Already in the *Logical Terms* Mendelssohn had taken issue with the Aristotelian conception of creation and Maimonides' treatment of Creation as the imposition of form on preexistent matter (see chapter 2 above).[42] Mendelssohn now followed Nahmanides in repeatedly pointing to the miracle of Creation and the fact that in natural, unlike artificial or artisanal, creation form permeates matter and is inseparable from it.[43] This miracle is fundamental for Mendelssohn: only God is capable of it and thus he is beyond nature and Aristotle's First Cause. Mendelssohn therefore scrupulously cataloged those acts in which God brought forth something "out of nothingness into being": Adam and Eve who were "not born but created ex nihilo" (Genesis 5:2),[44] the plague of lice (Exodus 8:13),[45] and the manna that the Israelites ate in the desert (Exodus 16:7).[46] Mendelssohn asserted that while on the seventh day creation ceased and a natural order obtained, God retained the right to intervene miraculously at any time, such as at the Exodus from Egypt and the creation of manna, especially in order to reward good or punish evil, without thereby abrogating the extant order of the world.[47] Moreover, because he knew God "face to face," Moses was able to perform miracles through him or on his behalf. Mendelssohn's insistence on the initial miracle of Creation and the possibility of future miracles brings them into the service of practical reason and the Commandments. The miracle of Creation also has a central and abiding place in the Commandments; honoring parents is an obligation since they participate in the act of *creatio ex nihilo* in bearing children.[48] In this emphasis on Creation Mendelssohn acknowledged his debt to the medieval exegete Nahmanides.[49]

Mendelssohn also took issue with Maimonides by bringing the issue of good and evil under the purview of practical knowledge. In keeping with his general philosophy, Mendelssohn asserted that there is neither absolute good nor absolute evil in the world. Rather Creation produced a combination of the two.[50] That God created man "in our image and likeness" means he was distinguished from other creatures by being endowed with "intelligence and understanding, reason and the aptitude to act."[51] Man is therefore faced with the choice between good and evil.[52] In this regard Mendelssohn was at odds with Maimonides. Mendelssohn contended that Maimonides followed Aristotle in seeing good and evil as a matter of "generally accepted opinions" that, unlike truth and falsehood, are not subject to reason.[53] In contrast, Mendelssohn sees those issues as belonging to the realm of reason in general and practical knowledge in particular: the choice is between desire guided by reason and desire propelling itself.[54] Adam and Eve's sin consisted in allowing desire free rein.[55]

For Mendelssohn man is not the sole participant in this contest between reason and desire: "the purpose of Creation [is] to mend evil and make it good."[56] Creation is designed to promote the good. The punishment God metes out is didactic, aiming to educate rather than merely to discipline the sinner—an idea that Mendelssohn had expressed earlier in his German and Hebrew writings and that he now illustrated with a rabbinic dictum.[57] Moreover, although man's desire is the result of free choice, God nonetheless attempts to direct it to ends that serve his own good purposes.[58]

Mendelssohn's commentary shows that he was not a Maimonidean. He consistently disagreed with the Aristotelian elements of the *Guide of the Perplexed*, though there were many other passages of the work he cited with approval, and he also followed numerous passages of Maimonides' legal compendium, the *Mishneh Torah*. While it should be noted that in the course of his commentary Mendelssohn took exception to one or another of the views of virtually all the major medieval exegetes and philosophers, his unyielding opposition to Maimonides' Aristotelianism was singular.[59]

Mendelssohn's opposition to theoretical knowledge also figured prominently elsewhere in his commentary. For example, Mendelssohn pleaded that a general disquisition on "science" had no place in a commentary on Creation.

> The Bible does not aim to discuss the four elements and their relationship to one another, which being higher and which lower according to the nature of their consistency, whether dense or fine, for this does not belong to the issue of Torah or of belief.[60]

We have already discussed how Mendelssohn took issue with Maimonides (Genesis 1:30), arguing that the nature of good and evil belongs under the purview of practical reason. Maimonides aimed to unburden reason of such matters since he considered truth to be a higher value than good and evil. Mendelssohn was at pains to deny that such theoretical knowledge of God was available to mankind. Moses' knowledge of God was unsurpassed and not to be attained by any other individual, yet ultimate knowledge of God remains beyond any mortal. In commenting on the multiple names of God (Exodus 3:15), Mendelssohn asserted that God's ineffability shows "His concealment and mystery from every intellect save His own."[61] On the episode (Exodus 33:23) in which God revealed his glory to Moses (albeit from the back), Mendelssohn elaborated:

> For this is the limit of what it is possible for a created being to know of the essence of His glory, may it be blessed. Moses attained [more knowledge] than any other person. Before him no person did, and after him no person will reach his exalted honor in attaining [knowledge of] His name and an understanding of the ways and means by which He guides His creatures. Beholding His visage is the attainment of His name and knowledge of His ways in and for itself. This is impossible for all created beings. Since an essence is realized in its own concepts, yet a concept cannot in and of itself be more elevated than he who holds it, therefore it is impossible for a mortal to attain the essence of His Holy name. God alone is capable of this.[62]

The inability of man to comprehend God is also manifest in the inability of the German language to convey the meanings inherent in the Hebrew names of God. Mendelssohn argued that German lacked a single word that could impart the three essential attributes of God's being: "His truth, His priority and eternity and that He rules and superintends everything," or eternity, necessity, and providence.[63] Mendelssohn therefore chose to substitute the part for the whole, arguing that the notion of "eternity" (German: *der Ewige*) suggests the other meanings as well. Mendelssohn's collaborator, Solomon Dubno, approved of this metonymic device.[64] Mendelssohn pointed out that earlier translators and commentators had faced similar problems with their respective languages—Onkelos with Aramaic; Saadya and Maimonides with Arabic—and that the Aramaic translation of Jonathan ben Usiel provided a precedent for resolving the problem by using the attribute of "eternity."[65] There were also extracanonical (the apocryphal Book of Barukh) and Christian (Calvin's Geneva Bible) sources that had used this appellation.[66] In this passage, in contrast to others, Mendelssohn did follow Maimonides' Aristotelian emphasis on God's "existence," which allowed him to offer an alternative to the Christian term "Lord" (German: *Herr*). His choice was in fact to become a fixture of German Jewish life, including the liturgy, in the nineteenth century.[67]

Mendelssohn's denial of ultimate knowledge or esoteric doctrine corroborates his decision to make commentary his medium of choice and to eschew a systematic exposition of Judaism. It further shows that whatever the external circumstances, his biblical commentary was an organic outgrowth of his understanding of Judaism and his general philosophy and not an artificial appendage. Since Mendelssohn thought the Bible offered practical knowledge in a form accessible and relevant to all Jews, his commentary contains no hint of the common distinction made by medieval rationalist exegetes between exoteric exegesis for the masses and esoteric exegesis for the initiates. In fact, Mendelssohn explicitly excludes from his own enterprise the esoteric speculations on Creation and the significance of the altar undertaken by Maimonides, Ibn Ezra, Nahmanides, and others.[68] Instead, as he put it in his introduction, "Light for the Path": "For us this Torah is a possession . . . to know the commandments which God has enjoined us to learn and to teach, to observe, and to fulfill; it is our life and the length of our days."[69]

LITERAL MEANING

Since Mendelssohn saw the Bible as the primary source of practical knowledge, the translator's and exegete's task was to make that knowledge available by translating and explicating the literal meaning. Yet in Judaism the notion of the Bible's literal meaning was neither fixed nor self-evident: even though *literal meaning* had designated the authoritative teaching or the meaning generally accepted and taught at least since the rabbinic period, its definition remained fluid.[70] For example, each of the three virtually canonical medieval literalist exegetes had understood the literal meaning in his own way. Rashi had understood it to combine grammar and homily; Ibn Ezra had introduced the notion of context to explain the meaning of words, verses, and metaphors; and Nahmanides thought literal meaning included philosophical allegory.[71]

Mendelssohn redefined literal meaning. He used the phrase the "profundity of literal meaning" to convey his basic premise that the Bible had a unique oral quality that made it the most effective means of transmitting practical knowledge.[72] He thought the Bible had been composed according to a set of principles that ranged from such basics as the singular qualities of the Hebrew language, including accents and grammar, to the "connectedness" of words, phrases, and the various genres of Pentateuchal literature—genealogy, legislation, narrative, or poetry.[73] These principles were known to the Jewish exegetical tradition and Mendelssohn relied on them. He considered the major literalist exegetes "our eyes in the interpretation of Scripture," and in his commentary he presented a digest of that tradition from the eleventh to the sixteenth century (from Rashi to Obadiah Seforno).[74] He also used rabbinic exegesis and utilized earlier translations, especially Aramaic ones. In addition, he employed homily (*derash*). Utilizing the concepts of "primary" and "secondary" intention he had introduced in his introduction to Ecclesiastes, Mendelssohn used the homiletical interpretation when it agreed with or enhanced the literal one or when rabbinic tradition deemed it authoritative.

Mendelssohn was convinced that because the Bible is essentially oral the practical knowledge it contains is transmitted in the most effective manner. The argument that Hebrew was a divine language distinguished by its oral quality had been made by Judah Halevi in the twelfth century.[75] Mendelssohn amplified Halevi's argument by asserting that the accents had a divine origin: God had vouchsafed them to Moses at Sinai. Moses had heard every word of the Torah from God, who pronounced the words with the full emotion, inflection, and intonation that made their meaning unmistakable and their impact indelible.[76] Moses duly noted all of these oral signs and transmitted them to Joshua, from whom they were communicated through the ages. This process was possible because of the singular nature of Hebrew. Hebrew is not only the language of God and the primordial language of all mankind (and on this point Mendelssohn echoes Dubno's introduction) but because of its system of accents recording the full range of expression it has the singular ability to preserve oral expression. All language was originally oral; Hebrew alone was able to remain so. The advantage of the spoken over the written word is immediate understanding. The speaker's voice makes the words comprehensible. Spoken language "enters the listener's heart to arouse and to instruct him." Spoken words are "stakes and nails" that are "implanted" in the auditor's heart.[77] In short, spoken language is the medium for the "vital" and "efficacious" knowledge that results in practice. Since Hebrew retains its oral qualities, word and thought agree so perfectly that meaning can be transferred directly from the "heart of the speaker" to the "heart of the auditor."[78] In the ideal situation the Hebrew text is read or sung according to the accents, making it understood immediately or, if not, then with the aid of a brief Hebrew commentary. Such a situation is the perfect conduit for the "living waters" of the Torah.[79]

This ideal of oral transmission in Hebrew had not always obtained. Beginning with the Babylonian exile, Hebrew ceased to be the living language of the people as the Jews lived out the dictum that subject peoples adopt "the language of the ruling nation."[80] In consequence, there has been a long history of Jewish translations of the Torah, and Mendelssohn chronicled the many efforts in many languages (Aramaic, Greek, Arabic, Spanish, and Yiddish). To be sure, this history vindicated yet another translation; more important, it also explained how a translation could preserve the oral character of the text.

Mendelssohn understood translation in relation to the categories of primary and secondary intention he had employed in his introduction to *Ecclesiastes*. The translator, like the commentator, aims to convey the sense of the text. The differences between languages make it impossible to do so without altering the words, their order, and their associative qualities. Such changes can substantially modify the impact the words then have on "auditors"; that is, the practical effect can be lost.[81] The most faithful translator is therefore one who "adds, subtracts, or changes the order of words" in order to capture the meaning of the "speaker."[82] Mendelssohn quotes the Talmudic equivalent of "traduttor, traditori": "Everyone who translates a verse literally fabricates."[83] Instead, Mendelssohn took as a model the Aramaic translation of Onkelos, which rabbinic tradition deemed authoritative.

Onkelos in particular did not deviate from the primary literal intention, except for those passages where he was forced to do so for the sake of the true meaning, or in those passages where it was necessary to remove obstacles to correct understanding.[84]

Mendelssohn translated according to Onkelos's model, aiming to preserve the Torah's oral character and impact as practical knowledge by conveying both the primary and secondary intention. Mendelssohn reiterated his conviction that these intentions do not contradict but alternate. In those cases where he was unable to render both intentions, he adhered to the primary one. If rabbinic tradition endorsed the secondary, homiletical meaning and he was unable to convey both, then he translated according to tradition.[85] In other words, Mendelssohn gave precedence to the literal meaning, yet where translation posed an unavoidable choice he accepted tradition's verdict.

As translator and exegete, Mendelssohn made the accents one of his chief guides to literal meaning. His reliance on the accents had precedents: some medieval exegetes had made frequent use of them; Ibn Ezra had made extensive use of them; others had written treatises about them.[86] Mendelssohn used accents more systematically than his predecessors, employing them to establish the meaning of words, the connection between words, the positioning of clauses, and the meaning of entire passages.[87] While Mendelssohn's use of accents to ascertain the meanings of individual words and clauses is too technical to discuss here, we can mention two important passages we have already considered. He used the accents to show that the "wonder" of Exodus 3:12 was not Moses' embassy, "as the majority of exegetes have interpreted," but rather the two promises that God made.[88] He also used the accents to demonstrate that the first two commandments in Exodus 20:2 were separated from the others.[89] Mendelssohn also employed the accents to highlight the oral quality of the text by taking account of the emotions and inflections they conveyed. In a number of cases he introduced exclamation points in the German translation to capture the emotions they communicated, while elsewhere he tried to render the pictorial or mimetic qualities they contained.[90]

In translating Mendelssohn was also acutely aware that the structure of the Hebrew language was fundamentally different from German. In the last section of his introduction to the Pentateuch, entitled "The Parts of Speech and Their Uses in Language," he provided a concise if detailed account of the grammatical principles informing his translation and commentary.[91] This section drew on Maimonides' *Logical Terms* and his own commentary, combining logic and grammar. It revealed the connection between the revival of Hebrew philosophy and biblical exegesis as well as the continuity of Mendelssohn's endeavors.

Mendelssohn asserted that without a knowledge of grammar, God's word, both literal and homiletical, remained incomprehensible. Grammar alone unlocks the tradition of Jewish scriptural transmission, and it is this tradition that prevents the Jews from being "like a blind man in the dark" (the same traditional metaphor Mendelssohn had applied to logic in the introduction to the *Logical Terms*; see chapter 2 above).[92] This need for grammar is especially acute in translation, which requires a thorough knowledge of both Hebrew and the language into which one is translating. Mendelssohn therefore undertook to delineate the singular nature of Hebrew vis-à-vis German: one encounters the recurring phrase "such is the case in all the vernaculars known to me, but in the holy language . . ."[93]

To take a few examples. After an explanation of subject and predicate and the difference between a "trinary" sentence (in which subject, predicate, and the connection or extension each has its own word) and a "binary" sentence (in which the predicate and its extension are combined in one word), Mendelssohn argues that Hebrew is able to use a binary sentence where other languages must employ a trinary (e.g., for "I will grow": Hebrew: *egdol*; German: *ich werde gross*). The translator must be careful to convert the binary Hebrew sentence into a trinary German one.[94] Similarly, in Hebrew both the adjective and the predicate follow the gender and number of the subject (for "the large man" Hebrew has *ha-ish ha-gadol*); in German the adjective changes according to the subject (German: *der grosse Mann*) while the predicate does not (*der Mann ist gross*).[95] Again, in the construct state in Hebrew the associated noun changes whereas in German the noun itself changes (e.g., for "the children of one man": Hebrew: *bnei ish ehad*; German: *Kinder eines Mannes*).[96] Finally, in passive constructions in Hebrew the subject is an accusative whereas in German the subject is a nominative (e.g., for "the apple is eaten": Hebrew: *ha-tapuach neekhal*; German: *der Apfel wird gegessen*).

In explaining the grammar of Hebrew vis-à-vis German, Mendelssohn obviously used a good deal of German (in Hebrew characters). He not only gave copious examples to exemplify his points, but here, as in the *Logical Terms,* he gave the German and often the Latin equivalents for grammatical terms. Even where he simply explained Hebrew grammar without comparison with German, he gave the German equivalents

of his examples as preparation for the Pentateuch translation.[97] He
patently aimed to teach the skills that would reveal the practical knowledge of the Torah. The translation, commentary, and introduction all
shared this goal.

> The reader will note that in many places in our commentary we have grasped
> the meaning of the text by employing these principles [of grammar]. For this
> reason I have decided that here was the time and place to give these princi-
> ples and issues a clear exposition in the introduction to the book, so that they
> will enter the heart of the student and will be preserved and inscribed there,
> before he comes to the passages of the book which are explicated through
> them.[98]

As he was thoroughly convinced of the indispensability of grammar, he
recommended that students spend an hour per day studying it (he had
recommended an hour per week for logic in the introduction to *Logical
Terms*): were they to do so for two years, they would be able to understand the Bible and the commentators without difficulty.[99]

Mendelssohn dealt with grammatical issues throughout the commentary. In Genesis 1:1 he analyzed the Hebrew word (*et*) that accompa-
nies a direct object, explaining that the German equivalent could be
either nominative or accusative. He cited passages from elsewhere in the
Bible to illustrate the various uses of the word and reminded his readers
to remember this important grammatical rule.[100] In Exodus 7:14 he returned to an issue he had treated in the grammatical section of the introduction, namely, those peculiar Hebrew verbs that indicate a state of
being rather than change. He cited additional instances from elsewhere
in the Bible and added that it was a form of eloquence in biblical Hebrew to put such verbs in the past rather than the present tense.[101] In
Exodus 39:28, finally, Mendelssohn explained the construct state.[102]

The degree of Mendelssohn's commitment to grammar can be seen in
his treatment of anthropomorphisms. How one reconciled corporeal im-
ages with divine incorporeality was a litmus test of exegetical method.
In Exodus 3:8 ("And I have *come down* to deliver them out of the hand
of the Egyptians") Mendelssohn argued that the verb that seemed to indicate God's physical motion, that is, descend, could also mean engagement with an issue or thought humbler than God, that is, condescend.
Mendelssohn therefore asserted that Maimonides' philosophical method
for dealing with anthropomorphisms in the *Guide of the Perplexed* was
mistaken; instead, he agreed with Rashbam who simply relied on the literal meaning as explained by grammar.[103] Mendelssohn continued this
line of thought in another passage (Exodus 19:20). Citing Ibn Ezra, he

argued that all language is the language of mankind. When people try to explain something lower than themselves they necessarily elevate it (for example, "the earth opened its mouth," Numbers 16:32); when they try to explain something more elevated than themselves they necessarily diminish it, which is the reason for all anthropomorphic references to God. In this passage as well ("And the Lord came down on Mount Sinai") Mendelssohn endorsed Rashbam's view: God's descending is actually His condescending.[104]

Mendelssohn offered similar explanations for other anthropomorphisms. He asserted that the verse "two tablets of stone written with God's finger" (Exodus 31:18) is an explanation "after the manner of men" intended to show that there was no human participation: it was "the desire and will of God alone," for "no action of man participated in it and no action of any creatures had a part in it."[105] Similarly, the phrase "face to face" (Exodus 33:11) does not mean that Moses literally saw God's face, but rather that "the speech came to him plainly, in waking and in sight, and not in a dream and night vision."[106]

"Connectedness"—denoting the logic, context, and structure that constitute units of meaning—was a key to literal meaning for Mendelssohn. He had lamented the failure of earlier exegetes to study it in the case of Ecclesiastes and in his own commentary had offered a corrective.[107] In his Pentateuch translation and commentary he systematically studied "connectedness" at a number of levels, since he was concerned with establishing meaning in all aspects of the text, whatever its form and content.

A critical problem for the translator and exegete was the paratactic syntax in the Bible: most clauses and sentences were connected with a simple "and" (the Hebrew letter *vav*). It was therefore left to the translator or exegete to decide the precise meaning of the conjunctions. Mendelssohn scrupulously distinguished the various sorts of conjunctions— the *vav* of continuity, division, condition—and translated accordingly: continuity became "and," division "or," condition "if."[108] The ambiguity extended beyond the conjunctions themselves: the relationships of subordination, causality, and sequence in time in various clauses were also left to the exegete's judgment. Here again Mendelssohn carefully analyzed the relationships according to the accents and the opinions of earlier exegetes before introducing the adverbs (such as "so," "thus," "subsequently," "beforehand," "en route," "namely," "in this way," "once," "finally," "at last") and conjunctions (like "because," "since," "then," "hence") that would clarify the German translation of a passage.[109] In keeping with his own pronouncements on translation, especially the model of Onkelos's Aramaic translation, Mendelssohn also rearranged the order of clauses, sometimes introducing parentheses, in order to render the meaning of passages, although in doing so he relied heavily on the accents and the opinions of earlier exegetes.[110]

In some instances Mendelssohn also introduced interpolations. In his translation of and commentary on the story of the Golden Calf, for example, in which he relied on Judah Halevi, Ibn Ezra, and Nahmanides, Mendelssohn contended that Aaron agreed to make the Golden Calf because the original intention was that it be a substitute for Moses, who had guided the Israelites in the desert and had now disappeared without a trace on the mountain: the people wanted "another Moses."[111] The Israelites initially had no desire to be released from worship of God and Aaron had no reason to refuse their request. Only subsequently did some Israelites begin to see the calf as a replacement for God. To make sure the reader did not miss this point, Mendelssohn inserted a parentheses in the translation (Exodus 32:5): "that they namely accepted the calf not as a guide but rather as a God."[112] Similarly, in the matter of *lex talionis* ("an eye for an eye"; Exodus 21:34–35), Mendelssohn discussed the views of numerous exegetes (Saadya, Nahmanides, Ibn Ezra, Rashi, and Kimhi) and the Talmud in order to justify his translation according to rabbinic law: the plantiff is due monetary compensation. To make this interpretation clear in the translation, Mendelssohn interpolated at the beginning of Exodus 21:24, "for legal purposes," and at the end of the passage (Exodus 21:25), "therefore the perpetrator is obligated to give money for it."[113]

"Connectedness" for Mendelssohn also applied to the structure of narrative. The key to biblical narrative for Mendelssohn was the principle of "general and particular," which he derived from a rabbinic source and from Rashi.[114] He considered this principle one of his most powerful exegetical tools.

> Keep this rule in mind since it is an essential and central principle for understanding the Bible. Using it allows us to comprehend several passages in the Bible which otherwise would entirely elude comprehension. In some instances all the exegetes wearied and these mighty men did not succeed in finding the literal meaning of the Bible. If you remember this method by which the Torah is explicated you will find them to be simple matters easily susceptible to understanding, as you will see, God willing, in this commentary in a number of places.[115]

Mendelssohn saw this principle at work in the first two verses of Genesis: the first verse is the "general" statement, the rest of the Bible the "particular" that explains it, though only one part of it. Mendelssohn asserts that the conjunction that begins the second verse ("And the earth") "resumes the narrative"—and he finds support for this view in the accents. The phrase thus means "But as for the earth that I mentioned"; that is, it refers to the "earth" in "God created the heavens and the earth," whereas the "heavens" receive no discussion whatsoever. The entire Bible is in fact devoted to the "earth," or, as Mendelssohn put it, "the world of existence and corruption which is subject to man."[116] Mendelssohn argues that the story of the creation of mankind is similarly structured around a general statement ("Let us create man in our image") followed by the particulars, such as the creation of Adam or the creation of Eve.[117] In a number of passages Mendelssohn explained the grammatical construction of this principle; namely, the connection of the general and particular was indicated by the addition of a particular Hebrew letter (lamed).[118]

Mendelssohn used this principle to solve some difficult cases as well. In the account of Moses ascending Mount Sinai to receive the tablets of the Law (Exodus 24:13–19), there was a knotty chronological problem: Were the six days that the cloud covered the mountain (verse 16) part of the forty days (verse 18), or were they separate and anterior? Ibn Ezra had opted for the latter, yet this solution seemed to entail a number of intractable problems. Mendelssohn asserted that this view

> did not suffice to elucidate appropriately the connectedness of the text and the duplication of statements. If, however, we explain the text as a "general statement" followed by a "particular," as is the manner of stories [i.e., narrative in the Bible]—and we have already recorded this in the introduction to the book ["Light for the Path"] and in a few places in the commentary— the connectedness and order of the verses are explained without any strain whatsoever.[119]

Mendelssohn employed another principle to explain a similar difficulty with chronology. When and why did Jethro's visit to Moses (Exodus 18) take place? Mendelssohn cited the contrasting rabbinic opinions (from the Mekhilta): some said Jethro came because of the Exodus from Egypt, others because of the war against Amalek, still others because of the giving of the Torah at Sinai. Another problem was the length of the visit: How long did he stay? Was he present at the revelation at Sinai? Mendelssohn argued that there were problems with all the interpretations, including those of Nahmanides and Rashbam. Nevertheless, he argued that Jethro had come prior to Sinai but remained during the giving of the Torah. Mendelssohn stressed the continuance of the story in accordance with the principle of biblical narrative.

We must admit that this entire story did not take place at one time. Rather, once the Bible had begun the story of Jethro it completed the story in order not to pause in the middle. For this is the manner of the Bible [in narrating a story]. In fact Jethro accompanied Israel from Refidim to Sinai to accept the Torah.[120]

Mendelssohn attempted to discover the compositional principles of all forms of biblical exposition, including such genres as genealogy. He adopted Ibn Ezra's insight that genealogy followed the vertical line: even if the members of the horizontal line were included, longevity was given only for the direct descendants (Exodus 6:14–26). He adopted Rashbam's insight that the direct vertical record structured other biblical genealogies, reaching backward to the patriarchs and forward to Joshua, Judges, and Kings.[121]

Mendelssohn also discovered principles in the structure of legislation. When God renewed the covenant of Abraham with Isaac, for example, instructing him not to go to Egypt to escape the famine, God promised to multiply Israel's descendants and give him the land because Abraham had "obeyed My voice and kept My charge, My commandments, My statutes, and My laws" (Genesis 26:5). Mendelssohn asserted that the accents showed this passage to be structured as a general statement followed by three particulars. "My charge" was a "general term for every injunction that informs man of an obligation to act that is incumbent upon him" and which also serves as the common basis of the others. The three particulars each represent a different sort of charge. "Commandments" are those performed out of desire derived from reverence and honor, as in the relationship of a son to a father. "Statutes" are those performed out of fear of punishment, as in the relationship of master to slave or ruler to nation. "Laws" are those performed for the welfare of the performer, as in the relationship of teacher to student. Divine law incorporated all three of these aspects, and for the divine legislator there was no distinction between them. Mendelssohn translated the passage accordingly, separating the general term from the particulars with the adverb "namely" (to wit: "my charge, namely, my commandments, my statutes, and my laws"). He reiterated the argument he had made elsewhere that performance of the Commandments, rather than understanding, was crucial: "In his capacity as man, the commandment is to perform them."[122]

With regard to the Decalogue he relied on Ibn Ezra and Nahmanides to discern a parallel pattern of descent and ascent. The gravity of sin descends from the First Commandment: not believing in God is graver than believing in other Gods and polytheism; the sin of polytheism is graver than the sin of taking God's name in vain. The ability of man to resist sin ascends from the last commandment, with it and the first being the foundations of them all.

> He who does not covet anything that is not his will never harm a fellow human being, since it is as a result of coveting that one is led to deal falsely and to lie, to steal and to murder, to commit adultery, to desecrate the Sabbath and holidays and to humiliate parents; and one will [inevitably] be led to hate mankind and envy others. He who is not covetous will love mankind and honor them, and he will be freed of worries, sorrows, and sighs. He will trust in the Lord his God to sustain him, and will cast his burden upon Him [paraphrasing Psalms 55:23]. The injunctions "I" [am the Lord your God] and "do not covet" are like keys to all the other commandments. They are the beginning and the end.[123]

Mendelssohn's interpretation of the last commandment was his own; reason was to guide desire, as he had argued in explicating Genesis. The enormous weight he placed on the sin of covetousness was in keeping with his view of man as a social being, a view that pervaded his German and Hebrew works as well as his understanding of the Bible. That he regarded the First Commandment as the basis of all morality ("He who does not believe in his heart in God does not accept any commandment or obligation of the heart at all") fit his general philosophy and the idea of natural religion.

Mendelssohn devoted special attention to the structure of biblical poetry because he thought it the most concentrated and effective medium for transmitting practical knowledge. He had laid the groundwork for this understanding in his translation of Psalms; he now elaborated it. Mendelssohn first attempted to explain the art of biblical poetry at the song of Lemah (Genesis 4:23), which he called "the first poem that has reached us from those ancient times."

> The essence of the composition of poetry in the holy language [Hebrew] is to divide every extended idea into parts, and to compose from them short phrases of almost equal length—which are called verses or "doors"—and to place "door" next to "door" until they are parallel in meaning. This is the beauty of [biblical] poetry.[124]

Using examples from elsewhere in the Bible, Mendelssohn explained how the parallel verses ("doors") could have the same meaning, repeat the same words with slight, if significant variations, show opposed meanings in similar words, or employ ellipsis in the second verse. In his translation he arranged Lemah's poem in appropriate verse form.

At the Song of the Sea (Exodus 14:31–15:1) Mendelssohn gave an extended account of biblical poetry. Biblical poetry is different in kind from either Greek and Latin poetry or contemporary Hebrew poetry since all these others are intended "for the ear alone": when set to music they must be altered and their meanings changed. In contrast, biblical poetry is intended

> not for the ear of the auditor alone, but for his heart. [The words] will remain inscribed on the tablets [of his heart], in order to produce in him joy and sorrow, timidity or trust, fear or hope, love or hate, as is appropriate to the intention, and to install in him the honorable attributes and the elevated characteristics as stakes and nails that are implanted, as a peg that cannot be moved.[125]

Biblical poetry not only fit its music but the two worked together to affect the auditor's soul: "The goal of biblical music was to penetrate the powers of the soul, to rule its capacities, and to alter its characteristics as it wished." Such music was widely known in ancient times and used to disseminate God's word in Israel. It has since been lost "in the duration of the dispersion." All that remains are the names of the instruments. Today's music bears no resemblance to biblical music because it aims merely to give sensual pleasure.

Biblical poetry and music were able to transmit God's word or practical knowledge because meaning was preeminent: "The entire aim [of biblical music] was to preserve the meaning, to arouse it." Music enhanced the ability of the short, balanced lines of the poetry to be understood. Once set to music, such poetry presents the kind of arguments that are comprehended and remembered and thus form the core of practical knowledge—as Mendelssohn had advocated in his early philosophical works.[126] Moreover, because biblical poetry is a poetry of meaning, it is translatable: even if its form is lost, its meaning can be preserved and still produce the desired effect on "the soul of the auditor."[127]

Mendelssohn then dealt with the specifics of biblical poetry. He first quoted a long passage from Azaryah de Rossi's sixteenth-century treatise on the workings of Hebrew meter.[128] He then showed how parallelism was not only aesthetically pleasing but also "awakened its intention in the auditor's heart."[129] In addition, he discussed the practice of doubling. The origin of the practice was oral: the poem was originally sung by a chorus, for which the accents served as a guide (especially to the use of ellipsis), as the two sides of the chorus sang the parallel verses in turn. Such doubling contributed to understanding, explaining the subject of the poem, from all sides, to the point that no matter will remain opaque or disguised, and in this way the teaching will be clear, distinct and transparent . . . with the result that it will arouse the auditor's spirit to receive the matters and to accept them into his heart. There they will gain strength and will rule his inclinations, and will penetrate the attributes and characteristics of his soul, and will guide them as it sees fit.[130]

Mendelssohn concluded his account with an apology for his lengthy digression and a paean to the form and content of biblical poetry.

I have already gone beyond the limits set by my purpose. I have transgressed the law of brevity which I had laid down for my commentary, and this I did from love for the subject. For I have not found in any of the commentators on the Torah a statement that sufficiently explains the matter and makes the reader aware of the glorious beauty of the poems in the Holy Scriptures. I notice how the youth among our people "supply themselves with the products of the gentiles" and take pride in the poetic art of alien nations, as if to them had been given the splendor and precious grace of poetic art. Hence my heart was burning with the zeal to show that "as far as the heavens are high above the earth," so are the ways of our sacred poetry high above the ways of secular poetry. This is true not only in regard to the excellence of the poets, who are the efficient cause; or the exalted phrases, which are the material of the poems; or the purpose, which is to guide us to eternal happiness and true felicity through the sublime matters they treat, namely, the prophecies, promises, blessings, and praises of God that lead man to life eternal; it also holds for the form, that is, the arrangement, composition, and order of the words. In this respect as well, our sacred poetry is vastly superior in splendor and beauty to all other poems that are so highly praised.[131]

Mendelssohn's understanding of literal meaning and what he called the "profundity of literal meaning" demonstrate his complete immersion in the Jewish exegetical tradition. In important or disputed passages Mendelssohn cited the opinions of the major medieval literalist exegetes (especially Rashi, Ibn Ezra, Nahmanides, and Kimhi) and on occasion the opinions of later ones (such as Abrabanel, de Rossi, and Obadiah Seforno). Where appropriate, he also summarized or quoted the opinions of the rabbis in the Talmud or midrash. He usually cited the Aramaic translation of Onkelos, which rabbinic tradition deemed authoritative. In some instances he also cited the Aramaic translation of ben Usiel, and on occasion the translation that appears in the Babylonian and even the Jerusalem Talmud. He would always cite other passages throughout the Bible in which the word or phrase in question appeared in order to ascertain the precise meaning or usage. Finally, he would give his own opinion, either directly or by agreeing with one of the authorities cited, and often prefaced with the phrase "and such is the German translation."[132]

The sources cited also varied with the nature of the material. In the legal section of Exodus (21–24), Mendelssohn constantly referred to rabbinic sources, especially the midrashic compilation devoted to law, the *Mekhilta*. At the outset Mendelssohn quoted Rashbam's comment on this passage: his first task was to explicate the literal meaning of the text, yet the laws nonetheless took precedence. He invoked the authority of his illustrious predecessor Maimonides—"we will take shelter in the shade of the wings of this great eagle"—and then continued in the same spirit.

> We will not diverge to the right or to the left from the literal meaning of Scripture. Yet we have also not forgotten the principle enunciated in the introduction to the book on the difference between alternation and contradiction, namely, that the literal meaning of Scripture can alternate with the tradition of the rabbis in our commentary but it cannot contradict in regard to rules and laws. For when statements alternate it is not impossible that both of them are true, whereas with statements that contradict, if one is true the other is necessarily false. Therefore in every passage in which the discoveries of the literal meaning apparently contradict the traditions of our rabbis of blessed memory with regards to rules and laws, it is the duty of the commentator to leave the path of literal meaning and to follow the road of true tradition or to mediate between them, if such is possible. This is the covenant that we have made for our commentary and we will preserve it, just as the good hand of the Lord protects us.[133]

The net result is a commentary that could stand on its own since it was both a digest of literalist exegesis and a reference work to rabbinic tradition and biblical usage. That the *Book of the Paths of Peace* was intended to be a self-contained, contemporary guide to the Jewish exegetical tradition can be seen in the original edition: it included the Hebrew text, the German translation (in Hebrew letters), technical notes on the Masoretic text (Dubno's "Tikkun Soferim"), and the commentary. As one later observer aptly put it, Mendelssohn "had grasped the torch of the great medieval commentators and rekindled it."[134]

HISTORY

One consequence of the Bible's being the primary source of practical knowledge was the need to make its literal meaning known. Another consequence was that history became the medium of belief. Mendelssohn established and defended his belief in Judaism through history. Belief required "certainty," and Mendelssohn found such certainty in the historical facts of the Exodus, the public revelation at Sinai, and the chosenness of Israel. At the same time, the historical-critical school of biblical study posed a fundamental challenge to such an interpretation of the Bible. Mendelssohn answered that challenge with a defense of the Bible based on its oral nature.

In all of his pronouncements on the nature of exegesis, Mendelssohn recognized the significance of history. He had insisted as early as a 1757 review that in addition to a knowledge of grammar and aesthetics, the exegete must also have the ability to understand and differentiate the "genius of various peoples."[135] In a 1770 letter to Lessing he similarly insisted that one cannot discuss biblical figures without understanding the times in which they lived, meaning the "morals, customs, and knowledge" of the age.[136] During the Lavater affair, Mendelssohn had asserted that the exegete required "knowledge of man in his particular circumstances."[137] And in a letter of 1771 he argued that to understand a book of the Bible one needed to know its "author, times, and circumstances."[138]

This recognition of history appeared in a number of ways in Mendelssohn's exegesis. He recognized the historical situation (in the later parlance of biblical exegesis, the *Sitz im Leben*) that informed a particular passage. He had already employed this technique in his commentary to Ecclesiastes: he understood the verse "Cast your bread upon the waters" (11:1) as the king's advice to shipping merchants to increase the nation's riches.[139] He explained Moses' second approach to Pharaoh as belonging to the customs of the nation: since the Nile's alluvium was the source of the country's wealth and well-being, the pharaoh would pay a visit during the spring, and for that reason God told Moses to meet Pharaoh at the river.[140] Mendelssohn evinced a similar use of history as custom in his account of the commandment of the "fringed garment" (Numbers 15:39): Mendelssohn cited the ancient Peruvians as using knots and ties as a means to remember past events, and he suggested that the custom enjoined on Israel had a similar origin.[141] In his peroration to the Book of Exodus Mendelssohn asserted that there is a point of balance (or "border") in each society between necessity and luxury which must be understood "according to time and history."

> This border is not the same for each and every nation and language. It varies according to the success of the nation, the number of its inhabitants, the blessings of the land, and its relationship with the surrounding nations.[142]

Mendelssohn also understood the origins and transmission of the biblical text historically. In this regard Mendelssohn's use of history should be compared to contemporary biblical scholarship, especially the nascent "historical-critical" school of which Johann Gottfried Eichhorn was the preeminent representative. For Mendelssohn history guaranteed the text's purity; for the historical-critical school history was the source of its corruption. Eichhorn's *Introduction to the Old Testament* offered an introduction to the historical-critical view of the Bible; Mendelssohn's "Light for the Path" was an innovative defense of the traditional Jewish view.

Eichhorn championed the notion of "higher criticism," which he regarded as a means to rescue the Bible from theological dogma on the one hand and Enlightenment rationalism on the other.[143] By applying the methods that had been developed to study classical and profane literature, he treated the Bible as a human document that was the product of history.[144] He rejected divine origins in favor of the "documentary" hypothesis: on the basis of textual evidence he recognized Moses as having authored the Pentateuch by weaving together earlier accounts as well as by adapting the Egyptian culture, especially its legislation, in which he had been educated.[145] While Eichhorn acknowledged that the text was genuine, he asserted that it had suffered "manifold and irremediable" corruption.[146] That the text has survived at all was miraculous: how many texts of other ancient cultures were still extant?[147] That it was corrupt was inevitable—it had been shaped by centuries of history: "It was through the contributions of many hundreds of years that the Hebrew text finally reached the internal and external form in which it now stands before our eyes in manuscripts."[148] Were Moses "to rise from the dead" he would hardly recognize what we know as the text of the Bible.[149] That text emerged between the sixth and tenth centuries when Jewish students of the Bible, the Masoretes, divided the words, introduced punctuation and accents, and in general attempted to establish the text. That effort prevented further corruption but was not authoritative; the corruption long predated the Masoretes' work and could not be corrected by it.[150] Similarly, the medieval Jewish exegetes—and Eichhorn mentioned Ibn Ezra, Rashi, Maimonides, and Kimhi—had made contributions in collating manuscripts and studying the text according to the Masoretes, but they were not to be trusted.[151] Rather, Eichhorn argued that all existing methods of correcting mistakes (whether parallel passages in various translations, later divergences, or the Masoretic traditions) were insufficient. The contemporary exegete must rely on his experience and historical sense to suggest emendations: this was the method of "higher criticism."[152]

Mendelssohn had voiced his opposition to the "higher criticism" as early as 1773. After mentioning two biblical passages to which scholars had recently suggested emendations he wrote:

> I do not know in fact when we will get to the end of this audacity. In the meantime, so long as the fashion has the charm of novelty, one must allow it to take its course. In time people will lose their taste for it; and then it will be time to redirect them to the path of healthy reason.[153]

Mendelssohn's account of the biblical text in his introduction ("Light for the Path") and commentary is a restatement of Jewish tradition that used history to counter "higher criticism." Just as in his introduction to *Ecclesiastes* he had provided a natural explanation for the multiple modes of rabbinic interpretation, so here he offered a natural explanation for the authenticity of the biblical text. He defended the Jewish tradition of scriptural transmission and notation: the peculiar endowments that enabled Hebrew to retain its oral character also safeguarded the text from corruption. Eichhorn had argued for multiple sources. Mendelssohn propounded the traditional Jewish argument that God had spoken every word of the Torah to Moses, which he duly recorded.[154] The oral tradition had preserved the knowledge of the way God had spoken and thereby precluded the text's corruption. Even the first exile had not altered this, as Ezra restored knowledge of the oral tradition after returning from Babylonia. Only during the period of the Second Temple when Greek and Aramaic began to be used for sacred as well as profane purposes did a declining knowledge of Hebrew threaten the oral tradition and make its recording imperative. At that point the various notations began to be written down.[155] Eichhorn had asserted that the Masoretes had invented these notations:

> To attribute the origin of these notations to Moses and the author of the Old Testament is ludicrous; to attribute them to Ezra and the men of the great synagogue improbable. Their first appearance patently belongs in the period between Ezra and the Talmud.[156]

In contrast, Mendelssohn saw the Masoretes merely committing pre-existing oral traditions to writing. What saved the biblical text from corruption then was the oral tradition peculiar to Hebrew, the same oral tradition that also accounted for the richness of the Bible's literal meaning. Mendelssohn characterized this tradition as the advantage of "scribes" over mere "books."[157]

Eichhorn's entire argument showed the Bible to be a profane book whose text had suffered corruption and therefore required emendation.

Mendelssohn demonstrated that it was a sacred book that had escaped corruption by virtue of a singular oral tradition. Emendation was not only unnecessary but unthinkable.[158]

Eichhorn and Mendelssohn were no less at loggerheads in their views of the medieval exegetes. Eichhorn had acknowledged their relative merits but disputed their authority: "We do not rely on their judgment for our understanding of the present composition of the Hebrew text, but rather on what experience and critical investigation of it teach us."[159] Mendelssohn, as we have seen, deemed them "our eyes in the exegesis of Scripture."[160] Though he recognized their fallibility and did not hesitate to disagree, he felt duty bound to justify his interpretation in relationship to theirs.

Mendelssohn's effort to assert Jewish tradition against contemporary historical-critical scholarship can also be seen in his commentary. Eichhorn had qualified Israel's originality as a people by emphasizing its Egyptian and nomadic origins: Moses' contribution consisted in his ability to fuse the elements of his Egyptian education with his experience of nomadic life in Midian.[161] Mendelssohn did not dispute this claim of Egyptian influence; rather, he treated it as providential, making history the medium for God's intervention.

> The ideas of God are deep; who can fathom His secrets. . . . Perhaps God ordained that Moses would grow up in the palace of the King so that his soul would be at the highest level of study and custom, and not humbled and accustomed to slavery. Remember, he killed the Egyptian because of his violence and rescued the daughters of Midian from the shepherds who committed violence in watering their sheep from the drawn water. And one further matter: if he had grown up among his brethren and was known to them from his youth, they would not have venerated him because they would have considered him to be one of them.[162]

Eichhorn also attempted to show that the biblical text had been knit together from different "documents" distinguishable by the various names of God. The first and perhaps most important such seam occurred in the Creation story (Exodus 2:4).[163] Mendelssohn marshaled his most powerful exegetical techniques to argue that no such seam existed. He implied that the use of the different names of God (Genesis 1–2:3 vs. Genesis 2:4) had no historical significance—and thus did not serve as evidence of different documents—by asserting that "according to the literal meaning" the two names are the same: "God (*Adonai*) is the Lord (*Elohim*)." He then cited the rabbis: the different names of God refer to different attributes of his being, one to "justice," the other to "compassion." Here he combined literal meaning and homily to counter the historical-critical view.

Mendelssohn also used the idea of oral tradition.

> It is likely that the passage from "In the beginning" (Genesis 1:1) to "he had done" (Genesis 2:3) was known to some exceptional individuals from the days of the holy fathers, possibly from the days of Adam and Seth. This was an oral tradition passed from father to son in which the holy men would teach their sons and students the secret of Creation and the renewal of the world. In this way such belief spread to all corners of the earth, to every nation and language, to the point that one could not find a nation or language that does not have some knowledge, or at least a hint of it. The tradition was in part corrupted by the vanities of the overly wise and the deceptions of writers who . . . devised falsehoods in order to capture the hearts of the masses on whom the light of God's teaching had not shown. Truth became mixed with lies, and all that remained to them were a few hints that shined like a light in the darkness of night and gloom.[164]

Here was an oral tradition gone awry. The tradition was restored when God gave the correct story to Moses; it was preserved in its pristine state through the uncorrupted transmission of the Bible.

Mendelssohn also invoked his principle of the general and the particular. The account that begins in Genesis 2:3 is a "particular": it details the creation of mankind, which had only been related in a general way earlier (Genesis 1:26–31). What Eichhorn saw as two versions or independent sources of the Creation story Mendelssohn understood as integral parts of a single coherent account. While Mendelssohn made limited use of history in his exegesis, he resisted any attempt to employ it to question the integrity of the Masoretic text.[165]

History helped establish Mendelssohn's faith. He argued privately during the Lavater affair that the public revelation of the Law to the entire nation at Sinai was a source of certainty that grounded Jewish practice and belief.

> Although witnesses contradict one another so often, they are all agreed that once a "certain" Moses was ordered directly by God to free a "certain" people from slavery; that this ambassador of God realized his project before the eyes and against the will of a great and powerful nation, and thereby performed miracles that transcend all human concepts; that the legislator of nature appeared to this entire people, which was assembled in one location, in His full majesty and gave them laws. Many thousands of witnesses saw this divine manifestation with their eyes and related it to their children. All miracles that occurred, or are supposed to have occurred anywhere else in the world, do not compare with this great manifestation worthy of God. And this event is not contradicted by any legitimate witness known to us.

> Here I have a matter of history on which I can rely with certainty. I can
> proceed from it. What contradicts this matter of history is false.[166]

Mendelssohn made some of these same points in his commentary. To
the verse "You have seen what I did to the Egyptians" (Exodus 19:4),
Mendelssohn paraphrased the midrash from the *Mekhilta* to emphasize
the quality of direct witness: "This is not a tradition that you possess; I
do not dispatch words to you; I do not appoint witnesses. Rather 'You
have seen.'"[167] He similarly emphasized direct witness in the passage
"that the people may hear when I speak with you" (Exodus 19:9).

> They will actually hear with their own ears and not according to the word of
> a spokesman; and not on the basis of signs and wonders alone, rather with
> the auditory power of the ear since I am sending you to them to offer my
> Torah. For this reason they will also believe in you forever. If a prophet or
> the dreamer of a dream will rise up among them, even if he will produce a
> sign or a wonder in order to abrogate one of the laws of the Torah, they will
> not listen to him and will contradict him immediately, since your embassy to
> them has been validated by a proof which brooks no doubt or retort, that is,
> the evidence of the senses publicly known.[168]

The corollary to Israel's direct witnessing of God's revelation was
its chosenness. Mendelssohn focused on the historical fact of the Exodus from Egypt in his comment on the first verse of the Decalogue, "I
am the Lord your God who brought you forth from the land of Egypt
from the House of bondage" (Exodus 20:2). The purpose of the first
two commandments (see the section "Practical Knowledge" above) was
not to confer belief in God but to bind Israel to God's commandments
through the historical fact of the Exodus from Egypt.

> We are His people since He brought us out of Egypt from the House of
> bondage and performed all of these miracles; [we are] to be His chosen and
> treasured people among all the nations. He will rule us with His own glory,
> without the intermediary of an angel, official, or star. Behold, we are His ser-
> vants and are obligated to assume the yoke of His kingdom and His govern-
> ment, and to uphold His laws, and He commanded us not to worship any
> other besides Him . . . The Exodus from Egypt, from slavery to freedom, is
> the reason [that we are obligated to perform His commandments] . . . To us
> alone did God, may He be exalted, give His Torah, commandments, and laws
> and injunctions, for He is our king and our legislator, and it is incumbent on
> us to observe His laws and precepts.[169]

Following Nahmanides, Mendelssohn argued that these factors of
direct witness and chosenness combine in God's unmediated delivery of
the first two commandments to make Israel a nation of "prophets in the

belief in God and in the interdiction of idolatry."[170] Here was the foundation of Mendelssohn's faith.

Mendelssohn's use of history should be put in perspective. Mendelssohn was historical without being historicist: he acknowledged history in the Pentateuch rather than the Pentateuch as a product of history. He recognized that the Bible had emerged in an ancient and foreign setting that had influenced its contents and therefore had to be elucidated: history was a matter of the character and customs of different peoples at different times.[171] That recognition neither qualified the Bible's validity and divine content nor entailed examining its sources and dating but rather set the exegete's agenda of extracting practical knowledge through a comprehensive study of the literal meaning. The peculiar oral qualities of Hebrew had preserved the text and its literal meaning from corruption. History made it necessary for that meaning to be made available in various languages and cultural milieus: translation was entirely feasible, indeed, the tradition of Jewish biblical translation provided outstanding models. At the same time, the basis of Israel's belief were the historical facts of the Exodus, the revelation at Sinai, and Israel's chosenness.

In this approach to the Bible Mendelssohn showed a conservatism that set him apart from the mainstream Enlightenment of the 1770s and 1780s.[172] In fact, Mendelssohn's approach had remarkable affinities to the exegesis of the preeminent theological Wolffian of the 1730s and 1740s, Siegmund Jacob Baumgarten.

Baumgarten became an adherent of Wolff's philosophy almost from the start of his academic career. In an early systematic work he reconciled Wolff's philosophical method (the coherence of knowledge, in which all truths are connected as in a "chain") and many of his key ideas (the agreement of reason and revelation, the best of all possible worlds) with a transcendent Christian belief that was fully orthodox through the pietist notion that the true end of all theology is practical: it must provide a "vital knowledge" that promotes the "union" of man with God. In emphasizing practice, Baumgarten rejected the Protestant scholastic primacy of speculation.[173]

Baumgarten did not remain with this formulation, however. In the late 1730s and 1740s he discovered that Anglican apologists had found in history the most effective means to defend belief against the attacks of deists and freethinkers.[174] This discovery appealed to him yet challenged his Wolffianism. Wolff had deprecated history as offering facts without certainty. Baumgarten wanted history to offer precisely such certainty, albeit within the confines of Wolffian philosophy. He tried to find a solution in his exegetical method. Baumgarten argued that through the application of an exacting hermeneutical method designed along Wolffian lines "divine truth" could be extracted from the Bible. A rigorous investigation starting with language and metaphors and continuing to the situation of the speaker, his audience, and the prevailing circumstances would allow the exegete to analyze all the elements that linked the Bible to a particular time and place, that is, what made it historical. Once these aspects had been analyzed and the connections between them demonstrated—and such demonstration of coherence was the centerpiece of Wolffian method—then the exegete could proceed to ponder the question of ultimate purpose. For Baumgarten denied that every word of the Bible was literally inspired: rather, it was infallible for the revealed truths that bear on the "union" of man with God, that is, the truths that contribute to the practical core of Christianity. Yet the Bible could not be expected to serve as a textbook of philosophy or natural science and much of its content was of merely local interest.[175]

Mendelssohn used history in the 1770s and 1780s in much the same way as Baumgarten had in the 1730s and 1740s. By recognizing history in the Bible they were both able to find the "certainty" Wolffian philosophy demanded and to garner the divine practical truth they thought to be the Bible's true message. Yet there was an important difference here as well. Baumgarten had pioneered the use of history in his day. Mendelssohn was deliberately resisting contemporary historicism, such as Eichhorn's. Comparison to another biblical exegete, Johann David Michaelis, further clarifies Mendelssohn's stand.

We have encountered Michaelis before: in his earliest work (1759) he had defended the christological interpretation of Psalms. In his major work of the 1770s, *The Mosaic Law,* Michaelis subjected the Mosaic legislation, as the "remains of the most authentic legislative wisdom," to an entirely historicist examination. Unlike Greek law, Mosaic law had not received the attention it deserved, yet knowledge of it was essential to a "genealogy of law" in general.[176] Michaelis therefore studied the Mosaic legislation using the categories Montesquieu had employed in his study of law, that is, climate and geography, morals and manners. He understood the law as a human creation. Moses used older legislative systems, especially the Egyptian and the nomadic. It was also entirely historical. Michaelis saw the Mosaic law "not as the best categorically, but under the prevailing conditions; not the best in a Platonic, but in an Israelite commonwealth."[177] Moreover, Michaelis limited the validity of these laws: "The laws of Moses conformed to the circumstances of the Israelites and are therefore not to be introduced to peoples living under different circumstances."[178] Yet these laws were also of limited duration and subject to change over time: "Even were God himself to write a 'politics,' the laws would be different according to circumstances, indeed, they would change over time and through time."[179] Michaelis's historicist position also led him to reject explicitly the rabbinic interpretation of the Mosaic law: "The oral traditions of in part ignorant rabbis which are collected in the Talmud can teach us the common law of the Jews in the time in which they [the rabbis] lived, but not the meaning of Moses' [laws]."[180] Michaelis historicized both the Bible's contents and its subsequent interpretation. In contrast, Mendelssohn asserted the absolute validity of biblical law for the Jews as well as deeming that law and its subsequent rabbinic interpretation one and the same. In his revival of biblical exegesis as in his revival of Hebrew philosophy, Mendelssohn was the Jewish counterpart to the theological Wolffians.

Mendelssohn's Bible project was integral to the Haskalah, and also characteristic of the religious Enlightenment. Mendelssohn aimed to reintroduce the independent study of the Bible into a curriculum dominated by Talmud study and Kabbalah. Reform Catholicism also attempted to revive the study of the Bible as part of its effort to replace baroque piety and scholasticism with a curriculum based on the Bible, patristics, and church history. Mendelssohn wanted the Bible to be understood properly, and his translation and commentary served the Hebrew original. The premier Reform Catholic pedagogue in central Europe translated the Bible into German for Catholic schoolchildren in the 1760 and 1770s because he wanted them to be able to study directly the key source of their faith.[181] Similarly, the 1774 reform of seminary education in Austria introduced a curriculum—under the slogan "to the sources" (*ad fontes*)—that rested on a foundation of direct study of the Bible and patristics as well as church history and theological literature.[182]

In the *Book of the Paths of Peace* Mendelssohn embraced history as a basis of faith, yet he rejected a historicism that subjected faith and the sources of faith to notions of process and development. In so doing he distanced himself from much contemporary exegesis and once again demonstrated his affinity to the theological Wolffians.

RECEPTION

Mendelssohn had conceived of the *Book of the Paths of Peace* as a means to instruct Jewish youth, and that pedagogical intention was at the heart of the work's early unfavorable reception. The opponents of the Haskalah attacked the book as the epitome of the Haskalah's pedagogical program, especially the attempt to promote knowledge of the vernacular. The attacks did not endure. In the 1790s editors and publishers began to recast the work as a pious text, following the pattern of Mendelssohn's translation of Psalms. Once recast, the *Book of the Paths of Peace* enjoyed long use, many reprintings, and wide acceptance.

Accompanying the first edition were a number of approbations from local rabbis who supported Mendelssohn's pedagogical intention. They pointed to the poor state of the study of the Hebrew language and the Bible among Jews; the deficiencies of the Yiddish translations and the dangers of the Christian ones (the rabbinic court of Berlin saw Mendelssohn's translation as an attempt "to rescue the youth of Israel from danger"); and Mendelssohn's reliance on rabbinic tradition to ascertain the literal meaning of the text.[183]

This positive view did not go uncontested. An influential if fleeting opposition did emerge, although a ban was never pronounced and the book was never burned. Perhaps the most famous instance was in Altona. The chief rabbi, Raphael Cohen, was known for his hostility to secular studies and his readiness to use the ban—though the political authorities, as we shall see in chapter 8 quashed his efforts. A newspaper report (subsequently retracted) that he was intending to pronounce a ban had the beneficial result that Mendelssohn acted preemptively and enlisted the king of Denmark (Altona was a Danish possession) and the Royal Library as subscribers.[184]

The first direct attacks on the book were a response to the controversy surrounding the emperor Joseph II's Edict of Toleration (1781–1782) and proposed educational reforms (see chapter 9). In a pamphlet suggesting a major reform of the curriculum of Jewish schools, Naphtali Herz Wessely (whose work on biblical synonyms was discussed in chapter 4) insulted the rabbinate and presumed to usurp their position as leaders.[185] At the same time he lavishly praised the *Book of the Paths of Peace* for setting a new standard in Jewish pedagogy. Wessely inadvertently made Mendelssohn a target for some of the ire he himself had aroused.

The first public assault came from the rabbi of Frankfurt, Pinhas ha-Levi Horowitz, who in a public sermon (June 1782) derided the *maskilim* as evil and Mendelssohn's commentary as fantasy and nonsense.[186] The chief rabbi of Prague, Ezekiel Landau, who at first had supported Mendelssohn, now attacked him for making the Torah a "maidservant to the German tongue": by using such difficult German, Mendelssohn forced students to concentrate on that language instead of the contents of the Bible. Landau subsequently endorsed a new word-by-word Yiddish translation.[187]

This sort of opposition remained vocal in the early 1780s yet appears to have subsided as the *Book of the Paths of Peace* was gradually turned into a traditional text and absorbed into the curriculum as *the* study edition of the Bible. The rudiments of this process can already be seen in the editions of the 1790s and the early nineteenth century. The original edition contained the Hebrew text, the German translation (in Hebrew characters), the *Biur*, and Dubno's notes on the Masoretic text. Subsequent editions added the authoritative Aramaic translation of Onkelos, Rashi's commentary, and the division of readings for the Sabbath and holidays while omitting Dubno's notes.[188] Other editions also included the liturgy.[189] While these modifications ran counter to Mendelssohn's aim of making the *Biur* an independent digest of the literalist tradition, they helped to make the work acceptable and useful to a pious audience. Indeed, the various editions of the *Book of the Paths of Peace* demonstrate that the work was widely accepted in orthodox and traditional circles throughout central and eastern Europe during the nineteenth century. Prominent rabbis subscribed to and wrote approbations for new editions and the book was used for pious study by children and adults. Even many vociferous opponents of religious reforms were to be found among Mendelssohn's subscribers and readers. In the case of Holland the book stimulated a veritable renaissance of biblical study.[190]

In contrast, the most consistent opposition in central Europe emanated first from the vigorous spokesman of Orthodoxy, the rabbi of Pressburg, Moses Sofer (1763–1839), though he exercised toleration when he discovered that his most eminent student, Moses Schick, studied the book. Another opponent was the founder of ultraorthodoxy, Akiva Josef Schlesinger (1837–1922), who exercised no such toleration.[191] In eastern Europe the Hasidic movement consistently opposed all of Mendelssohn's works as the symbol of Haskalah, whereas opposition from non-Hasidic or mitnagdic circles appears to have been concentrated on the official edition the Russian government published (Vilna, 1852) as part of its program of educational reform.[192]

PART THREE

Politics

The fact that "Germany" was a mosaic of some three hundred polities belonging to the Holy Roman Empire affected the political thinking of the German Enlightenment. In the face of the imperial pretensions of the Holy Roman Empire, Enlightenment thinkers regarded the states as the guarantors of freedom as well as of order, even if their rule was despotic, as was so often the case in the eighteenth century. Yet those same thinkers increasingly articulated ideas of individual and natural rights. In consequence, the onus of political thought in the German Enlightenment was to balance the claims of individual rights against the demands of the absolutist state.[1]

Mendelssohn was politically engaged virtually his entire career as a thinker and writer, and his thinking focused on this dialectic of state and individual rights, if with a significant difference: he addressed the issue from the position of a Jew living on sufferance. From the outset his political engagement involved questions about Judaism, whether its liturgy, law, or ritual practice.

Mendelssohn's thought developed in two phases. At first he used Enlightenment ideas to intercede with the absolutist state on behalf of various Jewish communities. The major political issues of Judaism in his day were the practice of early burial and the jurisdiction of the courts. In keeping with a shift in emphasis in German political thought, Mendelssohn later advocated legal equality, articulating a politics based on ideas of natural right which resembled the position of many theological Wolffians. Here the issue was whether the very nature of Judaism constituted an insurmountable obstacle to emancipation. Yet Mendelssohn's advocacy of rights was also a novel way of reinstating the dualism of the autonomous community, that is, of reconciling the positions of the intercessor and the theological Wolffian.

CHAPTER SEVEN

Intercession

Mendelssohn followed in the footsteps of his ancestor, Moses Benjamin Wulff, in serving his fellow Jews as an intercessor. Acting as lobbyist, petitioner, or spokesman with the powers-that-be to negotiate the best terms or to avert harsh measures and persecution was a recognized office among European Jews.[1] Moses Benjamin Wulff's ability to act as an intercessor was typical of the court Jews of the seventeenth and eighteenth centuries: it resulted from his wealth and service to a sovereign. In contrast, Mendelssohn's ability to intercede was unprecedented, since it rested on his prominence as a philosopher and man of letters. The authority he brought to his office was intellectual and moral, and from the start he employed Enlightenment categories.

The intercessor's undertaking rested on two assumptions: he recognized the necessity of cooperation, if not of a tactical alliance, with the political authorities, yet he understood his own actions as well as the consequences of his alliance with the authorities to be subordinate to God's will.[2] Mendelssohn articulated both of these assumptions early in his career. In an important passage in *Logical Terms* (1760–1761), he proclaimed his absolute obedience to Jewish law but declared its irrelevance to political matters because of the Jews' dispersion.

> For the Torah that Moses commanded us straightens our path in matters pertaining to God and in matters of justice between fellowmen, and we have no other duty but to contemplate it and to learn from it the actions which each of us must perform and by which we must abide. Yet in governance of the state, the Torah is of no aid and no purpose so long as Israel remains

dispersed among the nations and no leader in the nation or ruler of state is drawn from among our number.[3]

He thus renounced any presumption to Jewish political leadership, let alone sovereignty. Such a renunciation had direct implications for belief in the Messiah: while Mendelssohn steadfastly believed in the coming of the Messiah, he deferred his hopes from an imminent to a more distant future: "Succour your people, the remnant of Israel, and may the Redeemer come to Zion in our days."[4] Mendelssohn's renunciation also implied obedience to the powers-that-be. In an explanation of the term "law" in his commentary on Maimonides' *Logical Terms*, Mendelssohn asserted that the law of the state required obedience even if the subject could not fathom the justification.[5] He endorsed heteronomy in politics as well as in religion. In his commentary to Ecclesiastes (1768), he acknowledged that the sovereign's authority, whether justified by divine right or by right of law, must remain unquestioned.

> No one can judge the King aside from the ruler of all the earth. . . . It is an important principle of politics that the nation does not have the right to judge the King's deeds. For the King is the judge of the nation and not vice versa. Were this not the case there would be no end of rebels against the King. . . . There is none superior to him save God.[6]

The sovereign was of course subordinate to God and his providence; obedience to him and to God were one and the same. Mendelssohn made this point the centerpiece of the thanksgiving sermon he composed at the behest of the Berlin Jewish community after the Prussian victory over Austria at Leuthen in 1757. Mendelssohn maintained that this miraculous victory was an act of God, since all miracles, indeed all events, are divinely ordained. However great Frederick's military prowess, God was responsible. The victory was a cause not to celebrate human achievement but to thank God.[7] Mendelssohn similarly emphasized the role of providence in the sermon he was commissioned to write to celebrate the end of the Seven Years' War and the Peace of Hubertusburg in 1763. While Frederick had brilliantly discharged his duty, it was God, as a God of peace, who had turned the king's heart back to peace and created the conditions in which love of fellowman could be realized.[8]

These views were at one with Mendelssohn's Jewish thinking. An insistence on the divine ordination of events and the role of providence was central to Mendelssohn's understanding of Judaism as well as of natural religion. Professions of obedience and loyalty to the powers-that-be were a time-honored tradition that underpinned the politics of the autonomous community and the office of the intercessor.[9]

Necessity was the mother of intercession. The first community to call on Mendelssohn for assistance was Altona in 1769. Its rabbinic court had been accused of defaming Christianity in the community calendar and punitive action had been initiated. Mendelssohn was asked for advice and aid. His efforts were apparently successful, since a letter from the community offered profuse thanks. Mendelssohn's letters have not survived, yet the community's letter of gratitude significantly asserts loyalty to a righteous king as well as the role of providence: "The heart of Kings is in God's hands."[10]

Three years later Mendelssohn received an urgent letter from the community of Mecklenburg-Schwerin. The duke had issued a rescript on April 30, 1772, prohibiting the Jewish practice of early or same-day burial. The order commanded that since early burial was not essential to Jewish religious belief, in accord with contemporary medical practice a three-day waiting period would be instituted to prevent the burial of the comatose or others who exhibited symptoms of death but nevertheless remained alive.[11] The community protested the order and offered to procure certification of death from a doctor prior to burial. In response to that concession the duke temporarily suspended the rescript and gave the community three weeks to provide evidence that the proscription of early burial was contrary to fundamental religious beliefs. On the recommendation of Jacob Emden of Altona, one of the foremost rabbis of the day, who was first approached for a letter of support and in fact provided one, the rabbi of Schwerin wrote to Mendelssohn, imploring him to act as a "patron and advocate" by combining his command of the vernacular and knowledge of Jewish law to compose a letter that would convince the duke to change his mind.[12]

Mendelssohn's reply epitomized the politics of intercession. He attempted to find a compromise that would satisfy loyalty to God and the sovereign. Mendelssohn used the language of the Enlightenment to acknowledge that the duke's actions were taken in the best interests of his subjects: "This gracious order has the highest purpose of serving exclusively and only our own good, our own security." Yet he also asserted that "according to our religious laws we are obligated not to allow the dead to lie at home longer than is necessary."[13] From the outset Mendelssohn distinguished between "early removal" and "early burial," defending the former. Early removal of the dead is integral to Jewish belief, he argued, having both biblical foundations and rabbinic specifications. Since Jews were no longer able to practice the laws of purity as Moses had prescribed, they had to rely on the rabbis' interpretations. He invoked his characteristic argument for heteronomy yet gave notice of his reservations.

> Although this ruling [of the rabbis on the question of early burial] seems to be neither fully demonstrable nor beyond all objection, we as Jews are obligated by our present religious constitution fully to subject ourselves to the rabbis' statutes, to live according to their precepts, and to guide ourselves in all our actions according to their prescriptions and standards.[14]

The duke had granted the Jews the privilege of religious liberty; it was their duty to exercise it. Mendelssohn further conceded that rabbinic law recognized exceptions. Were even the slightest trace of life observable, then

> the Bible and the Rabbis agree with healthy reason and Your Highness's conscientious sovereign care to leave the dead unburied; it would be a shameful misuse of rabbinic teaching were we to extend it [early burial] to these cases as well.[15]

While acknowledging the exceptions, Mendelssohn argued that in most cases a few hours sufficed to ascertain death, and on that basis he proposed the compromise already in force: the Jews would continue early burial, but interment would be permitted only after a recognized physician had certified the death.

The duke found Mendelssohn's argument compelling, and on the strength of it he rescinded the original rescript and issued a new one (August 31, 1772): the Jews were to continue their traditional practice but were to obtain a physician's certification prior to burial.[16] Mendelssohn's intercession was successful and the official matter was put to rest.[17]

Yet the matter of early burial remained alive in another form. When Mendelssohn sent his compromise proposal to the Schwerin community, he also enclosed a Hebrew letter to the community leaders expressing his reservations about early burial. He confessed his inability to comprehend the leaders' consternation over the duke's rescript. He reproved them for treating the matter as an emergency and attempted to prove that there was rabbinic support for delayed burial. Should the duke not rescind his order, the community should abide by it. Mendelssohn also made this case to Rabbi Jacob Emden of Altona. As we have seen, the Schwerin community had originally approached Emden for a letter of support proving that early burial was essential to Judaism;

while he had recommended Mendelssohn, he had also hastily penned the testimonial.[18] In the meantime, Emden had had no reply from Schwerin, and he wrote to Mendelssohn asking for news. In replying Mendelssohn made his case for the ancient practice and asked Emden, whose learning he admired, for his opinion.

Just as he had tried to demonstrate the convergence of Wolffian philosophy and Judaism in his philosophy and exegesis, Mendelssohn now asserted the convergence of early Jewish practice and rabbinic principle on the one side with contemporary medical practice on the other: "Our Sages and the doctors are of one mind."[19] He tried to show that a concern with premature burial had informed Jewish practice from the start. His argument combined biblical example with rabbinic precept. In ancient times Jews had immediately removed the dead from their homes but had kept them in caves for three days where they were watched by guards. This practice had embodied two principles. Immediate removal of the dead preserved the purity of the living; he understood this to be the primary justification for the practice of early burial. Guarding the corpse for three days implemented the principle of "saving a life" by guaranteeing that premature burial would not take place. Mendelssohn advocated the revival of this ancient practice by the erection of morgues in cemeteries: this practice, which had been introduced by doctors in the 1760s and 1770s concerned with premature burial, would make it possible both to separate the dead from the living—thereby upholding the principle of purity—and to keep the corpse under surveillance—thereby precluding premature interment. He also cited a further reason. The well-established rabbinic principle of "saving a life" overrides all other considerations. Since rabbis in the past had postponed burials for various minor reasons, such as honoring the dead or awaiting the arrival of relatives, the compelling reason of "saving a life" justified delay. Mendelssohn was ready to accept the judgment of contemporary medicine that early burial put life at risk because he thought that this had been Judaism's view from the start.[20]

Mendelssohn thus made his case on three occasions. Despite differences of emphasis in the three pronouncements, his argument was consistent. In his public memorandum to the duke he upheld the importance of early removal on the basis of the principle of purity and stressed that in most instances death could be ascertained within a few hours, so that the concerns of contemporary doctors were germane only in exceptional cases. Mendelssohn had fulfilled the intercessor's obligation to defend religious freedom, yet he had also not withheld his reservations about the Jews' present practice. In his private letters to the Schwerin community and to Emden, he expressed dissatisfaction with the current practice and stressed the legitimacy of contemporary medical knowledge. Although he mitigated his recommendation to Schwerin by saying that he was only giving his opinion and did not expect it to be followed, he did assert that the original practice was the correct one since in following it the Jews did not "depart from the way of their ancestors, of blessed memory, either to the left or to the right."[21] In replying to Emden, Mendelssohn had also asked for instruction so he could be sure his opinion was correct.

Mendelssohn's suggestion was not well received. Emden defended early burial on the basis of his understanding of death as a form of judgment: whether one was to receive reward or punishment, the process could not begin until the body had been interred. The righteous are to be laid to rest on the same day so that they can enter paradise and enjoy their reward without delay. Sinners must be laid to rest so that they can begin their course of punishment.[22] Emden also argued that the universal practice of early burial among Jews attested to its legitimacy and he doubted that the ancient practice could be reinstituted. Emden accused Mendelssohn of violating a fundamental law of the Mishnah, of using the casuistic method he supposedly detested to support his position, and of admitting foreign medical knowledge into the fabric of legal argumentation.[23]

The vehemence of Emden's response to Mendelssohn can be attributed to a fundamental difference in their positions. Emden's primary concern was with the deceased's soul because he espoused the ideology of reward and punishment which had developed in rabbinic and medieval Judaism and the notion, laden with mystical baggage, that only with the corpse's interment could the process begin.[24] Mendelssohn clearly believed in the afterlife and judgment as well, as his philosophical and exegetical writings attest. While he did not dispute the notion that reward and punishment waited on burial, he also chose not to mention it. In contrast to Emden, his use of the rabbinic principles of "purity" and "saving a life" showed that he was concerned primarily with the welfare of the living.

Was Mendelssohn advocating a "reform" of Jewish practice that repudiated his own doctrine of heteronomy? Indeed not. He was simply following his own program for the renewal of Judaism in keeping with the Andalusian tradition. Just as he had tried to renew the traditions of philosophy and exegesis, he now tried to renew the understanding of ritual practice. He treated Jewish law as a form of practical knowledge. Emden's accusation that he was utilizing "vain dialectics" was misguided. Mendelssohn was not employing the casuistic method to reconcile seeming contradictions between unrelated passages in an exercise that had no bearing on practice.[25] Rather, he was concerned with the plain meaning of the Law following the Andalusian tradition: he aimed to derive the underlying principles in order to determine practice. In his view Jewish burial practice was informed by two principles. Immediate removal of the body was based on the law of purity—a novel derivation, to be sure, and one that was the reason for Emden's accusation—while guarding the dead in caves was based on the concept of "saving a life." Since original Jewish practice had been better able to uphold both precepts and had also been in keeping with contemporary knowledge—like Solomon's understanding of Harvey's law of circulation—it should be reclaimed. Mendelssohn's aim was not to "reform" but to restore an earlier and to his mind a more apt practice.

Mendelssohn's view was also in accord with his understanding of history, since it was historical without being historicist. During the Lavater affair he had conceded that Judaism, like all religions, had suffered "human additions and abuses."[26] Here he gave no account of how the ancient practice of burial had been altered, corrupted, or disappeared. He introduced no historicist notion of development, process, or teleology to explain the change. Instead, he pointed to the ancient practice as being truer to the precepts of Judaism, both biblical and rabbinic.

Renewing ritual practice was fundamentally different from renewing exegesis or philosophy, however, since it involved the community and the exercise of authority. From the start Mendelssohn thought that his suggestion was unlikely to be approved, let alone adopted, because of the "tenacity and power of custom."[27] That was certainly the case: the rabbi of Schwerin, for example, dismissed the suggestion out of hand. The disagreement with Emden remained a private affair and had no repercussions, and the two quickly resumed their amicable scholarly correspondence. Mendelssohn's views first became known—and as a result played a role in later public controversies—when an enterprising *maskil* published the correspondence in 1785.[28]

In 1775 Mendelssohn answered the appeal of the minuscule Jewish community of Switzerland, which was threatened with the prohibition of procreation. Despite the absence of contact between Mendelssohn and Lavater since their controversy, Mendelssohn overcame his misgivings and immediately wrote to him since his prominent position in

Zurich would presumably enable him to influence events. Mendelssohn employed the language of the Enlightenment. He addressed Lavater as a "venerable friend of humanity" endowed with a "humane way of thinking" and asked that he intervene on behalf of the community to prevent this violation of "God's first commandment" by having its "old established freedoms" restored. Lavater responded favorably, and the proposed legislation was withdrawn.[29]

In 1777 the Jews of Königsberg faced an irksome rather than an ominous situation. Since the fourteenth century the "Aleinu" prayer had been intermittently censored by Christian authorities because one line, "for they prostrate themselves before vanity and emptiness, and pray to a God who saves not," was thought to defame Christianity. In 1703–1704 Prussia had required that the line be omitted from the prayer, that a member of the congregation pronounce the prayer audibly, that Christian inspectors with a knowledge of Hebrew be appointed to visit the synagogue to prevent violations, and that failure to comply with the order result in expulsion.[30] While the Jews were careful to observe the royal edict, the practice of inspection soon lapsed throughout Prussia with the exception of Königsberg, where professors of theology and oriental languages enjoyed the lucrative sinecure. There the inspector in 1777 submitted an official complaint, largely out of pique because of the synagogue's attempt to shift him to what he considered a less desirable seat. He maintained that the Jews were no longer saying the prayer audibly so that he was unable to discern if the offending line was being omitted; he also asserted that he had not been informed in advance of special celebrations in honor of royal persons and was therefore unable to ascertain whether the psalms that were recited (especially Psalm 49) were free of ambiguity and offense. He asked that the Jews be held responsible for their infractions.[31] When the government formed a commission to investigate the complaint, the community asked Mendelssohn to write on its behalf.

Mendelssohn submitted a vindication of the prayer which was consistent with his view of history. He argued that the original charge (1703) against the prayer was mistaken since the prayer predated Christianity. He cited all of the relevant rabbinic sources for dating its origins—though he opted for a late dating, "after the period of the prophet Isaiah and not, as some would have it, the time of Joshua"—and argued that the true target of this "sublime" prayer was idolatry. He also defended the prayer's uncorrupted transmission, as he would later do for the Pentateuch. The prayer had suffered no change because of its

central place in the liturgy. The Jews had scrupulously counted its sylla-
bles and thereby preserved it from any corruption or emendation. That
the text was exactly the same for Jews living in Muslim lands as in
Christian ones was testimony both to its uncorrupted transmission and
to its intended target.[32] A passage in the inspector's generally acerbic rejoinder illuminates Mendelssohn's ability to use history without being
historicist: "Much knowledge is available to a Jew who believes everything that his old rabbis have stated; a Christian, in contrast, demands
solid historical proof."[33]

Mendelssohn relied on his own exegetical work to defend the community's use of Psalm 49 to honor royalty. He argued that Luther's
translation, which the inspector had cited, was inaccurate, but even
more he asserted that "this entire Psalm . . . has hitherto not been properly explicated by any exegete, let alone properly translated."[34] Mendelssohn provided a translation of the verses in question and argued that
this was one of the most important "didactic psalms" because of its
explicit treatment of "the doctrine of a future life, the resurrection of
the dead, and the retribution of good and evil in a future life."[35] The
psalm was therefore a centerpiece of the funeral liturgy, consoling the
bereaved and admonishing the wayward, and only someone totally un-
acquainted with Jewish practice could find anything "improper or dis-
respectful" in it.[36]

Mendelssohn's intercession was once again successful. The government decided to rescind the law of 1703 and to abolish the office of inspector (although the current inspector was to retain his stipend). The
government also accepted the community's double offer: the cantor was
to swear an oath to abide by the law of 1703, which would be administered by the inspector, and the proceeds from the sale of the inspector's seat in the synagogue would be donated to the chest of the local
university.[37]

In 1777 Mendelssohn also responded to a dire threat to the community of Dresden. According to the privilege granted in 1772, the Jews
had to pay an exorbitant annual tax or face expulsion. Mendelssohn
received an urgent letter in elegant Hebrew informing him that because
of straitened circumstances many upright members of the community
were unable to meet their obligation. As a result, almost half of the Jewish population had already been expelled.[38] Mendelssohn immediately
penned a letter to a privy councillor of the Elector of Saxony, who, after
a meeting in 1776 and some correspondence, had offered Mendelssohn
his good offices.[39]

Mendelssohn now confronted the Jews' parlous position to which he had merely referred during the Lavater affair. Appealing to his correspondent as a fellow adherent of the Enlightenment's ideal of humanity ("generous friend of humanity"), he asserted that the Jews were being excluded from this ideal solely because of their religion.

> Expulsion is for a Jew the harshest punishment: more than mere banishment, it is virtual extirpation from God's earth, for prejudice turns him away at every border with an iron fist. Must fellow human beings who are free of guilt and trespass suffer this harshest of punishments simply because they adhere to different principles of belief and through misfortune are reduced to poverty?

Mendelssohn blamed this dire situation on the laws that governed the Jews, condemning the mercantilist policy that recognized economic utility but not common humanity. That policy compromised the state and the Jews. Since mercantilist policy was concerned solely with the Jews' wealth, it involved them in a moral contradiction: "Can the Israelite be expected to be honest when his poverty is punished as harshly as his dishonesty?" The policy implicated the state in a fundamental inequity: it was forced to mete out "punishment" (banishment) where there was no "transgression" (poverty).[40]

Mendelssohn's intercession was again successful and the edict of expulsion was revoked.[41] Yet in making his argument he had begun to make the transition from the politics of intercession to the politics of emancipation by applying the Enlightenment concepts he had used throughout his intercession to the states' treatment of the Jews. In so doing he pointed to the Jews' natural rights and lack of civil rights, thus laying the groundwork for the argument that their legal condition required fundamental revision. A further act of intercession in this period reveals another aspect of this transition.

Between 1774 and 1776 Mendelssohn wrote a treatise on the Jewish laws of property (regulating inheritance, guardianship, wills, marriage) under the supervision of the rabbi of Berlin, Hirschel Lewin. The treatise was produced at the request of the Prussian government, which was attempting to change the status of the Jewish courts. The Prussian "Jewry law" of 1750 had aimed to restrict the jurisdiction of Jewish courts to a confirmatory role: legal decisions affecting property were to be the domain of the Prussian courts, which would rule on the basis of Jewish law in consultation with the Jewish authorities.[42] This regulation was part of the effort of the Prussian state to deprive the institutions of the Jewish community of their autonomy, an effort which belonged to the state's general program of leveling corporate institutions.[43] As a result of the growing importance of Jews in the Prussian economy and the growing number of cases Jews brought to the Prussian courts, the state in 1769–1770 asked the rabbi of Berlin to provide information on the Jewish laws regarding wills, contracts, and inheritance.

Supplying this information took some six years. The initial report, prepared by the assistant rabbi in Berlin and a community leader, was declared unsatisfactory because it was unsystematic and disagreed with the report presented by the rabbi in Königsberg. In October 1770 the government therefore asked for a systematic treatise to be provided within eight weeks. Pleading a deficient knowledge of German, community leaders successfully requested one extension and then several more. Still empty-handed in 1772, the government threatened to impose a fine. At that point the community leaders, citing the resignation of the vice-rabbi and the impending arrival of his replacement, received a further six-month reprieve. The new rabbi, Hirschel Lewin, who arrived a year later than expected (because of illness), immediately requested a six-month extension, pleading a deficient knowledge of German. He saw the matter to a successful conclusion, however, with the four sections of the work delivered between early 1774 and the spring of 1776. *The Ritual Laws of the Jews*, albeit misleadingly named, was published in 1778.[44]

Mendelssohn was asked to produce this work because of its nature as well as its language.[45] In requesting information on the Jewish laws of property the Prussian government had two related aims. It wanted a legal handbook that would allow the Prussian courts to function independently of the rabbis. For this to be possible, the handbook had to be a code, stipulating the unchanging law of Moses.[46] Lewin had a detailed command of the relevant laws; Mendelssohn alone was capable of organizing the sort of systematic digest the government wanted.[47]

What the government had ordered was without doubt inherently difficult to produce. But the six-year delay had another cause. The Prussian government wanted its courts to exceed the 1750 law to usurp the jurisdiction of Jewish courts by ruling without their consultation on property matters. The rabbi and community leaders wanted to retain that consultative role. When they submitted the handbook, they explicitly defended the Jewish court's role, contending that Prussian judges would still be incapable of rendering independent judgment on the basis of the new digest.[48]

This argument informs Mendelssohn's book. He defended Jewish law

as distinct, immutable, and binding. In his introduction he first surveyed
the nature of Jewish law: the division between written and oral law; its
"eternally binding force" aside from the commandments that pertain to
the Temple, the Holy Land, and the high court; and the elements that
comprise the oral law. He then sketched the Law's history: the unbroken chain of tradition from Moses to the Mishnah, from the Gemarah
to Maimonides' *Mishneh Torah,* and then the *Shulchan Arukh,* "which
contains the laws and customs that are now current."[49] To this point
Mendelssohn's introduction is a miniature of other such introductions
to the Law, most notably Maimonides' introduction to the *Mishneh
Torah.*[50]

Mendelssohn then addressed the current Prussian situation, arguing that adjudication was impossible on the basis of the new handbook alone. While he had derived the handbook's laws primarily from
the *Shulchan Arukh,* the sixteenth-century compendium of Jewish law,
those laws were neither infallible nor authoritative, despite the fact that
its authors were "men of very enlightened views and pious morals" who
were held "in great esteem by the nation."[51] To understand a law properly one must be able to consult the Talmud as well as subsequent legal
authorities. This is true for a number of reasons. There are often essential related materials in other parts of the Law.[52] One must be able
to consult the original source to ascertain whether the specific circumstances of a case affect a law's application.[53] In addition, the differing
opinions of various authorities must be consulted, and throughout the
body of the work Mendelssohn highlighted such differences.[54] Finally,
adumbrating a theme of his introduction to the Pentateuch, "Light for
the Path," Mendelssohn argued that the Law is language-bound. It cannot be understood properly without a thorough knowledge of Hebrew
since the nuances and associated meanings of some legal terms are simply untranslatable.[55]

While *The Ritual Laws of the Jews* obviously belonged to Mendelssohn's activities as an intercessor, it should also be seen as an integral aspect of his Jewish thought. The digest can be compared to the *Book of
the Paths of Peace,* on which he was already at work. There he treated
the Bible as the primary source of practical knowledge. Here he provided another handbook of practical knowledge, albeit limited to the
laws of property, which was in keeping with the Andalusian tradition:
he sought the literal meaning of the law—without a trace of dialectics
or casuistry—in order to determine its practical application.

The work also belonged to Mendelssohn's transition from the politics of intercession to the politics of rights insofar as it fostered the Jews' civic integration. Mendelssohn accepted the diminution of the Jewish courts' jurisdiction as a fait accompli; no matter what he or any other community representative might argue, the Prussian bureaucracy would not restore the courts' powers. Instead, he chose to defend the sanctity of Jewish law under a new set of circumstances. In the property cases brought before Prussian courts he insisted that there be consultation with the Jewish court. In other words, what Mendelssohn emphasized was that Jews be governed by Jewish law. It was immaterial whether that took place in their own courts or in those of the state.

The correspondence with Dresden and *The Ritual Laws of the Jews* showed the beginnings of a shift in the dialectic of Mendelssohn's political thinking from defense of the Jews through intercession with the state to an assertion of the Jews' natural rights. With the changing circumstances of the next decade Mendelssohn would complete that shift.

CHAPTER EIGHT

Rights

The balance in the dialectic of Enlightenment political thought changed over time. The early German Enlightenment emphasized the individual's duties to the state. This situation altered dramatically in the 1770s and 1780s. Not only did established Enlightenment journals and publications begin to discuss political issues but a new genre of political publications emerged which made available knowledge previously reserved to the state. These publications circulated in a burgeoning network of reading societies and secondary associations. The publications, reading societies, and associations together constituted a new political public that, without questioning loyalty to the state, heightened the sense of individual rights.[1]

Mendelssohn's participation in intellectual societies testified to these developments. In 1755–1756 he was a member of the Berlin "Learned Coffeehouse," a forum for philosophy and science. He contributed a paper on probability (which he had someone else read, though his authorship was revealed when the reader mistook a zero for the letter *o* and Mendelssohn corrected him) and he corresponded with another member on the subject of determinism. In 1783 Mendelssohn became a member of the Berlin "Wednesday Society," a group devoted to political subjects which the Prussian government also used to test ideas for reform. In this setting Mendelssohn gave such lectures as "What Is Enlightenment," "On the Freedom to Express One's Opinion," "On the Principles of Government," and "On the Best Constitution."[2]

The Wednesday Society provided Mendelssohn with an occasion to develop his political ideas. As early as 1761 he had reflected on the limitations of political thinking in the German states.

> Philosophy is at home in Germany; foreigners are slowly beginning to recognize this fact. We also have no dearth of theoretical systems of statecraft erected on philosophical foundations. Yet our political thinking displays the sort of timidity that can only be shed in a free state. There [in a free state] is political thinking's true home, where it fears to confront neither arbitrary authority nor hypocrisy. In contrast, under a limited regime Minerva must more than occasionally avert her eyes so that her penetrating vision does not see further than she is allowed. Perhaps this is the reason that political writers in Germany and France concern themselves more with the external than the internal perfections of human society. It is only with regard to the external ones that the subject [of a monarchy] is permitted to be wise, and therefore devotes himself entirely to them, leaving the investigation of the internal ones to the free republican.[3]

This early passage reveals two crucial features of Mendelssohn's political thought. Political thought was dependent on circumstance: the type of government and the individual's political status conditioned, if not determined, the individual's ability to think or write about politics. The "subject" and the "republican" were clearly neither political nor epistemological equals. In addition, Mendelssohn assumed a direct relationship between politics and metaphysics ("external" vs. "internal" perfections). Whether for good or ill, politics ineluctably impinged on the individual's metaphysical status.[4] These two features demonstrate that history—as time, place, and circumstance—plays an even more important role in Mendelssohn's political thinking than in his biblical exegesis since human understanding, rather than a divine work, was at issue.

In a fragment in 1769 Mendelssohn attempted for the first time to define the basic concepts of the natural law tradition he would later use to understand the state and its relationship to religion.[5] After distinguishing between three types of freedom—physical, moral, and civic—he then argued that a (social) contract limits freedom. It removes the individual from the untrammeled freedom of the state of nature by subjecting him to the will of another, thereby converting indefinite claims into inescapable duties (perfect duties).

> Men's actions are subject to moral laws yet without a contract are dependent for their determination entirely on individual volition and are therefore free. As the result of a contract they are subjected to the volition of another; thus through every contract a portion of freedom is renounced. All duties are based on laws. Fully stipulated laws yield perfect duties, unstipulated laws

imperfect duties. Positive duties toward others depend on closer determina-
tion, which nature assigns to our own volition. When through a contract we
transfer to another the right to make these determinations according to his
volition, then we have turned imperfect duties into perfect ones.[6]

Mendelssohn first attempted to understand the Jews' situation in terms
of rights in the mid-1750s when he translated Rousseau's *Discourse
on the Origins and Foundations of Inequality*. In a notebook he commented: "He whose rights are violated in an impermissible manner is being warred against. War is therefore interminably being waged against
the Jews."[7] This idea did not receive further elaboration until 1762
when, in declining an invitation to join a "patriotic society" devoted to
social issues, he applied to the Jews the categories he had used to define
the status of political thought in Germany.

> Birth, education, and mode of life reveal their influence on people's way of
> thinking the most when the issue is the nobler part of philosophy [politics].
> The fortunate republican surveys human society from a much higher point of
> view than the subject of a monarchy, and the subject of a monarchy is far
> above the position accorded me in civic life. To be sure, the freedom to think
> in almost republican fashion blossoms under the rule of a Frederick; but you
> well know how little my fellow believers are allowed to partake in all the
> country's freedoms. The civic oppression to which we are condemned by a
> far too prevalent prejudice rests like a dead weight on the intellect's wings,
> making it incapable of ever attempting the high flight of the freeborn.[8]

In contrast to the "republican" or the "subject of a monarchy," the
Jew suffers a "civic oppression" that renders him incapable of political
thought. Exclusion from the polity entails exclusion from political thinking. That Mendelssohn unequivocally declined an invitation to join a
"patriotic society" in 1762 but became a member of the Wednesday Society in the 1780s reflects the changes in the intervening decades.

In 1768 a famous pedagogue of the German Enlightenment wanted
his textbooks and curriculum introduced into Jewish schools. He wrote
to Mendelssohn but Mendelssohn declined, arguing that these pedagogical materials were inappropriate for Jews because of the Jews' la-
mentable civic position.

> You have educated reasonable people to respect the rights of mankind, love
> truth and reasonable freedom, and to have the will and capacity to serve the
> state in which they live. Precisely this the Jew ought not, indeed cannot do,
> if his mode of thought is to agree with his condition. He should learn to up-
> hold the rights of mankind? If he is not to be thoroughly miserable in his con-
> dition of civic oppression, then he should not know of these rights at all.
> Should he love truth and reasonable freedom so he can despair that all civic

institutions in many places are aimed to keep him from both? Should he be trained to serve the state? The sole service that the state accepts from him is money. To remit large sums from circumscribed forms of business is the only vocation for which my brothers need training. If your textbook teaches this discipline, then it will be welcome to my nation, since it needs no other. Enough of this, as these considerations are too depressing for me to be able to pursue them willingly.[9]

These passages demonstrate that from the start of his political thinking Mendelssohn maintained a balance between individual rights and the absolutist state. The passages further demonstrate that his understanding of the idea of rights was firmly in place by the time he began his activities as an intercessor (1769) yet was submerged during his early acts of intercession, only becoming discernible with the events in Dresden in 1777. This new emphasis came to the fore when Mendelssohn transformed the next occasion for intercession into a plea for rights.

The Jews of Alsace were heavily concentrated in moneylending and intermediary occupations, which led to constant tensions with the surrounding populace.[10] At the peak of tensions in 1779–1780, one leader of Alsatian Jewry asked Mendelssohn to write a memorandum in defense of his community. Mendelssohn agreed, but because he was then at work on his commentary to Exodus, he enlisted the services of a respected and prolific political journalist and Prussian civil servant, Christian Wilhelm Dohm (1751–1820). The Alsatian Jewish leader had provided some materials for the memorandum; Mendelssohn and Dohm reorganized and supplemented these.[11] The resulting memorandum briefly summarized the history of the Jews from their expulsion from Spain to their arrival in France, surveyed the current restrictive regulations, and argued in favor of commerce as a source of wealth and abundance which also had the capacity to improve relations between Jews and their neighbors.[12]

After cooperating with Dohm on the memorandum, Mendelssohn asked him further to aid the Jews of Alsace by writing a treatise on the subject of the Jews' admission to citizenship—a bold step indicating Mendelssohn's sense of a new political situation. His reasons for choosing Dohm were obvious. Dohm excelled at this sort of writing, and in addition, he was interested: he had already had it in mind to write a history of the Jews in the diaspora. Mendelssohn was not to be disappointed. By August 1781 the treatise was complete and its impact was to be overwhelming.[13]

Dohm's *On the Civic Amelioration of the Jews* advanced a number of arguments within a political framework justified by raison d'état.[14]

Mercantilist policy suffered from an internal contradiction: it aimed to maximize wealth by expanding the population, yet legally restricted the Jews' ability to produce wealth.[15] Such legislation was at loggerheads with the state's secular criteria of citizenship: "Our well-established states must find every citizen acceptable who observes the laws and increases the state's wealth by his industry."[16] Dohm's major premise was the Enlightenment notion of universal mankind: "The Jew is more a man than a Jew."[17] His conclusion proclaimed the Enlightenment faith in perfectibility: "When the oppression [the Jew] experienced for centuries has made him morally corrupt, then a more equitable treatment will again restore him."[18] Dohm also maintained the Enlightenment balance between state power and individual rights by making the state the guarantor of rights. Because "humanity and genuine politics are one and the same,"[19] the state should immediately grant the Jews rights and then superintend the "civic amelioration" that would make them "morally and politically better than they are now."[20] He recommended that the Jews abandon commerce for morally healthy occupations, especially artisanry and farming, and that they educate their children in a new spirit either by changing the curricula of their own schools or by sending them to state schools.

Dohm's tract fulfilled Mendelssohn's hopes by provoking a major debate that made the rights of Jews a public issue.[21] Dohm's tract appeared in September 1781. The following month the emperor Joseph II issued an edict for the Jews of Bohemia and in January of 1782 one for the Jews of Austria granting them freedom of residence, commerce, and admission to the schools but leaving in force many restrictions, such as those governing marriage and taxes. The preamble to the legislation of January 1782 is informed with much the same Enlightenment spirit as Dohm's proposals.[22] For the first time an absolutist state had recognized the Jews' claim to civil rights.

Mendelssohn aimed to reinforce the impact of Dohm's tract and Joseph's legislation (even though he was suspicious of Joseph's intentions).[23] In 1782 he published a German translation of one of the pamphlets Menasseh ben Israel had written in the seventeenth century to help the Jews gain readmission to England. A catalog of the most common charges and calumnies against the Jews (such as blood libel, blasphemy of Christianity, cursing of Christians), the *Vindiciae Judaeorum* (1656), was a perfect complement to Dohm's tract. Dohm had treated political issues; it addressed religious ones.[24]

Mendelssohn appended a preface to the translation in which for the

first time he publicly advocated "civic acceptance" or equal rights.[25] Yet
he also maintained continuity with his earlier thinking. At the outset he
adopted the pious stance of the intercessor: whatever his own efforts,
the outcome was in God's hands. Mendelssohn began by calling on Providence. "Infinitely beneficent Providence is to be thanked for having
allowed me at the end of my days to experience this happy moment
in which the rights of man are beginning to be heeded to their true extent."[26] Mendelssohn argued that whereas toleration had since 1648
been limited in the Holy Roman Empire to the three recognized religions—Catholicism, Lutheranism, and Calvinism—he understood three
events to demonstrate that the Jews were also gaining consideration:
Lessing's play *Nathan the Wise* (1779), Dohm's tract, and Joseph II's
legislation. He qualified his own contribution with a disclaimer: he had
lived, and continued to live, at a "dark distance" from the great and powerful and did not expect to participate in the "transactions of the active
world." Rather, he would wait to see what "the infinitely wise and infinitely good Providence" would decree.[27] He also maintained continuity with his earlier étatism, writing, for example, of "the motherly
bosom of the state."[28]

Mendelssohn's preface contained a threefold plea for freedom.[29] He
first argued for an end to the prejudice that impeded the granting of
rights. Since "age-old prejudice is deaf," the sorts of charges Menasseh
ben Israel had refuted still circulated in the German states, accusations
like the poisoning of a sovereign by a Jewish doctor, or the blood libel.[30]
Moreover, "prejudice changed its appearance with the centuries" and a
new secular prejudice had supplanted the religious one.

> Now we are reproached for superstition and stupidity; a lack of moral feel-
> ing, taste, and good manners; the inability to engage in arts, sciences, and
> useful occupations, principally in the service of war and the state; an incor-
> rigible propensity to deceit, usury, and lawlessness . . .

Once conversionary zeal had abated, the Jews were neglected and then
blamed for the consequences of that neglect.

> We are excluded from all arts, sciences, and useful occupations and activities
> of mankind; all the means to useful improvement are closed to us, and our
> lack of applied knowledge is made the cause of our continued oppression.
> Our hands are tied and we are rebuked for not using them.[31]

In the second part of his plea Mendelssohn turned the theme of economic utility into an argument for economic freedom. After pointing to
Menasseh ben Israel's effort in the *Vindiciae Judaeorum* to defend the

Jews' contribution to national prosperity,[32] Mendelssohn cited the example of Holland. Its combination of economic and religious freedom had made it an unrivaled model of prosperity.

> Nothing but freedom, liberality of government, legal justice, and the open arms with which people of all kinds—of every dress, opinion, custom, habit and religion—are accepted, defended, and allowed to go their way; nothing but these advantages have brought Holland the almost overflowing prosperity, the abundance of goodness for which it is so much envied.[33]

At the bottom of Holland's prosperity was commerce. Mendelssohn took issue with Dohm's notion—common in the eighteenth century, especially among the physiocrats—that artisanry and farming are the sole sources of wealth, reiterating the positive view of commerce he had expressed as early as the *Kohelet Musar*: "Not only making but also doing is productive."[34] Every merchant and middleman, no matter how large or small his business, contributes to wealth by stimulating production with new goods, methods, and markets. Commerce can only prosper, however, when it is allowed to develop freely. Competition is its sine qua non.

> Only through competition and rivalry, through unlimited freedom and equality of rights among all buyers and sellers—be they of whichever estate, appearance, or religion they may—only through these invaluable advantages do all things acquire their value.[35]

For Mendelssohn economic and civic freedom were inextricably linked.[36]

In the third part of his plea Mendelssohn took issue with Dohm over the relationship between civic freedom and religious autonomy. Dohm had argued that the Jews should be allowed to retain autonomy in civil matters (such as property) so that cases could be adjudicated by Jewish courts. Such autonomy was required by their religion and would distance them from their fellow citizens no more than a city's separate laws distanced it from the state.[37] In addition, the Jewish community should have the same power as other religions to issue the ban of excommunication, albeit on condition it not affect the excommunicant's civil status.[38]

Mendelssohn disagreed with both these positions. He extended the argument he had made in the *Ritual Laws of the Jews* for integration into the state's legal mechanism. He agreed that in civil cases between Jews Jewish law should be used, yet he asserted that the sole credential for the judge was his state office and not his religion.

The judge should be a conscientious man and understand the laws according to which he is to pronounce justice for his fellow men. In religious matters he can follow the persuasion of his choice. When the authorities have deemed him capable of a judgeship and appointed him, then his judgments are valid. We entrust our health . . . to a doctor without regard to religion; why not our property to a judge?[39]

Not only did Mendelssohn think the judge's religion inconsequential, he asserted that if Jews were willing to trust the judgments of Christian judges then the judges would take the trouble to learn the appropriate Jewish laws.[40] In the space of four years his position had subtly changed. In 1778 he had argued that a Jewish judge must be consulted; here he asserted that Christian judges would learn enough Jewish law to render decisions on their own. This optimistic shift functioned in the terms of Mendelssohn's political thought: the assertion of rights was predicated on trust in the state and its appointees.

Mendelssohn also disagreed with Dohm on the ban of excommunication. He employed the categories he had first discussed in his fragment of 1769 to assert that no religion should have power over its adherents. He argued that religion concerned opinions and beliefs that were not susceptible to any external authority. What made such authority permissible was a contract in which an individual transferred a right to a "moral person." Such a right first had to exist in the "state of nature" as an unspecified or "imperfect" right; when transferred to a "moral person," such a right then became a specified or "perfect" right that carried obligation. Unlike actions that were alienable, beliefs and opinions were inalienable: the notion of a contract by definition could not be applied to them. Beliefs and opinions were not "imperfect" rights in the state of nature; they could therefore not be made into "perfect" ones in society.[41] No one could legitimately claim to exercise authority over another's beliefs.

Mendelssohn also asserted that the power of the ban was inimical to the very goals of religion.

The purpose [of an ecclesiastical society] is collective edification, participation in the effusion of the heart, through which we acknowledge our gratitude for God's benefactions and our filial trust in His infinite beneficence. In what spirit would we want to deny entrance to the dissident, nonconformist, errant or recusant, to refuse the freedom to partake of this edification? . . . Reason's house of devotion requires no locked doors.[42]

The category "edification" that Mendelssohn had used in one of his earliest works to signal the reconciliation of faith and reason now justified his contention that institutional religion was not to wield authority over convictions.[43]

In addressing the problem of coercion Mendelssohn acknowledged that he was the philosopher who described the ideal "ought" whereas Dohm was the social observer who recorded what "was."

> The true divine religion arrogates to itself no authority over opinions and judgments; . . . recognizes no power other than the power of argument to convince and to persuade and through conviction to bestow felicity. The true divine religion has recourse to neither arms nor fingers; it is pure spirit and heart.[44]

The examples he used to demonstrate that Judaism did not need the power of excommunication—"the wisest of our ancestors," King Solomon, as well as some early rabbis—similarly evoked the ideal rather than the actual situation.[45]

The purpose of Mendelssohn's distinction was to accelerate the realization of the ideal, for the ban was already a virtual anachronism. Mendelssohn mentioned a recent incident in Altona in which the rabbi had issued a minor ban and threatened a major ban against a man who had shaved his beard and started to wear a decorated wig. The man had protested to the authorities, and at the time Mendelssohn wrote his preface the case was pending.[46] For Mendelssohn this case showed that Dohm's distinction between "civil" and "religious" was captious: religious excommunication necessarily impinged on civil status because it involved the political authorities. Yet even the rabbi's right to issue a ban was an anomaly; in most German states rabbis had been deprived of this power in the course of the eighteenth century as part of the process in which the state divested all ecclesiastical authorities of such powers.[47] This right persisted in Altona because the city was a Danish territory; even so, the power had not been exercised for a number of decades.[48] The authorities eventually ruled against the rabbi, prohibiting the major ban and requiring him to apply in writing for permission to use the minor one.[49] Mendelssohn concluded by appealing to the rabbis to depart from their oppressors and renounce the power of the ban. In so doing he was asking them to abjure powers they had already substantially, if not completely, lost.

In this discussion of excommunication and the nature of institutional religion, Mendelssohn had begun to delineate his own understanding of issues that had been exhaustively treated by scholars of ecclesiastical law. His principled denial of religion's right to excommunication set him apart from the mainstream of that scholarship.[50] Since he further developed these views in *Jerusalem, or On Religious Power and Judaism*, we will continue the discussion when considering that work (see chapter 9).

Mendelssohn's advocacy of rights was fundamentally new, yet there was also substantial continuity with his earlier thought—not only in his appeal to Providence and his étatism but also in the connection between politics and metaphysics. This connection was paramount in Mendelssohn's applause for Lessing, Dohm, and Joseph II.

> Lessing and Dohm, the former as a philosophical poet the latter as a philosophical politician, have considered in conjunction the great goal of Providence, the vocation of man, and the rights of mankind, and it is an admirable monarch who at this very time has carefully reflected on these principles in their entirety but also . . . has conceived of a plan . . . and begun to act on it.[51]

For Mendelssohn the grant of civil rights would not only release the Jews from oppression but would also allow them to realize their "vocation" as men. Throughout his preface the philosophical implications of political change were unmistakable: Mendelssohn consistently employed key metaphysical terms. In another passage in which he took issue with Dohm, for example, he argued that limiting the growth of a state's population did more damage to "the culture of its inhabitants, the vocation of men, and their felicity" than did a population surplus.[52] In *Jerusalem* Mendelssohn would further develop these implications.

A month after the appearance of the *Vindiciae Judaeorum* (1782) Mendelssohn decided to publish his translation of Psalms. He had begun the translation in 1770 in the hope of reinforcing the triumph of toleration in the Lavater affair, aiming to restore the true meaning of the psalms as models of the "sublime" and thereby contribute to practical knowledge and edification. In 1782 he wanted to bolster the campaign for rights by showing that the Jews in King David's day had enjoyed a period of enlightenment which could now inspire them.

> If only our brethren could be made aware and be inflamed to become students of the books of prophets and writings. In those holy days the nation's situation must have been entirely different, since one could declaim these things to the entire nation and have hopes of being understood. Perhaps our children's children will experience such a century![53]

Not only did Mendelssohn's later intention go unrealized; it also vitiated the original one. The translation received little attention, and the most substantial review complained that the effort to use Psalms for an ulterior purpose—to show something about the state of the Jews' culture in the Davidic period—was not only ludicrous but, even worse, subverted the entire project since it was no more valid than the efforts of Christian theologians to interpret the Psalms christologically.[54]

Unlike the translation of Psalms, the preamble to the *Vindiciae Judaeorum* did have an impact, though not the one Mendelssohn had envisioned: it elicited a more serious challenge to his faith than Lavater's. In September 1782, five months after the publication of the preamble, a pamphlet appeared under the title "The Search for Truth and Right in a Letter to Moses Mendelssohn, occasioned by his Remarkable Preamble to Menasseh ben Israel." In order to be taken seriously the pamphlet masqueraded as the work of a famous Austrian statesman; in fact, it had been written by a minor writer, August Cranz.[55]

Cranz wanted to revive Lavater's public challenge but with a difference. Since "the indiscreet Lavater" had inadvertently put himself at the center of the controversy, Mendelssohn had managed to circumvent the issues.[56] Cranz asked for a full accounting since he thought that in the preface Mendelssohn had essentially repudiated Judaism. For Cranz, Judaism's "ecclesiastical system" and its punitive powers were all that separated it from Christianity. Since Mendelssohn had called for the abrogation of the ban, what could be left of his faith?

> Armed church law has always been one of the principal foundation stones of Judaism and a main tenet of the belief system of your fathers. To what extent can you remain steadfast in the faith of your fathers . . . when, in taking issue with the church law given by Moses on the basis of revelation, you remove one of its foundation stones and shake the entire building? The public has been aroused by you and has the right to expect enlightenment and instruction on this most important point.[57]

Cranz portrayed Mendelssohn as being on the horns of a dilemma. Either he had realized that Christianity was the true religion and was prepared to convert, or he thought Judaism was imperfect and in need of fundamental reform.[58] In either case, Mendelssohn should give a full exposition of his views. Such an exposition became urgent given the current discussion of rights. While Cranz shared Mendelssohn's hopes for rights, he also asserted that Judaism itself was at least partially responsible for the condition of the Jews because it separated them from the rest of society.

> In the faith of your fathers itself there is a powerful cleavage that prevents your nation from that full participation in the general and private benefits of society which puts men on an equal footing in the state.[59]

Cranz pointed to the conflict between the Sabbath and the duties of citizenship as well as to the prohibition on intermarriage. Since Mendelssohn had renounced the ban, could he not subordinate the Sabbath to the law of the land as well as permit intermarriage as a civil relationship?[60]

Accompanying Cranz's pamphlet was a postscript, written by an obscure chaplain, Mörschel, which presented Mendelssohn with a somewhat different problem. The author wondered whether Mendelssohn had renounced revelation altogether and become a naturalist? He asked for a clarification: "I am a Jew, I am a Christian, I am neither."[61]

With his preface to the *Vindiciae Judaeorum* Mendelssohn had tentatively entered the political arena. With the publication of Cranz's pamphlet he was at the center of it. Mendelssohn was forced to elaborate the arguments he had merely broached in his preface, and he did so by developing the political ideas he had explored on various occasions since the 1760s.

CHAPTER NINE

Credo

Jerusalem, or On Religious Power and Judaism was to be Mendelssohn's fullest elaboration of his views on rights and the nature of Judaism. Yet Mendelssohn wrote the work neither as a commentary nor as an effort at systematic philosophy but as an answer to Cranz's pamphlet. This is manifest in its structure, for each of its two parts grapples with a central issue Cranz had posed. In so doing Mendelssohn drew upon the views of Judaism he had expressed from his earliest works. The Andalusian tradition of pietist rationalism was fully in force in *Jerusalem,* but it was yoked to an argument for the separation of church and state which was intended as a novel means to preserve liberty of conscience and gain equal rights.

PART 1

In part one of *Jerusalem* Mendelssohn addressed Cranz's contention that in repudiating the ban of excommunication he had repudiated Judaism. In his preface to the *Vindiciae Judaeorum* he had used the distinction between "perfect" and "imperfect" rights to argue that religion was not authorized to coerce belief. He now embedded these ideas in a general theory of church-state relations. By guaranteeing freedom of conscience, he also made possible equal rights for Jews.

Mendelssohn contended that ever since the Reformation had shattered Catholicism's "consistent" and "despotic" answer to the question of church-state relations, the issue had not received a satisfactory solution. Mendelssohn criticized the ideas of the two foremost English political theorists of the seventeenth century as examples of what was awry in the contemporary understanding of church-state relations. Hobbes had sacrificed liberty for the sake of security by subordinating the church to the state and he had failed to recognize the existence of duties, albeit "imperfect," in the state of nature. Locke had secured freedom of conscience at the cost of an unbridgeable distinction between the temporal and the eternal—the state was concerned with temporal, the church with eternal welfare—which had grave "practical consequences."[1] While Mendelssohn acknowledged Hobbes to be the father of "moral philosophy" and expressed great sympathy for Locke, he proposed his own theory of church-state relations based on his Wolffian understanding of man's benevolence.

For Mendelssohn individuals achieved "inner felicity" and perfection by voluntarily fulfilling their duties.[2] There was no distinction between temporal duties to man and eternal ones to God, as Locke had proposed, since "one is inseparable from the other." In support of this view Mendelssohn cited a rabbinic dictum: "This life . . . is a vestibule in which one must comport oneself in the manner in which one wishes to appear in the inner chamber."[3] The true distinction was rather between actions and convictions.

Mendelssohn's theory of church and state is rooted in his notion of benevolence. This quality gives rise to the mutual bonds necessary for felicity and perfection: "Improvement is inseparable from benevolence."[4] In solitude man can fulfill his obligations neither to God nor to his fellowman; sociability is essential to the development of the faculties, including language (a notion that pervaded his German and Hebrew works, including the *Book of the Paths of Peace*). That benevolence is the link between politics and metaphysics testifies to Mendelssohn's fundamental optimism.[5]

In consequence of man's innate need for benevolence, actions and convictions contribute to the commonweal as well as to individual perfection.

> Actions and convictions thus belong to the perfection of mankind, and society should, as far as possible, take responsibility for both through collective efforts, that is, it should direct the actions of its members toward the common good and promote convictions that lead to these actions. The former is the "government," the latter the "education" of man as a social being.[6]

Mendelssohn thought there were two kinds of actions and convictions, each of which came under the purview of a separate institution. Those that arose in relationship to one's fellowman were the province of the state; those that arose in relationship to God were the province of religion. In Mendelssohn's distinction, unlike Locke's, there were bridges between the two—benevolence and also education.

Mendelssohn thought that the best state was one whose members were able to govern themselves through "education." There the individual would act voluntarily because he recognized that in joining society his gain outweighed his loss.[7] The institution capable of providing such education was religion.

> Here it is that religion should aid the state and the church should become a pillar of civil felicity. It is the church's business to persuade the populace most emphatically of the truth of noble principles and convictions; to demonstrate to them that duties toward men are also duties toward God . . . ; that serving the state is true service of God.[8]

Religion can accomplish this task since it is preeminently practical. Mendelssohn defined the church as a "public institution for the formation of man that concerns his relation to God," and he defined the "formation of man" as "the effort to arrange both actions and convictions in such a way . . . that they will *educate* and *govern* man."[9] These definitions accord religion a practical task, and this task is accomplished through "*collective edification*": religion has the ability, "through participation, to animate the at times lifeless concepts of reason, [turning them] into soaring sensations."[10] In other words, religion has the singular ability to turn abstract ideas into the vital knowledge that guides action. Its contribution to the state was to "teach and console."[11] To define religion Mendelssohn once again employed the concept of edification, which from his earliest works had implied the reconciliation of faith and reason.[12]

Mendelssohn was fully aware that the ability of religion to "educate" and "govern" mankind was an ideal. In the second part of the essay he would argue that ancient Judaism but no other polity had been able to realize the ideal. To account for actual conditions he invoked history (in a manner reminiscent of his peroration to the Book of Exodus). Once education could no longer govern, coercion took its place.

> Yet if the character of a nation, the level of culture to which it has ascended, the growth in population which has accompanied prosperity, the increasing complexity of relations and connections, excessive luxury, and other factors make it impossible to govern the nation exclusively by convictions, the state will have to have recourse to public measures, coercive laws, punishments of crime and rewards of merit.[13]

Under these circumstances the state must rest content with governing actions through law, the individual with obedience to the law.[14] In keeping with his German and Hebrew works, then, Mendelssohn endorsed heteronomy.

In the preface to the *Vindiciae Judaeorum* Mendelssohn had argued that the social contract converts imperfect rights into perfect ones. Here he made that argument in relationship to benevolence. In the state of nature all duties and rights are imperfect: "man in the state of nature is independent, that is, he has no positive duties towards anyone."[15] No claims can be made on benevolence; all acts are entirely voluntary.

The state of nature is first transcended through parenthood. Begetting an offspring obligates parents to educate it to the felicity of which it is capable; parents thus enter into a sort of contract.[16] Since Mendelssohn had posited that government by education was universally desirable, it was appropriate that the first contract concerned education, aimed at felicity, and was motivated by benevolence.

The contract between parents adumbrated society. True society emerged when one person voluntarily promised to transfer a physical or spiritual possession to another. Once the promise was accepted, the imperfect right to the object was converted into a perfect one whose owner was entitled to use compulsion to enforce his claim. In transforming an act of intentional benevolence into law, this conversion of imperfect into perfect rights constituted a contract. Such contracts were the basis of society: they enabled individuals to exercise benevolence and pursue felicity.[17]

How did Mendelssohn apply this notion of contract to church-state relations? He asserted that God has no claim on our benevolence. God neither needs nor asks for our benevolence, and no special division of duties exists toward God since "all man's duties are obligations towards God."[18] The church also has no claim on our benevolence or on any of its members' possessions. Mendelssohn reiterated the argument he had made in the preface to the *Vindiciae Judaeorum*: "The right to our convictions is inalienable."[19] As convictions do not involve benevolence, so there is no imperfect right that can be converted into a perfect one. Hence neither contract nor compulsion is applicable to convictions and the church has no legitimate claim to either:[20] "The church's only rights are admonition, instruction, reassurance and consolation; and the citizens' duties towards the church are an attentive ear and a willing heart."[21]

The state's lack of contractual power over convictions has two implications. The state has no right to coerce convictions or to influence them by granting privilege or prerogative: "Neither state nor church are authorized judges in matters of religion; for the members of society could not have vouchsafed them that right by any contract whatsoever."[22] The state may legitimately be concerned only with natural religion's three beliefs—"God, providence, and the future life"—which guarantee morality. Without them "felicity is a dream and virtue itself is no longer virtue."[23]

In addition, the state has no right to administer oaths in regard to convictions since no contract has granted the state such a right and oaths "do not create new duties."[24] Moreover, oaths are neither effective nor appropriate for matters of conviction. They should be used only to "awaken" the conscience of the average person about matters of external sense such as hearing and seeing. In matters of conscience language is too imprecise and susceptible to change over time for oaths to have any meaning. Here Mendelssohn voiced an objection to fixed formulations of belief or dogma; this position would recur in the second part of the book as a general critique of written traditions.

While Mendelssohn's defense of liberty of conscience was uncompromising, he maintained the dialectic between the individual and the state characteristic of his political thought and that of the German Enlightenment. His general position placed him at the conservative end of the spectrum of natural law theory in the closing decades of the eighteenth century. Throughout the eighteenth century natural law theory had been used to justify state absolutism: through the social contract the individual repudiated his "natural rights" for a "civil liberty" that required unquestioned obedience to the state.[25] As part of the political turn of the 1770s some thinkers began to adapt the theory to emphasize individual rights: since the individual's "natural rights" were inviolable, the state's duty was to secure them.[26] Mendelssohn generally followed Wolff in espousing the older theory of natural rights which emphasized the state's authority: the individual renounced the primordial rights of the state of nature by accepting the social contract.[27] Only in respect to liberty of conscience did Mendelssohn establish an inviolable individual right beyond the state. Yet to make this argument he used ecclesiastical rather than secular natural law theory.

Ecclesiastical natural law had also grappled with the dialectic between the state and the individual. In the aftermath of the Reformation the powers of Catholic bishops had often been transferred directly to Protestant sovereigns. In the late seventeenth century the "territorialist" school of Protestant ecclesiastical law used natural law to justify this domination of the church by the absolutist state. The territorialists subordinated the church to the state by acknowledging the temporal sovereign as the church's head, even though they recognized that state and church were institutions different in kind. In contrast, the "collegialist" school used natural law to create a theoretical basis for separation. Collegialists grounded the church's rights in those of its individual members by holding the church to be a voluntary society (*collegium*). Their separation of church and state had two aims: by recognizing the church as a distinct, voluntary society, they established freedom of conscience for the individual and made a case for toleration for the various churches.[28]

Mendelssohn was in good company in using collegial theory, for it was the common property of the religious Enlightenment. The theory first appeared among Calvinist sectarians in the second half of the seventeenth century in Holland, found significant expression among latitudinarians in the Church of England from the turn of the century, became current among German Protestants by the 1720s, and was taken up by central European Catholic scholars at the same moment that Mendelssohn used it in the 1780s.[29] Collegial theory offered religious Enlighteners of all persuasions a means to embrace toleration without relativizing belief.[30] The theological Wolffians were among its proponents. Siegmund Jacob Baumgarten, for example, used collegial theory in a tract of 1745 to defend freedom of conscience in general and toleration of Jews in particular. He recognized Judaism as a legitimate religious association whose rights were to be respected by the state: the state could only exercise control over those matters that did not infringe on the Jews' freedom of conscience (such as defamation of Christianity or commerce on Christian holidays).[31]

While Mendelssohn's use of collegialism was in keeping with his affinity to theological Wolffianism and the religious Enlightenment, he also revealed his characteristic independence by reconstruing it in a radical direction.[32] Both territorialists and collegialists had granted the church the power of the ban so long as it did not impinge on the individual's civil status. Dohm had followed the collegialists in his discussion of the ban.[33] Although Mendelssohn subscribed to the fundamental collegialist premise that the church/synagogue was a voluntary religious society and "a moral person," he denied that it could be based on a contract that vouchsafed the right of coercion.[34]

In short, Mendelssohn's answer to Cranz was that he had renounced excommunication not to repudiate Judaism but in order to argue for liberty of conscience. Mendelssohn wanted to secure liberty of conscience, toleration, and equal rights. A state that had no power to coerce religion and whose interest was limited to natural religion's triad of truths would be indifferent to the religious beliefs of individuals and capable of tolerating all religions. Moreover, such a state would be able to grant equal rights to Jews. Mendelssohn's discussion of church-state relations was also an argument for the political conditions that would make emancipation possible.[35]

Such a state belonged to the future. Cranz had cited a case in the Habsburg Empire: a Jew who had converted to Christianity after his marriage and the birth of his children asserted that there was no reason for a divorce and that the childrens' religion and religious education remained undetermined. Mendelssohn objected on the basis of his argument that the obligation to educate children was the first contract. The husband's desire for freedom should not be allowed to injure his wife's prior right to the fulfillment of their contract to raise the children as Jews. Were there "impartial," secular schools, then education would not be a problem. Since such schools do not exist, the childen must be educated in Jewish schools. Whereas Mendelssohn considered secular schools desirable, the state capable of erecting such schools, which was also the state capable of granting the Jews equal rights, had yet to appear.[36]

In this regard Mendelssohn differed from other *maskilim*. The 1780s saw the end of the early Haskalah. In 1783 a society was formed, "The Society for the Exponents of the Hebrew Language," and the following year a journal was issued in Hebrew, the *Me'asef* (Assembler). Political developments (such as Dohm's tract and Joseph II's reformist legislation) encouraged the formation of an organized society; indeed, within a few years a faction emerged with an agenda of social and political change.[37] A *maskil* such as Naphtali Herz Wessely, for example, thought the existing state capable of emancipating the Jews. He invested the acts of rulers like Joseph II with providential, even messianic status and advocated that the Jews reform their schools by introducing secular subjects.[38] A few years later David Friedländer would argue for an improvement of the Jews' political position, combining an argument from utility with an appeal to the beneficence of the tutelary Prussian state.[39]

Mendelssohn, in contrast, thought equal rights should be granted unconditionally. The state rather than the Jews had to change. The Jews' claim derived from their natural rights. To qualify for rights they needed only to reconstitute themselves as a voluntary community divested of all coercive power—a process already well under way. While Mendelssohn also favored secular in addition to religious education, he thought the Jews' efforts in this regard played no role in the emancipation process. The intellectual renewal of the Jews was an aspect of their liberty of conscience with no bearing on their claim to rights. The state, in contrast, had to alter its relations with the church to accord with natural rights. Since Dohm's argument for rights rested on notions of utility and raison d'état, "civic amelioration" involved reciprocity—both the state's grant of rights and the Jews' regeneration. Since Mendelssohn argued on the basis of natural right, the onus of "civic acceptance" lay with the state.[40]

In sum, Mendelssohn presented a theory for the separation of church and state which linked the eternal and the temporal through the concept of benevolence, and he asserted that liberty of conscience was necessary for the realization of man's eternal vocation. Here was a liberalism built on Mendelssohn's version of Wolffian metaphysics. Those same ideas, and especially the concept of benevolence, were to figure prominently in Mendelssohn's exposition of Judaism.

PART 2

The second half of *Jerusalem* confronted Cranz's contention that Mendelssohn had abandoned the religion of his fathers and Mörschel's assertion that Mendelssohn had forsaken revealed religion altogether. Mendelssohn answered as a philosopher, just as he had during the Lavater affair: he supported his understanding of Judaism with the appropriate philosophical views. In consequence, the argument of the second part of *Jerusalem* contains numerous digressions.[41] In fact, its pattern is to alternate between his exposition of Judaism and the digressions on various subjects needed to advance the argument.*

---

*The argument may be divided as follows:

1. The Problem and Practical Knowledge	8:152–156 (Arkush, p. 84f.)
2. Typology of Truths in Judaism	8:156–160 (Arkush, p. 89f.)
3. Practical Knowledge and Antihistoricism	8:160–164 (Arkush, p. 94f.)
4. Judaism as Revealed Legislation	8:164–168 (Arkush, p. 97f.)
5. Transmission of Knowledge, Oral vs. Written	8:168–183 (Arkush, p. 101f.)
6. Judaism as Ceremonial Law	8:183–186 (Arkush, p. 117f.)
7. Benevolence and Refutation of Christianity	8:186–191 (Arkush, p. 120f.)
8. Judaism	8:191–204 (Arkush, p. 126f.)

The first few pages—8:145–151 (Arkush, pp. 77–84)—summarize and conclude the argument of part 1.

The result of this argumentative structure is that Mendelssohn transcends his dualism of treating general philosophy in German works and Judaism in Hebrew ones. Here is a wide-ranging German-language discussion of Judaism which goes well beyond the focused treatment of specific issues characteristic of his intercessions. The proximate cause for the unprecedented expansive nature of this discussion was the challenge posed by Cranz and Mörschel. The final cause was the potential for a new relationship of the Jews to the state which, by abrogating the autonomous community, would render such dualism superfluous. Yet Mendelssohn paradoxically embraced rights as a means to reinstate a new version of that dualism.

PRACTICAL KNOWLEDGE

The second part of *Jerusalem* rests on two main arguments. First, Mendelssohn asserted that Judaism is the nonpareil religion of practical knowledge because it is a "divine legislation," not a "revealed religion."

> To state it briefly: I believe that Judaism knows of no revealed religion in the sense in which Christians understand this term. The Israelites possess a divine *legislation*—laws, commandments, ordinances, rules of life, instruction in the will of God as to how they should conduct themselves in order to attain temporal and eternal felicity. Propositions and prescriptions of this kind were revealed to them by Moses in a miraculous and supernatural manner, but [God conveyed through Moses] no doctrinal opinions, no saving truths, no universal propositions of reason.[42]

What distinguishes Judaism are the actions its laws prescribe. Judaism consists of a set of acts aimed at the "will" rather than a set of beliefs.[43] These acts, as Mendelssohn had shown in the *Book of the Paths of Peace,* are to be found in the Pentateuch, which is a "book of laws containing ordinances, rules of life, and prescriptions."[44] The Pentateuch is more than a sourcebook of laws, however: it is also "an inexhaustible treasure of rational truths and religious doctrines which are so intimately connected with the laws that they form but one entity."[45] Mendelssohn elucidated this point through a typology of truths.

Truths were either "eternal" or "historical." God established the eternal truths, which are of two kinds. The truths of pure mathematics and logic are "necessary" since God's "infinite reason" has made them so. These laws are immutable for God as well as for man. The truths of nature—physics and psychology—are "contingent." God has chosen them as the best (reflecting the Wolffian concept of the best of all possible worlds), yet he could also alter them, and on occasion he does so through miracles.[46] "Historical" truths, in contrast, are those that

> occurred once and may never occur again; propositions which have become true at one point in time and space through a confluence of causes and effects, and which, therefore, can only be conceived as true in respect to that point in time and space.[47]

Judaism was grounded in historical truth. As Mendelssohn had argued in his commentary to Exodus 20:2, the God who granted his legislation at Sinai was the God who had liberated the Jews from Egypt rather than the God of universal truth.

> *"I am the Eternal, your God, who brought you out of the land of Mizrayim, who delivered you from bondage, etc."* A historical truth, on which this people's legislation was to be founded, as well as laws, was to be revealed here, commandments and ordinances, not eternal religious truths. "I am the Eternal, your God, who made a convenant with your fathers, Abraham, Isaac and Jacob, and swore to make of their seed a nation of my own. The time for the fulfillment of this promise has finally come. To this end, I redeemed you from Egyptian slavery with unheard-of miracles and signs. I am your Redeemer, your Sovereign and King; I also make a convenant with you, and give you laws by which you are to live and become a happy nation in the land that I shall give you." All these are historical truths which, by their very nature, rest on historical evidence.[48]

Mendelssohn's insistence on the centrality of the Exodus and the revelation at Sinai reveals his proximity to Judah Halevi and thus his distance from Maimonides. Following Halevi, Mendelssohn grounded Judaism in the self-evident truth of Scripture. Maimonides had required that the truth of such teachings also be demonstrated by rational proof.[49]

The importance of the historical truths can be seen in Mendelssohn's understanding of the relationship between the component parts of Judaism. Ancient Judaism was tripartite. It contained "eternal truths about God, and his government, and providence, without which man cannot be enlightened and happy" and which are recommended to his reason rather than being forced on him on pain of punishment.[50] Judaism's foundation was natural religion. To illustrate this point Mendelssohn quoted from the Psalms, in keeping with his notion that they are a source of general "edification." Mendelssohn posited that God had endowed man with a faculty of reason sufficient to give him knowledge of all those truths needed for his temporal and eternal felicity. He thus reiterated what he had shown in his commentary (Exodus 20:2): Judaism

confirmed eternal truths already known but did not confer ones otherwise unknown. Mendelssohn thereby laid the basis for toleration. The
means to salvation were universal and innate; no religion could claim a
monopoly.[51]

Judaism also contained historical truths about the genesis of the nation and Israel's relationship to God which are "the foundation for national cohesion." Finally, Judaism was composed of the "laws, precepts,
commandments, and rules of life" that God gave to the Jews as a result
of his relationship with them. The laws were "peculiar to this nation"
and were designed to bestow "national . . . as well as personal felicity."[52]

The Pentateuch's laws bridge the historical truths of Judaism and the
eternal truths: they derive from God's relationship to his people and are
filled with eternal and historical truths. The laws "guide the inquiring
intelligence to divine truths, partly to eternal and partly to historical
truths. . . . The ceremonial law was the bond which was to connect action with contemplation, law with theory."[53] Moreover, "All laws refer
to, or are based upon, eternal truths of reason, or remind us of them,
and rouse us to ponder them. Hence, our rabbis rightly say: the laws
and doctrines are related to each other like body and soul."[54] The performance of Judaism's symbolic acts leads then to the eternal and historical truths.[55]

What is especially significant is that these laws and actions impart
practical knowledge. Throughout *Jerusalem* Mendelssohn echoed his
earlier works in asserting that abstract knowledge is inadequate and in-
effectual. For example, he argued that to force upon an opponent all the
consequences derived by pure logic from a particular theological position engenders needless controversy that leads away from the truth.[56]
Mendelssohn also advanced an argument he had made during the controversy with Lavater. He would refrain from attacking Christianity because its practical benefits outweigh purely theoretical considerations,
as it is a "religion from which so many of my fellow men expect con-
tentment in this life and unlimited felicity thereafter."[57] In addition, Mendelssohn argued that abstract philosophy had limited practical value. God
has endowed all men at all times with the reason that brings felicity. In
all ages he has also bestowed exceptional powers of reason on some
individuals, yet "not at all times is this necessary or useful." The simple unlettered person might intuitively understand more than the most
sophisticated philosopher; the man who derives his concept of God's
providence from his unmediated observation of nature might be better

served than the philosopher who knows the difference between "direct and indirect causality."[58]

This critique of abstract philosophy also informed Mendelssohn's dissent from Lessing's notion of the "education of mankind." Lessing had argued for mankind's progress by applying the ontogenic metaphor of individual development—from a conceptual childhood through adolescence to maturity—phylogenetically to the collective. Mendelssohn's objection displayed his general resistance to historicist teleology. Lessing's view implied that later forms of philosophy were more effective in guiding people's lives than earlier ones. Mendelssohn rejected this roseate view of abstract knowledge, arguing that when the masses were in thrall to idolatry abstract philosophy had failed to liberate them; indeed, the philosophers' efforts had made matters worse.[59] Lessing assumed that philosophy and abstract knowledge were capable of improving man's collective well-being. Mendelssohn held that philosophy and abstract knowledge were impotent in this regard since all progress toward felicity was individual. Lessing's theory was also a thinly veiled secularization of the Christian conception of salvation history by which a later and higher form of belief (that is, Christianity) superseded a prior and lower one (that is, Judaism). Finally, Lessing assumed that man was able to comprehend the direction of history. Mendelssohn reiterated the view he had taken from his earliest works, setting distinct limits to abstract knowledge: as ultimate knowledge was God's alone, history defied human comprehension. Progress was in the hands of a "Providence" that "never misses its goal."[60]

Judaism's essential difference was its reliance not on a set of abstract doctrines but rather on a "ceremonial law" in which "religious and moral teachings were to be connected with men's everyday activities."[61] The Law addressed man's will and never forced his belief.

> All these excellent propositions are presented to the understanding, submitted to us for consideration, without being forced upon our belief. Among all the prescriptions and ordinances of the Mosaic law, there is not a single one which says: *You shall believe or not believe*. They all say: *You shall do or not do*. Faith is not commanded, for it accepts no other command than those that come to it by way of conviction. All the commandments of the divine law are addressed to man's will, to his power to act.[62]

Mendelssohn supported this view by turning to his commentary on those passages in Genesis and Exodus where he had drawn a distinction between "trust" and "belief."

> The word in the original language [Hebrew] that is usually translated as *faith* actually means, in most cases, *trust, confidence,* and firm reliance on pledge and promise. *Abraham trusted in the Eternal and it was accounted to him for piety* (Gen. 15:6); *the Israelites saw and trusted in the Eternal and in Moses, his servant* (Exod. 14:31). Whenever it is a question of the eternal truths or reason, it does not say *believe,* but *understand* and *know*. . . . Nowhere does it say: *Believe, O Israel, and you will be blessed; do not doubt, O Israel, or this or that punishment will befall you.*[63]

Israel's adherence to these laws was the basis of its election. The observance of the Law was the fulfillment of Israel's divine mission as a "priestly nation": the Law did not merely indicate the path of virtue, it was that path.

> [The patriarch's] descendants were chosen by Providence to be a *priestly* nation; that is, a nation which, through its establishment and constitution, its laws, actions, vicissitudes, and changes, was continually to call attention to sound and unadulterated ideas of God and his attributes. It was incessantly to teach, to proclaim, and to endeavor to preserve these ideas among the nations, by means of its mere existence.[64]

That the Jews were a priestly people by virtue of the Law was in keeping with Halevi's view of the Law as an end in itself and the sole means to God.[65] This idea also echoed Mendelssohn's commentary to Exodus 20 and his peroration to the Book of Exodus in which he asserted that the Law was designed to insulate Jews from the vices of society.[66]

ORAL TRANSMISSION

The law made the Jews a priestly people not only through its contents but also through its means of transmission. Mendelssohn's second argument in this part of *Jerusalem* was that oral transmission made the law "vital" knowledge. The oral transmission that made the Bible so readily comprehensible that it immediately penetrated an auditor's heart as well as preserved the text from corruption also made the law an effective instrument of individual and collective life. The Mendelssohn who spent so many hours happily conversing on philosophical matters with his friends and who employed dialogue to such good effect in his philosophical works believed in the efficacy of oral teaching.

Mendelssohn's belief in oral transmission was linked to his typology of truth. Each category of truth has its own form of transmission. For the "eternal" truths the appropriate divine form of communication was nature itself ("nature and thing") since it was universal. While the "necessary" truths (mathematics, logic) required reason alone, the "contingent" truths (physics, psychology) depended on observation as well as reason.[67]

Historical truths, in contrast, admitted of a human form of communication. Appropriate to this form of truth was "word and script," the comprehension of which is limited to a specific people at a specific time. Moreover, since historical events occurred but once, being available to the senses only of those present at the time, the truths they establish become dependent on the "authority and credibility" of the narrator. Miracles are therefore a means to confirm the veracity of historical truths.[68]

Mendelssohn had formulated important aspects of this argument in earlier works. In *Logical Terms* he had defended the transmission of historical knowledge by a properly attested tradition.[69] In his private writings during the Lavater affair he had defined the relationship of history to revelation. On the one side he had responded to Lavater by asserting that miracles could not persuasively be cited as proof for an exclusive revelation of truth. Christianity's contention that only through the acceptance of its "historical witness" could men be blessed and achieve salvation was at odds with reason and natural religion.[70] On the other side, the revelation at Sinai achieved certainty by virtue of its content being limited to historical truth and its form being public—the witness of the entire nation.[71]

Here is another example of Mendelssohn's proximity to Halevi. Mendelssohn followed Halevi in considering Sinai a direct revelation to the entire nation. In contrast, Maimonides argued that Moses, not all Israel, experienced the revelation directly because he alone possessed the requisite intellectual perfection.[72]

For Mendelssohn "truths of reason" could not be attested by miracles.

Miracles and extraordinary signs are, according to Judaism, no proofs for or against eternal truths of reason. We are, therefore, instructed in Scripture itself not to listen to a prophet if he teaches or counsels things contrary to established truths, even if he confirms his mission by miracles; indeed, we are to condemn to death the performer of miracles if he tries to lead us astray into idolatry. For miracles can only verify testimonies, support authorities, and confirm the credibility of witnesses and those who transmit tradition. But no testimonies and authorities can upset any established truth of reason or place a doubtful one beyond doubt and suspicion.[73]

Miracles had bearing on historical, not eternal, truths. Although Mendelssohn did not press the point, this was an obvious criticism of Christianity.

Mendelssohn thought that the use of an inappropriate form of transmission could have grave consequences: employing the human form of written words ("words and script") for divine, eternal truths, for example, had promoted idolatry. His understanding of this issue can be elucidated from an early essay on the origins of language. Language had arisen naturally. In order for mankind to transcend sense experience and to be able to express and transmit concepts, an oral language based on mimetic signs emerged which was then replaced by one consisting of abstract or arbitrary signs.[74] The development of language aided the growth of knowledge by providing a means to differentiate as well as to communicate concepts. In *Jerusalem* he argued that written language also had distinct disadvantages: the common people mistook the signs for the things themselves. Through a combination of ignorance and clerical chicanery, the people transformed written signs into idols. However innocent the invention of writing may have been, by being applied to divine truth, "written characters [became] the first cause of idolatry."[75] Idolatry was inherent in the very nature of writing—though Mendelssohn was careful to point out that not every mythology and religion that used writing was by definition idolatrous.

Judaism serves as a bulwark against idolatry by employing oral tradition to transmit historical truths. The historical truths Judaism imparts are the laws and ordinances in which every word is of import: "Laws cannot be abridged. In them everything is fundamental; and in this regard we may rightly say: to us, all words of Scripture, all of God's commandments and prohibitions are fundamental.[76]

In ancient Judaism only the laws were written. Doctrines and convictions, in contrast, were "entrusted to vital, spiritual instruction." The Law itself was "a kind of vital script,"

> rousing the mind and heart, full of meaning, never ceasing to inspire contemplation and to provide the occasion and opportunity for oral instruction. What a student himself did and saw being done from morning till night pointed to religious doctrines and convictions and spurred him on to follow his teacher, to watch him, to observe all his actions, and to obtain the instruction which he was capable of acquiring by means of his talents, and of which he had rendered himself worthy by his conduct.[77]

The very means of transmission made the Law a form of "vital," practical knowledge.

That the Law was vital knowledge had a number of consequences. The actions the Law prescribes inherently resisted idolatry since "there is nothing lasting, nothing enduring about them which, like hieroglyphic script, could lead to idolatry through abuse or misunderstanding."[78] For this very reason Mendelssohn could happily proclaim that Judaism contains no "dogmas." The absence of dogma did not mean that it lacked central principles and truths, but rather that its truths were not expressed in fixed formulations.[79] In part 1 of *Jerusalem* Mendelssohn had argued that oaths should be used for matters perceptible to the senses and not for belief.[80] Here he objected to oaths as "shackles of faith."[81] In attempting to articulate eternal truths in fixed formulae, dogma creates the potential for idolatry: the words themselves, rather than their contents, are in danger of becoming objects of worship. This reification is a cardinal example of the inappropriate application of human means of communication to divine truths. Moreover, written transmission itself was also inappropriate. Whereas language is constantly in flux, the fixed formulae are not and they are therefore in danger of becoming incomprehensible.[82] Mendelssohn thought that oral transmission alone was appropriate to the eternal truths since it was able to renew language and keep the truths comprehensible.[83]

Unlike written doctrines, actions also inherently promoted the social relations that throughout his works Mendelssohn had argued were imperative for man's development: they propel him "to social intercourse, to imitation and to oral vital instruction."[84] In addition, oral instruction created an intimate connection between thought and action, the abstract and the practical.

> The unwritten laws, the oral tradition, the vital instruction from man to man, from mouth to heart, were to explain, enlarge, limit, and define more precisely what, for wise intentions and with wise moderation, remained undetermined in the written law. In everything a youth saw being done, in all public as well as private dealings, on all gates and on all doorposts, to whatever he turned his eyes or ears, he found occasion for inquiring and reflecting, occasion to follow an older and wiser man at his every step, to observe his minutest actions and doings with childlike attentiveness and to imitate them with childlike docility, to inquire after the spirit and the purpose of those doings and to seek the instruction which his master considered him capable of absorbing and prepared to receive. Thus teaching and life, wisdom and activity, speculation and sociability were most intimately connected.[85]

In Judaism the Law and its oral transmission created a unity of "life and doctrine."[86]

THEOCRACY, BENEVOLENCE, AND
CEREMONIAL LAW

The unity of life and doctrine was so complete that in ancient Judaism "state and religion were not conjoined, but *one*; not connected, but identical." In part 1 Mendelssohn had argued that the best state was one whose members were able to govern themselves through education. He now asserted that ancient Judaism was the example of such a state precisely because of the identity of religion and politics.

> In this nation civil matters acquired a sacred and religious aspect, and every civil service was at the same time a true service of God. The community was a community of God, its affairs were God's; the public taxes were an offering to God; and everything down to the least police measure was part of the *divine service.*[87]

Mendelssohn thereby confronted Spinoza's understanding of a theocracy as being an impediment, if not the chief impediment, to religious freedom, an idea that was the stock-in-trade of eighteenth-century liberal thought. Mendelssohn turned Spinoza on his head: he accepted his categories but reversed his judgments.[88] For Mendelssohn pristine ancient Judaism represented an ideal of government through education/religion. It also corresponded to the ideal for politics Mendelssohn had articulated in his early philosophical works insofar as no conflict existed between individual interest and the commonweal.

> In God's wise and harmonious government the goal for which human politics strives is achieved to the fullest extent, namely, that every individual furthers the common good in pursuing his own well-being; then no reasonable being can pursue his own true well-being without being a benefactor of all of creation, since the particular and general interests are so exactly, so indivisibly connected.[89]

In so portraying ancient Judaism, Mendelssohn was able to respond in yet another way to Cranz's contention that in abjuring the ban he had undermined Judaism. All punishments that ancient Judaism meted out were civil infractions. Beliefs were subjected to neither scrutiny nor punishment.

> Every sacrilege against the authority of God, as the lawgiver of the nation, was a crime against the Majesty, and therefore a crime of state. Whoever blasphemed God committed lese majesty; whoever sacrilegiously desecrated the Sabbath implicitly abrogated a fundamental law of civil society. . . . Not unbelief, not false doctrine and error, but sacrilegious offenses against the majesty of the lawgiver, impudent misdeeds against the fundamental laws of the state and the civil constitution were punished; and these were punished

only when the sacrilege exceeded all bounds in its unruliness, and came close to rebellion; when the criminal was not afraid to have the law quoted to him by two fellow citizens, to be threatened with punishment and, indeed, to take the punishment upon himself and commit the crime in their presence. Here the religious villain becomes a sacrilegious desecrator of majesty, a state criminal.[90]

The elaborate precautions surrounding the Law mitigated its apparent harshness, rendering it just and equitable. Moreover, punishment was didactic rather than vindictive. Mendelssohn tried to correct the hoary image of a wrathful Jewish God. Restating a position he had taken in a number of earlier works, Mendelssohn asserted that punishment stemmed from God's benevolence since its aim was to help the individual by contributing to his "moral improvement."[91]

Mendelssohn turned this discussion of God's benevolence into an unequivocal rebuttal of Cranz's hope that his views on Christianity had changed since the Lavater affair. In part 1 of *Jerusalem* Mendelssohn had argued that whereas the innate human need for benevolence was the foundation of society, God has no need for our benevolence, with the result that religion can have no claims on us. He now asserted that idolatry, by ascribing human passions and vices to the gods, assumed that "without benevolence . . . [the gods] would not be happy in their heavenly abode."[92] The one God has no need for our benevolence since he is infinitely benevolent. To support this idea Mendelssohn cited the crucial passage in Exodus (33:15f.) that in the *Book of the Paths of Peace* he had used to discuss the limitations to human knowledge.[93] He argued that what God revealed to Moses on that occasion was his "infinite benevolence." Since God's benevolence dictates that all punishment must be didactic, there can be no vicarious suffering: "In God's state no individual suffers merely for the benefit of others."[94] Such vicarious suffering would contradict the notion that God cannot leave a sin unpunished—which derives from his aim to educate and improve us through punishment. Using central points of his overall argument, then, Mendelssohn unmistakably demonstrated his critical view of Christianity. He showed that his belief in Judaism was in keeping with his understanding of society whereas Christianity was at odds with it. Moreover, he illustrated his view with quotations from two psalms, using them in a manner entirely consistent with his translation, since they illuminated a point at which Judaism and natural religion converged.[95]

Mendelssohn was quick to acknowledge that the ancient Judaism in which state and religion were identical was unique and short-lived. Its unity had begun to unravel with the appointment of an earthly king and the subsequent abuses of the priesthood and had disappeared entirely with the destruction of the Temple; here, as with other historical developments (such as the case of early burial), Mendelssohn made no attempt to offer an explanation beyond the simplest enumeration of causes.[96] With the collapse of the "Mosaic constitution" the harmony of interests as well as the unity of religious and civil law ceased. Ancient Judaism was the exception that proved Mendelssohn's argument in part 1 that religion should have no coercive powers.

> As the rabbis expressly state, *with the destruction of the Temple, all corporal and capital punishments and, indeed, even monetary fines, insofar as they are only national, have ceased to be legal.* Perfectly in accordance with my principles, and inexplicable without them! The civil bonds of the nation were dissolved; religious offenses were no longer crimes against the state; and the religion, as religion, knows of no punishment, no other penalty than the one the remorseful sinner *voluntarily* imposes on himself. It knows of no coercion, uses only the staff [called] *gentleness,* and affects only mind and heart. Let one try to explain rationally, without my principles, this assertion of the rabbis![97]

Given that autonomous Jewish communities had exercised precisely such punitive powers for many centuries and that such powers were integral to the community's existence, Mendelssohn's assertion appears strange indeed. Yet one should read this passage carefully: Mendelssohn did not make an assertion about history but about an ideal situation and the principles that should inform it ("to explain rationally, without my principles"). He did not create a fictional account of the past; instead, he projected a timeless ideal of what should be even if it obviously had not occurred.

After the destruction of the Temple and the exile of the nation, the laws pertaining to the land and the Temple fell into abeyance. What remained was the "ceremonial law."[98] Having argued for Judaism as the exemplary religion of practical knowledge made "vital" by oral transmission, Mendelssohn then made his characteristic argument for heteronomy (with his resistance to historicism central to it).

> I cannot see how those born into the House of Jacob can in any conscientious manner disencumber themselves of the law. We are permitted to reflect on the law, to inquire into its spirit, and, here and there, where the lawgiver gave no reason, to surmise a reason which, *perhaps,* depended upon time, place, and circumstances, and which, *perhaps,* may be liable to change in accordance with time, place, and circumstances—if it pleases the Supreme Lawgiver to make known to us His will on this matter, to make it known in as clear a

voice, in as public a manner, and as far beyond all doubt and ambiguity, as He did when He gave the law itself. As long as this has not happened, as long as we can point to no such authentic exemption from the law, no sophistry of ours can free us from the strict obedience we owe to the law; and reverence for God draws a line between speculation and practice which no conscientious man may cross. I therefore repeat my earlier protestation. Weak and shortsighted is the eye of man! Who can say: I have entered into God's sanctuary, gauged the whole system of his designs, and am able to determine its measure, goal and boundaries? I may surmise, but neither pass judgment nor act according to my surmise. If in things human I may not dare to act contrary to the law on the mere strength of my own surmise and legal sophistry, without the authority of the lawgiver or custodian of the law, how much less may I do so in matters divine?[99]

While Mendelssohn recognized the inevitable temptation to find explanations for the Law, especially historical ones ("time, place, and circumstances"), he resolutely denied such explanations any authority.[100] He instead introduced his characteristic distinction between "speculation" and "practice" which dictated that all such explanations were no more than a "surmise." Once again Mendelssohn set clear limits to speculative or theoretical reason, rejecting a contemplative ideal that might affect practice. The observance of the Law lay beyond the reach of abstract reason. Only through a second revelation, comparable to the one at Sinai in content (absolute clarity) and in form (public nature), could God establish the authority necessary to introduce changes into the practice of the Law.

RIGHTS, LAW, AND THEISM

The Law also lay beyond the debate on rights. In part 1 of *Jerusalem* Mendelssohn had argued for an unconditional grant of rights on the basis of natural right. He now argued that the grant of rights should not be made conditional on changes in the "divine legislation" or its observance. The Jews were duty bound to observe the law. As a true son of Israel Jesus had obeyed the Law; Christians cannot expect Jews today to act any differently. Jews could become part of the surrounding society only to the extent that it did not impinge on their observance of the Law.

No wiser advice than this can be given to the House of Jacob. Adapt yourselves to the morals and the constitution of the land to which you have been removed; but hold fast to the religion of your fathers, too. Bear both burdens as well as you can! . . . remain unflinching at the post which Providence has assigned to you.[101]

Should this not suffice to gain rights, then there is no choice but to forgo them.

> If civil union cannot be obtained under any other condition than our departing from the laws which we still consider binding on us, then we are sincerely sorry to find it necessary to declare that we must rather do without civil union; then that friend of mankind, Dohm, will have written in vain, and everything will remain in the melancholy condition in which it is now, or in which your love of mankind may think it proper to place it. It does not rest with us to yield on this matter. . . . We cannot in good conscience depart from the Law, and what good will it do you to have fellow citizens without conscience?[102]

Mendelssohn's devotion to the Law could brook no exception. If rights were to be given contingent on changes in, or abrogation of, the Law, then they could not be accepted. A quid pro quo of religious observance for rights was unthinkable.[103]

Mendelssohn's final concern was that the numerous attempts at unification of the faiths were a threat to freedom of thought and liberty of conscience, the central theme of part 1 of *Jerusalem*. In this crucial respect Mendelssohn departed from many Christian religious Enlighteners in central Europe who aimed to reunite the churches. Some Protestant religious Enlighteners hoped to develop a new Christian sensibility that would transcend the Lutheran-Calvinist divide and pave the way for a comprehensive Protestant church.[104] Some Catholic religious Enlighteners hoped that by introducing reforms to remove the grievances that had originally led to schism, Protestants would return to the church.[105] These hopes did not remain entirely theoretical, since at various times representatives of the churches met to try to find common doctrinal ground.

Mendelssohn regarded these efforts with horror. He understood the differences between the religions to be divinely ordained:

> In order to be under the care of this omnipresent shepherd the entire flock need neither graze in one pasture nor enter and leave the master's house through a single door. This is neither what the shepherd wants nor advantageous to the prosperity of the flock . . . diversity is evidently the plan and purpose of Providence.[106]

In Mendelssohn's view the diverse yet coherent world envisioned in Wolffian metaphysics meshed with the inherited Jewish view of religious multiplicity. What was at stake in religious diversity was liberty of conscience in general and theism in particular. The efforts at unification turned on finding verbal formulae to which all parties could agree. Mendelssohn considered this a shallow commerce in doctrines. Yet even worse, he thought it threatened "barbarism": fixed formulations of divine truths in the human medium of words would become binding as oaths. Still worse, were such a unification of faiths to succeed, it would result in tyranny of conscience since any dissent would then be a threat to civil peace.[107] Instead, Mendelssohn understood Judaism to play a special role: it sustained true theism through a law that enjoined actions rather than through doctrines that depended on words.

> Even had [the ritual laws] lost their use as a significant script or symbolic language, their necessity as a unifying bond would not cease, and to my mind this unity would remain part of Providence's system so long as polytheism, anthropomorphism and religious usurpation dominate the world. As long as these tormentors of reason are united, the true theists must maintain a unity of some sort lest the former bring everyone to heel. In what should this unity consist? In principles and opinions?—which, as doctrines of faith, symbols and formulas, fetter reason. Rather in actions, that is, ceremonies.[108]

Judaism was the bulwark of theism against all forms of idolatry. As we have seen in his commentary to Exodus, in which he argued for Israel's election but also for the validity of other forms of worship for other people, Mendelssohn's view was compatible with toleration. The contents of Judaism were identical with natural religion even while its form was historical. As a result, it was best for the Jews but not for everyone.

> The internal divine service of Judaism contains no other precepts than those of natural religion. These we are obligated to disseminate; and to the best of my ability, I attempt to fulfill this duty. . . . In contrast, our external divine service is not at all fit to be disseminated since it contains precepts that are linked to persons, times and circumstances. To be sure, we believe that our religion is the best, since we consider it to be divine. Yet it does not follow that it is therefore absolutely the best. It is best for us and our progeny, the best for specific times and circumstances and under specific conditions.[109]

At this point it is worth reflecting on the relationship between "divine legislation" and eternal truths. Did Mendelssohn hollow out the ceremonial law by separating the two? Mendelssohn certainly did not understand the issue as the medieval Jewish philosophers had. Living in a world of competing faiths, each of which laid exclusive claim to truth, the medieval philosophers understood Sinai to be a revelation of universal truths and Judaism to be the absolute religion. Mendelssohn's recognition of a common or universal foundation of belief in the form of natural religion was characteristic of the Enlightenment and set him apart from the medieval thinkers.[110] Moreover, his willingness to recognize a universal foundation of faith to which positive religion added the specific truths of revelation was integral to the religious Enlightenment.[111] Mendelssohn's insistence that the truths needed to attain eternal life were universally accessible led him to reconstrue the relationship between the universal and particular, yet he did not thereby render the ceremonial law hollow or, in the end, superfluous. Rather, he laid particular emphasis on Israel's election and its historical role. Adherence to the ceremonial laws not only guided the Jews to the eternal truths, but this intimate connection between action and belief safeguarded those truths for all mankind. Far from being hollow, then, the ceremonial law preserved and protected the eternal truths that informed it, a notion clearly derived from the Andalusian tradition.[112]

Mendelssohn's concluding plea was for "our noblest treasure," liberty of conscience. It was to be secured by a "universal toleration" that was "the height of culture" and for which "reason still sighs in vain."[113] For Mendelssohn toleration was a matter neither of economic expedience nor of political pragmatism: it was providentially ordained, metaphysically grounded, and required by natural right.

What was the relationship between the two parts of Jerusalem? Was Mendelssohn a "sophist" in part 1 and a "typical Jew" in part 2, as was reputedly charged?[114] Mendelssohn used a number of themes developed in part 1 in his discussion of Judaism in part 2: the rejection of oaths was elaborated into a general consideration of the unsuitability of the written word for divine truth; the preference for government through education was echoed in the portrayal of "ancient Judaism" as the embodiment of that ideal; "benevolence" as the primordial motive of society became a defining characteristic of idolatry as well as of the argument against Christianity; and the argument for liberty of conscience through natural right was founded in a providential justification of diversity. These themes knit together the two parts: there was a seamless transition between natural philosophy and Judaism which resembled such early works as the *Preacher of Morals* and *Logical Terms*. In part 1 Mendelssohn argued entirely on the basis of natural right; in part 2 he argued on the basis of revealed legislation. Mendelssohn had in fact reflected on the relationship between a natural ("earthly") and revealed ("heavenly") politics toward the end of *Jerusalem*.

> Just as, according to Plato, there is an earthly and also a heavenly Eros, there is also . . . an earthly and a heavenly politics. Take a fickle adventurer,

a conqueror of hearts, such as are met with in the streets of every metropolis, and speak to him of the *Song of Songs*, or of the love of erstwhile innocence in Paradise, as Milton describes it. He will believe that you are raving, or that you wish to rehearse your lesson as to how to overwhelm the heart of a prude by means of Platonic caresses. Just as little will a politician a la mode understand you if you speak to him of the simplicity and moral grandeur of that original [Mosaic] constitution. As the former knows nothing of love but the satisfaction of base lasciviousness, the latter speaks, when statesmanship is the subject, only of power, the circulation of money, commerce, the balance of power and population; and religion is to him a means which the lawgiver uses to keep the unruly man in check, and the priest—to suck him dry and consume his marrow. I had to remove from the eyes of my reader this false point of view, from which we are in the habit of regarding the true interest of human society.[115]

Despite the obvious differences, the two parts were informed with a single vision consistent with his earlier works.

Jerusalem also recalled Mendelssohn's earlier works in its affinity for the Andalusian tradition and theological Wolffianism. Mendelssohn affirmed his adherence to the Andalusian tradition in his emphasis on practice and observance. The primacy of practical knowledge, the "divine legislation," was supported by his uncompromising endorsement of heteronomy and the unquestioned authority of the revelation at Sinai, his rejection of a contemplative ideal and the limits he set to abstract knowledge as well as his espousal of historical truth yoked to his principled resistance to historicism. The oral transmission that guaranteed the authenticity of the Masoretic text also ensured that the knowledge the legislation imparted was not only practical but indeed "vital." His kinship with theological Wolffianism was expressed in his use of ecclesiastical natural law ("collegial") theory, which enabled him to reconcile natural religion and the "divine legislation" in order to endorse revelation as well as toleration. It was also expressed in his turn to history as a means to attain certainty of belief. While Mendelssohn wrote *Jerusalem* as a polemical response, the work was not only in harmony with his earlier works but elaborated many of their major themes. Nevertheless, *Jerusalem* was not, and was not intended to be, a systematic account of Jewish belief and observance.

THE HASKALAH AND POLITICS

Mendelssohn's answer to Cranz and Mörschel was unequivocal. He was neither a naturalist nor was he tempted by Christianity: he remained steadfast in his loyalty to Judaism. Judaism was a "divine legislation" established by the historical truth of Sinai and sustained by oral transmission. As the religion of practical knowledge, it provided protection against two related dangers: the descent into idolatry suffered by revealed religions whose doctrines, once recorded in writing, became dogma; and the infringement of liberty of conscience by revealed religions that exercised coercion.

As a religion of practical knowledge, Judaism was also entirely suited to a society that vouchsafed equal rights. Since Judaism prescribed actions rather than convictions, therefore not requiring coercion of any sort, it was entirely compatible with the state grounded in the separation of church and state, the state that Mendelssohn thought capable of recognizing the Jews as equal citizens.

In this regard Mendelssohn can be said to have used novel means to a conservative end: he tried to reinstate the dualism of the autonomous community through the means of equal rights. The autonomous community had remitted taxes and rendered obedience to the sovereign in exchange for an independent religious and social life. Mendelssohn tried to accomplish something similar with his plea for an unconditional grant of rights. In exchange for loyalty to the state in the form of a "civil union," the Jews would be able to preserve their religious independence in the form of a voluntary society.[116] In this manner Mendelssohn reconciled the role of the intercessor with that of the theological Wolffian: through toleration and rights the religious freedom of the Jews could best be defended.

Jerusalem represented the culmination of Mendelssohn's thinking on politics and rights. In the course of some two decades Mendelssohn had shifted the balance in his political thinking toward rights—although without questioning the importance of the state or his loyalty to it. In the 1760s he developed political categories that he also applied to the Jews' general situation ("civic oppression"). From his first act of intercession in 1769, Mendelssohn was forced to confront the specifics of the Jews' political situation, yet it was only with the general politicization of German life and of the Haskalah in the 1770s that he slowly began to apply his political categories to the Jews' actual circumstances. In the 1780s he encouraged Dohm to enter a plea for the rights of Jews and he supported it with his preface to the translation of Menasseh ben Israel. In response to Cranz's challenge he published *Jerusalem*. In other words, Mendelssohn was gradually drawn into the debate on rights by the turn of events of the late 1770s and early 1780s. This undertaking grew out of his activity as an intercessor and relied on his Enlightenment thinking. Yet it represented a diversion of the Haskalah into politics.

To be sure, *Jerusalem* was Mendelssohn's most sustained presentation of his beliefs on Judaism—his credo—and it was fully in harmony with his earlier works. Yet the work's main ideas about Judaism had been developed earlier, as part of his efforts to renew the Andalusian tradition through the revival of the cognate disciplines of philosophy in Hebrew and biblical exegesis as well as in his private writings during the Lavater affair. These ideas predated his argument for rights, even if he utilized and amplified them in making that argument. In other words, Mendelssohn developed his version of the Haskalah independently of the political question of rights, though he made full use of it once he started to address that question.

Mendelssohn's case suggests that the Haskalah was first and foremost an autochthonous effort at intellectual renewal. In this respect the movement was typical of the eighteenth-century religious Enlightenment. Yet it was also typical of the religious Enlightenment in being diverted from its initial religious and intellectual program by the politicization of intellectual life in the 1770s and 1780s. We have already seen the late Enlightenment's development of a political public in the 1770s and 1780s. The entire religious Enlightenment underwent a thoroughgoing politicization that threatened to alter its very nature. This development is especially evident in the case of Reform Catholicism.

Reform Catholicism was an indigenous effort at intellectual and religious renewal, a second humanist reform or "counter-Counter Reformation" that first appeared in certain monasteries (ca. 1720) and then in some universities and academies (ca. 1740). After the accession of a conservative pope (Clement XIII) in 1758 and the Habsburg defeat in the Seven Years' War in 1763, Reform Catholicism increasingly became allied with the state and the secular Catholic Enlightenment in a program of religious and pedagogical reform. As a result of that alliance there was a growing co-optation of Reform Catholic personnel into the government bureaucracy in the 1770s and 1780s which threatened to dilute the movement's original intellectual and religious character and also endangered its effort at internal church reform by turning it into a faction. In the 1780s some Reform Catholics protested against these developments by leaving government service to return to their monasteries and intellectual pursuits. Others remained and experienced a radicalization that took them far from their Reform Catholic origins toward the secular Enlightenment and, in some extreme cases, to an unalloyed rationalism.[117]

It was the promise of a new relationship with the absolutist state which drew Mendelssohn into the political arena and away from his original agenda of the intellectual renewal of Judaism. Exercising his characteristic independence of mind and displaying his readiness to embrace novel means for conservative ends, he saw the acquisition of civil rights for Jews as a way to safeguard the freedom of Judaism.

Conclusion

While Mendelssohn's works in the last three years of his life (1783–1786) were devoted to political and philosophical issues relevant to his Jewish thought, his specifically Jewish writing effectively ended with *Jerusalem*. In a series of essays first delivered as talks at the Wednesday Society, he expanded on many of the key political notions broached in *Jerusalem*, including his famous definition of "Enlightenment" in which he distinguished between its practical ("Kulture") and theoretical ("Aufklärung") components.[1] The controversy over Lessing's alleged Spinozism, which was the cause célèbre of German intellectual life in the 1780s, resulted in Mendelssohn's final and most sustained philosophical work, *The Morning Hours, or Lectures on God's Existence.* He reiterated the central ideas of natural philosophy that underpinned his understanding of Judaism and expressed his preference for practical reason ("common sense") over speculative thought.[2] Whereas the ideas in these works were consonant with, perhaps even derived from, his Jewish allegiances, the works themselves did not deal specifically with Jewish issues and should not be considered contributions to his Jewish thinking.[3]

Mendelssohn had been active as a Jewish thinker throughout his career. His writing, translating, and commenting were not limited to discrete periods but rather stretched from the very beginning to virtually the end of his adult life.[4] In the 1750s and 1760s he produced the *Kohelet Musar, Logical Terms* (1760–1761), the Hebrew essays posthumously published as *The Book of the Soul,* and the commentary to Ecclesiastes (1769–1770). After the Lavater controversy he produced his translation of Psalms, *The Book of the Paths of Peace,* the preface to the translation of Menasseh ben Israel, and *Jerusalem.* If Mendelssohn's production on Jewish matters ever slackened, it was during the peak period of the 1760s when he was most productive in the world of German letters. Yet even then he did not cease entirely to write on Jewish subjects, and he had embarked on the new project of biblical commentary prior to the Lavater affair.

If Mendelssohn's production stayed constant, so did his positions. He staked out his primary positions at an early stage and stayed with them. The emphasis on practical knowledge and the repudiation of a contemplative ideal, the endorsement of heteronomy and resistance to historicism, as well as the defense of rabbinic exegesis and the Masoretic text of the Bible were formative ideas he maintained throughout his career. Whether addressing philosophy, exegesis, or politics, these ideas allowed Mendelssohn to reconcile faith and reason by rearticulating the Andalusian tradition of practical rationalism in a manner comparable to the Protestant theological Wolffians of the second quarter of the eighteenth century. To be sure, at various points in his career he elaborated ideas in new areas, for instance, in aesthetics and in biblical exegesis. He also changed his mind on some secondary or tertiary issues, such as the extent to which Prussian judges should rule on the basis of Jewish law. His primary views on Judaism and metaphysics, however, remained unchanged. While his argument for rights was in harmony with these, it resulted from the increasing politicization of German intellectual life in the 1770s and 1780s rather than being the logical next step of his program of Haskalah.

Mendelssohn's reputation suffered from the accelerated change at the close of the eighteenth century. He was a figure of the religious Enlightenment, yet in central Europe an alliance with the state transformed that religious and intellectual movement and during the Revolutionary and Napoleonic era it vanished or went subterranean. He was the preeminent *maskil,* but contemporary and later observers tended to confuse the Haskalah with the processes of embourgeoisement and assimilation which the Jews in central and western Europe subsequently experienced. The disappearance of the religious Enlightenment and the misinterpretation of the Haskalah meant the anchors of Mendelssohn's thought were lost, allowing the legend and symbol to float rudderless through history.

The result was that Mendelssohn became the symbol of the modern Jew. Successive interpreters shaped an image of Mendelssohn accord-

ing to the conflicts that filled the next two centuries. These interpretations of the two faces of Mendelssohn were creative misreadings of
his life and work. They concentrated on the externals of his career and
his novel methods: Mendelssohn the German philosopher, the friend of
Lessing, the supposed follower of Maimonides, the defender of Judaism
in German. They either neglected, ignored, or misunderstood the inner
workings and conservative ends of his thought.

The one face resulted from the celebration of Mendelssohn's novel
techniques and his life, making him the symbol of the fusion of Judaism
with modern culture. This symbol had already been created during his
lifetime in the idealized figure Lessing had modeled on him (Nathan) in
his drama of toleration, *Nathan the Wise*. In the biography of Mendelssohn Isaac Euchel wrote in Hebrew in 1788 he declared Mendelssohn a
model for all Jews: "His life should be our standard, his teaching our
light."[5] In 1829, on the centenary of Mendelssohn's birth, a preacher in
Hamburg declared him to have proved that "a son of Israel could also
soar upward to the height of pure morality and virtue, that he could
reach this height even on his own, without direction or guidance."[6]
That same year another preacher declared him to be "as a man and as
a writer, both teacher and model."[7]

It also became commonplace in the nineteenth century to date the beginning of the modern period in Jewish history from Mendelssohn. In
an important 1846 essay, for example, the most durable and significant
Jewish historian of the nineteenth century, Heinrich Graetz, dated the
final phase of the diaspora period, the "theoretical-philosophic," from
Mendelssohn.[8] In his eleven-volume history he also attributed the modern "renaissance" of the Jews to Mendelssohn:

> This rejuvenescence or renaissance of the Jewish race . . . may be unhesitat-
> ingly ascribed to Mendelssohn. . . . He produced this altogether unpremed-
> itated glorious result . . . without either knowing or desiring it: involuntarily
> he aroused the slumbering genius of the Jewish race. . . . The story of his life
> is interesting, because it typifies the history of the Jews in recent times, when
> they raised themselves from lowliness and contempt to greatness and self-
> consciousness.[9]

Mendelssohn was not only German Jewry's "patron saint" but also the
"ideal figure" of its subculture. All of the religious adaptations of Judaism in the nineteenth century—whether Reform, Positive-Historical,
or Neo-Orthodox—claimed his authority.[10]

Throughout Europe the rhetoric of emancipation advanced the idea
of a quid pro quo of regeneration for rights—the very idea Mendelssohn

had rejected. As the exemplar of the fusion of Judaism with modern culture, Mendelssohn ironically served as the symbol for that regeneration for non-Jews and Jews, governments and philosophers.

In the first systematic and far-reaching report on the Jews of Russia (1802), for example, the poet and politician Gavriil Derzhavin pointed to Mendelssohn to show that Jews could be regenerated.

> Everyone knows . . . that in many times and places a multitude of laws have been passed in an attempt to raise up the Jews or to eliminate them. . . . Nowhere, however, was any care taken to see to their political or moral education, no attempt was made to lift them out of darkness and barbarism. Only lately have we been given the example of the German Jew Mendelssohn, who is proving that the Jews are capable of something else, and whose work is recognized as the successful crowning of this attitude, especially in the purification of language, for he has translated the holy books into pure German and made them available to the simple people. . . . It is possible to open the eyes of the Jewish people . . . and to restore their religion to the pure source whence it originated.[11]

In eastern Europe Mendelssohn became the symbol of the Haskalah and belief in him became virtual dogma. "I believe with perfect faith that Mendelssohn was the greatest mind and father of the *maskilim,* that his doctrine is a doctrine of truth that admits of no change and that his path is a holy path without twists or turns."[12]

One of the first petitions in the Pale of settlement (Umam, 1822) to open a school with a dual secular and religious curriculum asserted that it would be "based on the system of Mendelssohn."[13] The two private elementary schools of the Haskalah that opened in Vilna in 1841 both used Mendelssohn's *Book of the Paths of Peace* to teach the Bible.[14] And *Jerusalem* was first published in Hebrew for an eastern European audience at the height of the Haskalah's hopes for emancipation (1867).[15]

In France Mendelssohn had been associated with change since Mirabeau's 1787 pamphlet *Sur Moses Mendelssohn, sur la réforme politique des Juifs,* which, as its title indicates, advanced arguments similar to Dohm's alongside an account of Mendelssohn's life and accomplishments. His example played a role both in the Assembly of Notables and the Sanhedrin that Napoleon convened in 1806–1808, and when consistory schools offering a dual secular and religious education were introduced in Alsace in the 1840s and 1850s, for example, the students were offered a didactic biography of Mendelssohn as a model of how to combine Judaism and modern culture.[16]

In England (1798) Mendelssohn was hailed as an unexpected Jewish entrant to the pantheon of world literature.

. . . a sublime genius; an Israelite, who feels no degradation when associated with a Locke and a Leibniz was hardly expected to arise. . . . By the force of his reasoning Germany calls him the Jewish Socrates; and by the amenity of his diction, the Jewish Plato.[17]

The translator of Mendelssohn's letters (1825) held him aloft as a model for contemporary Jews:

. . . the harbinger of better days to a fallen—but not an irreclaimable— people . . . [who has] pave[d] the way for the reestablishment of the people in its natural inheritance of wisdom, knowledge and individual and national consideration.[18]

Mendelssohn's friendship with Lessing was used to demonstrate the ability of Jews and non-Jews to live harmoniously under the new legal conditions. Gabriel Riesser, the chief advocate of Jewish emancipation in the German states in the 1830s and 1840s, declared that friendship a model of social relations: "Where are we to find a purer and more sublime model than in Lessing's and Mendelssohn's friendship?"[19] Moritz Oppenheim's painting of Mendelssohn and Lessing playing chess (1856) became the iconic symbol of that relationship. This symbol could even be invoked as a defense against anti-Semitism. As one lecturer put it at the height of political anti-Semitism in 1893:

We German Jews above all have only too much cause to remind ourselves of these two great intellectual benefactors. If we defend ourselves with the exalted words *Law* and *Humanity* against the afflictions of a cruel, hate-filled and perplexed time, to whom else should we Israelites be grateful for the inner meaning and true understanding of these words than this noble pair of friends?[20]

Mendelssohn's other face resulted from the denigration of his life and the novel means he employed, a critical view that made Mendelssohn the symbol for everything thought to be amiss with Judaism and the Jews. As early as 1783 Joseph II reportedly decided to exclude Mendelssohn's works from the empire: Mendelssohn was a "naturalist" and that was not the future he wanted for his Jews.[21] The conversion to Christianity after Mendelssohn's death of four of his six children fed this image.[22] In his ethical testament the leader of Orthodoxy, Moses Sofer, coined the admonition "Do not touch the works of Rabbi Moses of Dessau."

Mendelssohn's demotion to the symbol and false prophet of assimilation came in the closing decades of the nineteenth century with the rise of postliberal ideologies. Since these ideologies repudiated emancipation, they also rejected Mendelssohn as its most visible symbol. Peretz

Smolenskin virtually identified the Haskalah with modern Jewish life in Europe. When in the 1870s he lost faith in emancipation and began to rediscover the Jews as a nation, he subverted the eastern European Haskalah's dogmatic reverence for Mendelssohn by traducing him as the first assimilationist. This symbol subsequently became a commonplace within the Zionist movement and the other postliberal ideologies.[23]

The ideologue of Jewish autonomism and eminent historian Simon Dubnow, for example, treated Mendelssohn as the protagonist of emancipation and assimilation, and he deemed proponents of both Mendelssohn's followers. In the early twentieth century he wrote:

> ... the cultural assimilation was mounting. One of the most important manifestations of assimilation lay in the fact that the German and Alsatian Jews had repudiated their own national language, and instead spoke German or French. This was brought about by the propaganda of the Mendelssohn epoch; and the Old Testament was even translated for that purpose. The state language Germanized or Frenchified all modes of life, intruded into the family and the school, into the literature that Jews had created and even into the synagogues. The young generation became gradually alienated from Judaism: first the generation of Henrietta Herz, of Mendelssohn's daughters ... ; second, the generation of Börne and Heine; third, the generation of Marx and Lasalle. In each of these three stages the alienation gradually intensified.[24]

The Marxist historian Raphael Mahler held Mendelssohn and the *maskilim* responsible for the cultural collapse of Judaism.

> Mendelssohn's contempt for the spoken language of the people expressed the view of the new Jewish middle class, its hope of resembling the country's ruling classes in all things. . . . Neither he nor all of the *maskilim* who followed him realized that by jettisoning Yiddish, they were destroying one of the chief foundations of a distinct Jewish culture and thereby endangering the basis for the existence of Hebrew.[25]

Mendelssohn's reception as a thinker paralleled his fate as a symbol. The very fact that he wrote about Judaism in German using philosophical categories was of overwhelming importance. He was the magnetic pole to the compass of nineteenth-century Jewish thought, providing the point of reference and orientation. Yet the substance of his thought was more often refuted than accepted, more often creatively misread than critically evaluated. His understanding of Judaism remained an "ephemeral solution" to the problem of the philosophical articulation of Judaism. A major factor in this regard was that his philosophical position was virtually untenable during the last years of his life and became more so with time. Two stages in this process deserve mention.[26]

After the publication of Kant's *Critique of Pure Reason* (1781) Mendelssohn was fully aware that his Wolffianism was under siege: he confessed that he ceased to be current with philosophical developments and, in a phrase that has since become famous, dubbed his erstwhile competitor "the all-destroying Kant."[27] By introducing a new method into philosophy, Kant also altered the focus of concern about Judaism. He criticized Judaism by reviving Spinoza's view of Judaism as a theocracy. He denied Judaism the status of a religion, understanding it instead to be a political constitution inimical to the development of his ideal—a religion that promoted morality by being grounded purely in autonomous reason.[28] Whereas Mendelssohn has been concerned to show that Judaism was fully congruent with natural religion, Jewish thinkers after Kant were concerned to establish Judaism's status as a religion of morality and belief, an effort for which Mendelssohn's notions of "divine legislation" and heteronomy were an impediment. Hence Saul Ascher, one of the first thinkers to attempt a systematic presentation of Judaism in the 1790s, understood Judaism as a revealed religion that could educate reason and promote morality better than Christianity if only it were subjected to a reform that would restore its status as a religion of belief by eliminating the preponderance of law.[29]

This emphasis on morality and belief was buttressed by the emancipation process. Emancipation required a regeneration in which the Jews proved their ability to be moral citizens worthy of rights. In addition, emancipation required that the Jews be recast as a confession and cease to be a political or social group. One theological consequence of emancipation was that Judaism was understood to be a system of belief with a definable "essence," for example, monotheism. As a result, Mendelssohn's definition of Judaism as a "divine legislation" served more as a foil than a model. Even those who considered themselves to be working in Mendelssohn's spirit and continuing his project of renewal, for example, the preachers and teachers who were the ideologues of emancipation in the first decades of the nineteenth century in Germany, in fact did not accept his understanding of Judaism.[30] And Solomon Ludwig Steinheim, the most original of the Jewish thinkers of the 1830s and 1840s, argued against Mendelssohn that Judaism's uniqueness consisted in its doctrinal revelation of God's transcendence and creation of the world ex nihilo, which human reason was incapable of comprehending.[31]

An additional stage in this process came with German idealist philosophy: the historicism Mendelssohn had resisted became fundamental to the nineteenth-century understanding of Judaism. The language of immutable truth gave place to that of dynamic process, development, and the realization of an essence or teleology. Lessing's notion of the "education of mankind" which Mendelssohn had resolutely rejected now became widely accepted in various forms among Jewish thinkers.[32] The programmatic statement (1822) for the academic study of Judaism (*Wissenschaft des Judentums*), for example, combined the notions of essence and development: the idea of the transcendent divinity ("the unity of all being in eternity") unfolds through history, attaining ever greater clarity and universality.[33] Nachman Krochmal, the foremost philosopher of Judaism in eastern Europe and a student of German idealism, grappled with the implications of the historicist position that, just as all cultures develop over time, so the Judaism of the Bible and rabbinic literature had changed as well.[34]

The way in which Mendelssohn's Jewish thought was understood was significantly influenced by the fact that his German works, and primarily *Jerusalem,* were far more consistently read than his Hebrew ones. It was the rare thinker who attempted to come to grips with the full scope of his Jewish thought.[35] This tendency to emphasize the "German" Mendelssohn was canonized by the first edition of his collected works (1843–1845). Only the German works were republished. There was no trace of the Hebrew works, and the *Book of the Paths of Peace* was transformed into a German work: the translation that had originally been published in Hebrew characters was transcribed into Latin letters and published without the commentary, and only short excerpts in German translation from the Hebrew introduction, "Light for the Path," appeared in the editor's introduction.[36] That the full scope of Mendelssohn's Jewish thought was normally not engaged can be seen in the case of the founder of Neo-Orthodoxy, Samson Raphael Hirsch. Hirsch distinguished between the practical (Nahmanides, Halevi) and speculative (Maimonides) traditions in medieval Jewish thought and then, basing his judgment on *Jerusalem* alone, rued the fact that Mendelssohn had opted for the speculative, Maimonidean tradition.[37] Mendelssohn's symbolic status as a German thinker clearly influenced the assessment of his Jewish thought.

The reception of Mendelssohn's thought and the varied and conflicting versions of the symbol belonged to nineteenth- and early twentieth-century Europe. They should not be allowed to color our understanding of Mendelssohn's thought. Mendelssohn was a transitional figure whose position depended on a delicate and highly wrought balance between old and new. He represented not a departure from previous Jewish tradition but an effort to renew it, not rupture but self-conscious continuity. We should resist the temptation of trying to make him into something he was not—as a symbol a vindication of emancipation or an indictment of assimilation, as a thinker either wholly modern or wholly medieval.

His Jewish thinking might best be described by a metaphor. His thought is like a much-viewed and abused master painting that has been covered with many layers of varnish and grime. Some who applied varnish felt the original needed embellishment or improvement, others thought that conserving the original meant altering it to fit their own taste. Still others applied varnish in the hope that the original might be repudiated, disfigured, or forgotten. The passage of time brought the inevitable grime. The purpose of this study has been to strip away some of the accumulated layers of varnish and grime so that Mendelssohn's Jewish thought can be seen as a creation of the eighteenth-century religious Enlightenment which, while closer in time to the subsequent symbol or later Jewish thinkers, was closer in manner to the thought of the theological Wolffians and closer in matter to the Andalusian tradition of Jewish thought.

Biographical Notes

Baumgarten, Siegmund Jacob (1706–1757). Professor at Halle and a "theological Wolffian." The preeminent theologian of his age, he used Wolff's philosophy to articulate Protestant doctrine.

Cranz, August (1737–1801). Political pamphleteer whose accusations prompted Mendelssohn to write *Jerusalem*.

Dohm, Christian Wilhelm (1751–1820). Prussian civil servant and political journalist. At Mendelssohn's request he wrote the most influential tract advocating emancipation of the Jews.

Dubno, Solomon (1738–1813). Hebrew scholar who served as tutor to Mendelssohn's children. Played a major role in the Pentateuch edition.

Eichhorn, Johann Gottfried (1752–1827). Professor in Göttingen. One of the most important exponents of the historical-critical study of the Bible.

Emden, Jacob (1697–1776). Learned rabbi. A figure of the early Haskalah in his tolerant attitude to Christianity and his secular studies.

Friedländer, David (1750–1834). Mendelssohn's self-proclaimed "friend and disciple," he was instrumental in radicalizing the Haskalah and propagating the myth of Mendelssohn.

Gumpertz, Aaron Salomon (1723–1769). A medical student in Berlin who tutored Mendelssohn in French and English.

Halevi, Judah (1075?–1141). Poet and philosopher. His *Book of the Kuzari* was the most important source of Mendelssohn's view of Judaism.

Ibn Ezra, Abraham (1089–1164). Biblical exegete, poet, philosopher. A major figure in the "literalist" tradition of biblical exegesis.

Kisch, Abraham (b. 1728). A medical student in Berlin who tutored Mendelssohn in Latin.

Lavater, Johann Caspar (1741–1801). A Swiss Protestant pastor whose millenarianism led him to attempt to convert Mendelssohn. The effort resulted in a public controversy.

Leo, Hartog (d. 1784). A *maskil* and secretary of the Berlin and later the Breslau community with whom Mendelssohn corresponded. Leo contributed comments to Mendelssohn's commentary on Ecclesiastes.

Lessing, Gotthold Ephraim (1729–1781). Playwright, critic, and religious thinker who was a central figure of the German Enlightenment and Mendelssohn's closest friend. His play *Nathan the Wise* (1779) idealized Mendelssohn (in the character of Nathan) and advocated religious toleration.

Locke, John (1632–1704). *The* philosopher of the Enlightenment in England. An exponent of empirical philosophy, he championed the theory of natural law and religious toleration.

Lowth, Robert (1710–1787). Anglican scholar, later bishop of London, who published a pioneering work on the nature of biblical poetry, *The Sacred Poetry of the Hebrews* (1753).

Maimonides (1135–1204). Philosopher and scholar of Jewish law. The Aristotelian Jewish philosopher of the Middle Ages, he also produced the most celebrated compilation of Jewish law, the *Mishneh Torah*.

Michaelis, Johann David (1717–1791). Biblical scholar and professor at Göttingen. He and Mendelssohn were at odds at various times over a number of issues, including the interpretation of Psalms, the significance of law in the Pentateuch, and the feasibility of granting the Jews equal rights.

Nahmanides (1194–1270). Biblical exegete, scholar of Jewish law, and philosopher. He wrote an extensive commentary to the Pentateuch which belonged to the "literalist" tradition of Jewish biblical exegesis.

Rashi (1040–1105). Biblical and Talmudic commentator. The central figure in the "literalist" tradition of biblical interpretation.

Reinbeck, Johann Gustav (1683–1741). The most prominent "theological Wolffian" in Berlin whose work exercised considerable influence on the young Mendelssohn.

Samoscz, Israel (1700–1772). Born in Galicia. A key figure in the effort of the early Haskalah to revive the tradition of medieval Jewish philosophy. One of Mendelssohn's early tutors.

Spinoza, Benedict (1632–1677). Archrationalist of the seventeenth century. In his *Theological-Political Treatise* he questioned whether Moses had written the Pentateuch and defined ancient Judaism as a "theocracy."

Wessely, Naphtali Herz (1725–1805). Poet and exegete of the early Haskalah. Wessely wrote the commentary to Leviticus for Mendelssohn's Pentateuch edition. He also wrote an important educational tract, *Words of Peace and Truth,* in response to Joseph II's Edict of Toleration.

Wolff, Christian (1679–1754). *The* philosopher of the German Enlightenment in the second and third quarters of the eighteenth century. He combined the mathematical method with scholastic comprehensiveness.

Abbreviations

SOURCES

GS Moses Mendelssohn. *Gesammelte Schriften.* 7 vols. Leipzig, 1843–1845.

JubA *Gesammelte Schriften. Jubiläumsausgabe.* 27 vols. in 36. Stuttgart, 1972– .

UbV Christian Wilhelm von Dohm. *Über die bürgerliche Verbesserung der Juden.* 2 vols. Berlin, 1781–1783.

MENDELSSOHN'S WORKS

Abhandlung *Abhandlung über die Evidenz in Metaphysischen Wissenschaften* (Treatise on Evidence in Metaphysical Philosophy, 1763)

BMH *Biur Milot Ha-Higayon* (Commentary on the Logical Terms, 1760)

BMK *Biur Le-Megillat Kohelet* (Commentary on the Scroll of Ecclesiastes, 1770)

Chamäleon *Aus der moralischen Wochenschrift Der Chamäleon* (From the Moral Weekly The Chamäleon, n.d.)

E&N *Über das Erhabene und Naive in den schönen Wissenschaften* (On the Sublime and Naive in the Fine Arts, 1758)

Jerusalem	*Jerusalem, oder über religiöse Macht und Judentum* (Jerusalem, or On Religious Power and Judaism, 1783)
KM	*Kohelet Musar* (Preacher of Morals, date uncertain)
Morgenstunden	*Morgenstunden, oder Vorlesungen über das Dasein Gottes* (Morning Hours, or Lectures on God's Existence, 1785)
OlN	*Or la-Netiva* (Light for the Path, 1782)
Orakel	*Orakel, die Bestimmung des Menschen betreffend* (Oracle, or Concerning Man's Vocation, 1763)
PG	*Philosophische Gespräche* (Philosophical Dialogues, 1754)
Rhapsodie	*Rhapsodie, oder Zusätze zu den Briefen über die Empfindungen* (Rhapsody, or Additions to the Letters on the Sentiments, 1761)
Schreiben	*Schreiben an den Herrn Diaconus Lavater zu Zürich* (Letter to Pastor Lavater in Zurich, 1770)
Sendschreiben	*Sendschreiben an den Herrn Magister Lessing in Leipzig* (Open Letter to Mr. Lessing, M.A., in Leipzig, 1756)
UdH	*Über die Hauptgrundsätze der schönen Künste und Wissenschaften* (On the Leading Principles of the Fine Arts and Sciences, 1771)
UE	*Über die Empfindungen* (On the Sensations, 1755)
Vorrede	*Manasseh ben Israel, Rettung der Juden, nebst einer Vorrede von Moses Mendelssohn* (Menasseh ben Israel, Deliverance of the Jews, with a Preface by Moses Mendelssohn, 1782)

SECONDARY SOURCES

BLBI	*Bulletin des Leo Baeck Institut*
HUCA	*Hebrew Union College Annual*
MGWJ	*Monatsschrift für Geschichte und Wissenschaft des Judentums*
MMBS	Alexander Altmann, *Moses Mendelssohn: A Biographical Study* (Philadelphia, 1973)
PAAJR	*Proceedings of the American Academy of Jewish Research*
YLBI	*Yearbook of the Leo Baeck Institute*
ZFGJD	*Zeitschrift für die Geschichte der Juden in Deutschland*

Notes

INTRODUCTION

1. Isaac Euchel, *Toledot Rabeinu he-Hakahm Moshe ben Menahem* (The Life of Our Sage Rabbi Moses Son of Mendel) (Berlin, 1788), 113.

2. Meyer Kayserling, *Moses Mendelssohn: Sein Leben und seine Werke* (Leipzig, 1862), 284, 484.

3. "Am Olam" (The Eternal People), in *Ma'amarim*, 3 vols. (Jerusalem, 1925–1956), 1:41. Quoted in Isaac E. Barzilay, "Smolenskin's Polemic against Mendelssohn in Historical Perspective," PAAJR 53 (1986): 11–14.

4. "Die Bauleute," *Kleinere Schriften* (Berlin, 1937), 110. English quotation in "Teaching and Law," in Nahum N. Glatzer, ed., *Franz Rosenzweig: His Life and Thought* (New York, 1953), 238.

5. Heinrich Heine, "Zur Geschichte der Religion und Philosophie in Deutschland," in *Heinrich Heine: Beiträge zur deutschen Ideologie* (Frankfurt, 1971), 65.

6. S. L. Steinheim, *Moses Mendelssohn und seine Schule* (Hamburg, 1840), 37. English quotation in Michael A. Meyer, *Response to Modernity: A History of the Reform Movement in Judaism* (New York, 1988), 69.

7. Alexander Altmann, "Moses Mendelssohn as the Archetypal German Jew," in Jehuda Reinharz and Walter Schatzberg, eds., *The Jewish Response to German Culture* (Hanover and London, 1985), 17–31, esp. 17–18.

8. All biographical materials are derived from Alexander Altmann's authoritative account, MMBS.

9. For a brief overview of the religious Enlightenment and a comparison of the Jewish and Catholic versions in central Europe, see David Sorkin, "From Context to Comparison: The German Haskalah and Reform Catholicism," *Tel Aviver Jahrbuch für deutsche Geschichte* 20 (1991): 23–58.

10. For Ashkenazi Judaism of the baroque period see the recent study by Jacob Elbaum, *Petihut ve-Histagrut: Ha-Yetsira ha-Ruhanit-Sifrutit be-Polin*

ube-Artsot Ashkenaz be-Shalhei ha-Meah ha-Sheish Esrei (Openness and Insularity: Literary and Religious Literature in Poland and the Ashkenazic Lands at the End of the Sixteenth Century) (Jerusalem, 1990). For a survey of the literature see Joseph M. Davis, "The Cultural and Intellectual History of Ashkenazic Jews, 1500–1750: A Selective Bibliography and Essay," YLBI 38 (1993): 343–390.

11. On this phenomenon see Ismar Schorsch, "The Myth of Sephardic Supremacy," YLBI 34 (1989): 47–66.

12. Bernard Septimus, "Nahmanides and the Andalusian Tradition," in Isadore Twersky, ed., *Rabbi Moses Nahmanides (Ramban): Explorations in His Religious and Literary Virtuosity* (Cambridge, 1983), 34.

13. Bernard Septimus, *Hispano-Jewish Culture in Transition: The Career and Controversies of Ramah* (Cambridge, 1982), 89–115. For an illuminating comparison of the "speculative" Maimonides with the "practical" Halevi see Harry Wolfson, "Maimonides and Hallevi: A Study in Typical Jewish Attitudes towards Greek Philosophy in the Middle Ages," *Studies in the History and Philosophy of Religion*, 2 vols. (Cambridge, Mass., 1973), 2:120–160.

14. Allan Arkush, *Moses Mendelssohn and the Enlightenment* (Albany, N.Y., 1994), 200.

15. Dominique Bourel, "La purification ou Spinozisme chez Mendelssohn," *Archivo di Filosofia* (1978): 133–145.

FOUNDATIONS

1. Eliezer Landshut, *Toledot Anshei Shem u-Fe'ulotam* (History of Renowned Men and Their Activities) (Berlin, 1884), 36. Biographical information from Alexander Altmann, "Moses Mendelssohns Kindheit in Dessau," BLBI 40 (1967): 237–275.

2. Menahem Schmelzer, "Hebrew Printing and Publishing in Germany, 1650–1750," YLBI 33 (1988): 371–372; Moritz Steinschneider, "Hebräische Drücke in Deutschland," ZFGJD (1892), 168.

3. Max Freudenthal, "R. David Fränckel," in M. Brann and F. Rosenthal, eds., *Gedenkbuch zur Erinnerung an David Kaufmann* (Breslau, 1900), 575–589.

4. Altmann, "Mendelssohns Kindheit in Dessau," 257f. On his early relationship to Maimonides see Simon Rawidowicz, "Mendelssohns handschriftliche Glossen zum More Nebukim," MGWJ 78 (1934): 195–202.

5. On the founding of the "Beit Ha-Midrash" in 1743–1744 see Moritz Stern, "Das Vereinsbuch der Berliner Beth Hamidrasch," *Beiträge zur Geschichte der Jüdischen Gemeinde zu Berlin* 4 (1931), and Steven M. Lowenstein, *The Berlin Jewish Community: Enlightenment, Family, and Crisis, 1770–1830* (New York, 1994), 14.

6. Lowenstein, *The Berlin Jewish Community,* 1–68; H. Seeliger, "Origins and Growth of the Berlin Jewish Community," YLBI 3 (1958): 159f.

7. Altmann, "Mendelssohns Kindheit in Dessau," 273.

8. David Sorkin, "From Context to Comparison: The German Haskalah and Reform Catholicism," *Tel Aviver Jahrbuch für deutsche Geschichte* 20 (1991): 21.

9. MMBS 22–25.

10. Lewis White Beck, *Early German Philosophy: Kant and His Predecessors* (Cambridge, Mass., 1969), 118–126.

11. This position has been characterized as an "interaction between western ideas and Leibnizian assumptions." See Peter Hans Reill, *The German Enlightenment and the Rise of Historicism* (Berkeley, 1975), 7.

12. E. A. Blackall, *The Emergence of German as a Literary Language,* 2d ed. (Ithaca, 1978), 26–48.

13. Beck, *Early German Philosophy,* 276–296.

14. *Vernünftige Gedancken von Gott, der Welt und der Seele des Menschen* (Leipzig, 1729), "Vorrede zu der anderen Auflage," n.p. See also Jean Ecole, "Wolff," in Y. Belaval and D. Bourel, eds., *Le siècle des lumières et la Bible* (Paris, 1986), 805–822.

15. *Vernünftige Gedancken von Gott, der Welt und der Seele des Menschen,* passim. On Wolff see Mario Casula, "Die Theologia naturalis von Christian Wolff: Vernunft u. Offenbarung," 129–138, and Günter Gawlick, "Christian Wolff und der Deismus," 139–147, in Werner Schneiders, ed., *Christian Wolff, 1679–1754: Interpretationen zu seiner Philosophie und deren Wirkung* (Hamburg, 1983); and Thomas P. Saine, "Who's Afraid of Christian Wolff," in Alan C. Kors and Paul J. Korshin, eds., *Anticipations of the Enlightenment in England, France and Germany* (Philadelphia, 1987), 102–133.

16. *Allgemeine Deutsche Biographie,* 56 vols. (Leipzig, 1875–1912), 28: 2–5; D. A. Tholuck, *Geschichte des Rationalismus: Geschichte des Pietismus und des ersten Stadiums der Aufklärung* (Berlin, 1865), 142–143.

17. *Betrachtungen über die in der Augsburgischen Confession enthaltene und damit verknüpfte Göttliche Wahrheiten,* 2 vols. (Berlin and Leipzig, 1733), 1:xxi.

18. Ibid., 1:9.

19. Ibid., 1:115–193.

20. Ibid., 1:47–48. Compare with Wolff, *Vernünftige Gedancken,* 623–629.

21. For Mendelssohn's familiarity with contemporary Protestant theology see his letter to Bonnet, JubA 7:319, in which he mentioned Cranz, Baumgarten, and Sack. See also the inventory of his library, *Verzeichniss der auserlesenen Büchersammlung des seeligen Herrn Moses Mendelssohn* (Berlin, 1786), which contained volumes that ranged from the Cambridge Platonist Cudworth (p. 4, nos. 67–68) to the Dutch collegiant Limborch (p. 14, no. 212) as well as to contemporary German theologians such as Mosheim (p. 11, no. 140, p. 47, no. 566), Spalding (p. 32, no. 249), and Jerusalem (p. 40, no. 376).

22. Rudolf Vierhaus contends that "popular philosophy" reached its height in Mendelssohn and Garve. See "Moses Mendelssohn und die Popularphilosophie," in Michael Albrecht, Eva J. Engel, and Norbert Hinske, eds., *Moses Mendelssohn und die Kreise seiner Wirksamkeit* (Tübingen, 1994), 25–42. On the tradition of popular philosophy see Johann van der Zande, "Popular Philosophy and the History of Mankind in Eighteenth-Century Germany," *Storia della storiografia* 22 (1992): 37–36, and Doris Bachmann-Medick, *Die ästhetische Ordnung des Handelns: Moralphilosophie und Ästhetik in der Popularphilosophie des 18. Jahrhunderts* (Stuttgart, 1989).

23. UE, JubA 1:43. Cf. Schreiben, JubA 7:16.

24. Ibid., 1:64–65. Cf. Schreiben, JubA 7:9.

25. Ibid., 1:65.

26. Abhandlung, JubA 2:306; cf. *Phaedon*, JubA 3,1:118.

27. Abhandlung, JubA 2:306.

28. UE, JubA 1:68–69.

29. *Phaedon*, JubA 3:113. Cf. Orakel, JubA 6,1:19–20.

30. Abhandlung, JubA 2:322.

31. UE, JubA 1:98.

32. Rhapsodie, JubA 1:404. Cf. UE, JubA 1:56, *Phaedon*, JubA 3:110, Schreiben, JubA 7:16, Orakel, JubA 6,1:19–20.

33. UE, JubA 1:99.

34. Abhandlung, JubA 2:276–278.

35. *Phaedon*, JubA 3:111–112. For man's innate sociability see Sendschreiben, JubA 2:83–109.

36. Abhandlung, JubA 2:317. Cf. Orakel, JubA 6,1:20.

37. Beck, *Early German Philosophy*, 335.

38. Chamäleon, JubA 2:121. On system see *Phaedon*, comments to 2d ed., JubA 3,1:131.

39. Abhandlung, JubA 2:271 and 329.

40. PG, JubA 1:24–25. He reiterated the fallibility of all philosophical systems in Morgenstunden; see JubA 3,2:114.

41. Abhandlung, JubA 2:296–297. He would reiterate this during the Lavater controversy. See *Nacherrinerung*, JubA 7:47.

42. PG, JubA 1:22.

43. *Phaedon*, JubA 3:16 and 128.

44. Abhandlung, JubA 2:317. Cf. Chamäleon, JubA 2:144–145.

45. *Phaedon*, JubA 3,1:15.

46. Abhandlung, JubA 2:315.

47. Leo Strauss, "Einleitung," JubA 2:L-LIII. For Wolff's related assumption of the unproblematic transition between "is" and "ought," see Anton Bissinger, "Zur metaphysischen Begründung der Wolffschen Ethik," in Schneiders, ed., *Christian Wolff, 1679–1754*, 151.

48. Abhandlung, JubA 2:311–312, 328–329; Rhapsodie, JubA 1:413–423. In one of his final works Mendelssohn would use the term "vital knowledge" to describe God's knowledge. See Morgenstunden, JubA 3,2:101–102.

Mendelssohn acknowledged the preeminence of the English in practical philosophy. See "Anweisung zur spekul: Philosophie" (1774), JubA 3,1:307. On the influence of English philosophy in general see Fritz Pinkuss, "Moses Mendelssohns Verhältnis zur englischen Philosophie," *Philosophisches Jahrbuch der Görres-Gesellschaft* 42 (1929): 449–490.

Some of Mendelssohn's key terms, including "edification" and "vital knowledge," were originally used by the Pietists but were later adopted by theological Wolffians and other religious Enlighteners. In German Protestantism in the eighteenth century the language of applied religion had largely been re-created by the Pietists. On these Pietist origins see August Langen, *Der Wortschatz des deutschen Pietismus*, 2d ed. (Tübingen, 1968), 36 (*erbauen*), 39 and 42 (*erbaulich*), 35 (*lebendig*).

A theological Wolffian who used the terms was Siegmund Jacob Baumgarten. For example, see his *Evangelische Glaubenslehre*, ed. Johann Salomo Semler, 3 vols. (Halle, 1759), 1:78–84. On this aspect of Baumgarten see Martin Schloemann, *Siegmund Jacob Baumgarten: System und Geschichte in der Theologie des Übergangs zum Neuprotestantismus* (Göttingen, 1974), 59–66, 79–95.

49. Rhapsodie, JubA 1:420–421; cf. Abhandlung, JubA 2:325.

50. Abhandlung, JubA 2:328; Rhapsodie, JubA 1:421–423. For this distinction see also "Sendschreiben an einem jungen Gelehrten zu B," JubA 1: 139–142.

51. Abhandlung, JubA 2:306.

52. Abhandlung, JubA 2:292–293.

53. *Phaedon*, JubA 3,1:119.

54. Ibid., 3,1:81.

55. Ibid., 3,1:80; cf. 3,1:116.

56. "Anweisung zur spekulativen Philosophie, für einen jungen Menschen von 15–20 Jahren," JubA 3,1:307. For the origins of this sketch see JubA 3,1:lvii–lviii.

57. GS 5:544 (Letter to Monsieur le Baron de Ferber, 22 September 1777).

58. Gershom Scholem, "Revelation and Tradition as Religious Categories in Judaism," in *The Messianic Idea in Judaism* (New York, 1971), 289–290.

EARLY WORKS

1. Wolfgang Martens, *Die Botschaft der Tugend: Die Aufklärung im Spiegel der deutschen Moralischen Wochenschriften* (Stuttgart, 1968), 15–99, 141–160.

2. There is a continuing controversy over dating and the existence of a collaborator. See Jacob Toury, "Problems of *Kohelet Musar*" (in Hebrew), *Kiryat Sefer* 43 (1968): 279–284; Meir Gilon, *Kohelet Musar le-Mendelssohn al Reka Tekufato* (Mendelssohn's *Kohelet Musar* in Its Historical Context) (Jerusalem, 1979), 5–21; and MMBS, 83–91. I think that the collaborator was fictitious and that the entire work was Mendelssohn's.

3. I will cite the *Kohelet Musar* according to Gilon's critical edition, giving the essay number and line numbers followed by the page number. Here: KM 4:109–112, p. 172. For these views in Mendelssohn's German works see, for example, Rhapsodie, JubA 1:406–407.

4. The passage is from Sotah 31a.

5. Gilon, *Kohelet Musar le-Mendelssohn*, 150.

6. Martens, *Die Botschaft der Tugend*, 231–246, 302–321.

7. KM 2, p. 162–164. For another discussion of providence and trust in God at about this time see Mendelssohn's thanksgiving sermon (1757), "Dankpredigt über den Sieg bei Leuthen," JubA 10,1:279–288.

8. Bava Kama 38:1; Bereshit Raba 9:5.

9. KM 5:83, p. 176. In the Rhapsodie Mendelssohn rejects asceticism and isolation; see JubA 1:393 and 405–408. He argues for the necessity of social relationships for individual development in "Über die Sprache," JubA 6,2:7–8.

10. Mendelssohn remained an unabashed advocate of commerce during the discussions of the 1780s; see, for example, Vorrede, JubA 8:13–16.

11. KM 2:25–37, pp. 160–161. For the career of this verse see Mordechai Breuer, "Manu b'naichem min ha-Higayon" (Keep your Sons from Logic), in Yitschak Gilat and Eliezer Stern, eds., *Mikhtam le-David: Sefer Zikaron ha-Rav David Oks* (Ramat Gan, 1977), 242–261.

12. KM 2:3–24, 38–50, pp. 160–161.

13. KM 6:34–72, pp. 178–180.

14. Isaac Euchel, *Toledot Rabeinu he-Hakham Moshe ben Menahem* (Berlin, 1788), 13. For Mendelssohn's disdain of *pilpul,* see p. 115.

15. For Maimonides, KM 1:52–53, p. 159; for Judah Halevi, KM, 2:7, p. 160, and 5:52, p. 175; for Ibn Tibbon, KM 6:17, p. 177.

16. For Maimonides' treatise see Israel Efros, "Maimonides' Treatise on Logic," PAAJR (1937–1938), 3–65. For its significance see Raymond L. Weiss, "On the Scope of Maimonides' *Logic* or What Joseph Knew," in Ruth Link-Salinger, ed., *A Straight Path: Studies in Medieval Philosophy and Culture: Essays in Honor of Arthur Hyman* (Washington, D.C., 1988), 255–265.

17. BMH, JubA 14:28–29.

18. Ibid., 14:28 and 52.

19. Ibid., 14:29. Mendelssohn obviously borrowed this image from Maimonides, who had used it to make a similar point. See *Guide of the Perplexed,* I,71. The image appeared in the Talmud: see bTalmud Hagiga 15b. Mendelssohn might also have been aware that David Gans had used the image to defend his own use of foreign sources. See *Zemah David,* part 2, introduction 2b (Prague, 1592).

20. BMH 14:28.

21. Ibid., 14:48.

22. Ibid., 14:49 and 51. For Halevi see *Kuzari* 1, 95f. For Halevi's notions of prophecy see Harry Wolfson, "Hallevi and Maimonides on Prophecy," *Studies in the History of Philosophy and Religion* (Cambridge, Mass., 1973), 2:60–119. For a similar assertion of the need to use God-given reason see Mendelssohn's thanksgiving sermon, JubA 10,1:287.

23. BMH 14:30.

24. See, for example, "Das erste Register, Darinnen einige Kunstwörter Lateinisch gegeben werden," in *Vernünftige Gedancken von Gott, der Welt und der Seele des Menschen* (Leipzig, 1729), 672–678.

25. BMH, JubA 14:80.

26. Ibid., 14:84, 94, and 117.

27. Ibid., 14:99. Mendelssohn would return to this issue in one of his last works. See Morgenstunden, JubA 3,2:89–94.

28. *Ruah Hein* (Jessnitz, 1744), inside front cover. The publisher lamented that the present "poverty" of Hebrew necessitated such a commentary.

29. MMBS 21–22. Some early *maskilim* opposed philosophy. Wesseley is perhaps the most prominent example. See his *Levanon,* 2 vols. (Amsterdam, 1765–1766).

30. Johann Gustav Reinbeck, *Betrachtungen über die in der Augsburgischen Confession enthaltene und damit verknüpfte Göttliche Wahrheiten,* 2 vols. (Berlin and Leipzig, 1733), 2:vi.

31. Ibid., 2:xl–xliii.

32. Ibid., 2:xliii–xlv.

33. Ibid., 2:viii–ix and xxxii.

34. Ibid., 2:xviii and xxxv–xxxvii.

35. Ibid., 2:Liii.

36. Amos Funkenstein makes this mistake by comparing the Haskalah's relationship to medieval philosophy only to Protestants. See "Das Verhältnis der jüdischen Aufklärung zur mittelalterlichen jüdischen Philosophie," *Wolfenbütteler Studien zur Aufklärung* 14 (1990): 13–21.

37. MMBS 179f.

38. "HaNefesh" (part 2, paragraph 2), JubA 14:127.

39. Ibid., 14:143. Cf. Gegenbetrachtungen, JubA 7:96, and Jerusalem, JubA 8:189.

40. "HaNefesh," 14:125. He would use the same language in his commentary on Ecclesiastes. See BMK, JubA 14:154 and 195.

41. *Sefer HaNefesh* (Berlin, 1787), vi.

42. "HaNefesh" (part 2, paragraph 22), JubA 14:127.

43. Ibid., 14:130.

44. Ibid., 14:138.

45. MMBS 181. Hartog Leo's comments are included in Mendelssohn's commentary to Ecclesiastes. See BMK, JubA 14:160f.

46. *Sefer HaNefesh*, vi.

"A GOLDEN BRIDGE"

1. Fritz Bamberger, "Einleitung," JubA 1:xxvi; Alexander Altmann, *Moses Mendelssohns Frühschriften zur Metaphysik* (Tübingen, 1969), vi.

2. Barukh Mevorah, "The Background of Lavater's Appeal to Mendelssohn" (in Hebrew), *Zion* 30 (1965): 158–170; Simon Rawidowicz, "Einleitung," JubA 7:xiii–xvii; MMBS 207f.

3. For Lavater's report of Mendelssohn's expression of "philosophical respect" see JubA 7:3. For the "philosophical Jews" of Berlin see JubA 7:327. For the phrase "golden bridge" see JubA 7:329.

4. On Bonnet see Jacques Marx, *Charles Bonnet contre les lumières,* vol. 156–157 of *Studies on Voltaire and the Eighteenth Century* (Oxford, 1976), esp. pp. 559–581.

5. JubA 7:3.

6. Lavater used the term "philosopher" or "philosophical" four times in the dedication; see JubA 7:3.

7. Schreiben, JubA 7:10. Cf. JubA 7:15 and 99.

8. Schreiben, JubA 7:10.

9. Ibid., JubA 7:12.

10. Ibid., JubA 7:13.

11. Mendelssohns Nacherinnerung, JubA 7:47.

12. Schreiben, JubA 7:13.

13. Ibid., JubA 7:13–14. Cf. JubA 7:74 and 76.

14. Schreiben, JubA 7:11.

15. Gegenbetrachtungen, JubA 7:95f.

16. JubA 7:341.

17. For Lavater's other conversionary efforts see Rawidowicz, "Einleitung," JubA 7:xvii. For Bonnet's disapproval see JubA 7:326. For Altmann's reconstruction of events see MMBS 223–234.

18. For his objections see JubA 7:31–35; for his continuing hopes of conversion see 7:36–37 and 367.

19. JubA 7:28–29.

20. For the autonomous community see Jacob Katz's classic, *Tradition and Crisis: Jewish Society at the End of the Middle Ages* (New York, 1993).

21. Nacherinnerung, JubA 7:47–48.

22. Schreiben, JubA 7:8. For his application to the Berlin Consistory see GS 1:20. Rawidowicz discusses it in "Einleitung," JubA 7:xxiv.

23. Schreiben, JubA 7:15.

24. Nacherinnerung, JubA 7:41.

25. *Dichtung und Wahrheit* in *Johann Wolfgang Goethe Sämtliche Werke*, ed. Klaus-Detlef Mueller, 40 vols. (Frankfurt, 1986), 14:660–661 (vol. 3, book 14). See Franz Götting, "Die Christusfrage in der Freundschaft zwischen Goethe und Lavater," *Jahrbuch der Goethe Gesellschaft*, n.s. 19 (1957): 28–49.

INTRODUCTION TO PART TWO

1. KM in Meir Gilon, *Kohelet Musar le-Mendelssohn al Reka Tekufato* (Jerusalem, 1979), 2:25–37, pp. 160–161.

2. Jacob Elbaum, *Petihut ve-Histagrut: Ha-Yetsira ha-Ruhanit Sifrutit be-Polin uve-Artsot Ashkenaz be-Shalhei ha-Meah ha-Sheish Esrei* (Jerusalem, 1990), 67–153; Peretz Sandler, *Ha-Biur le-Torah shel Moshe Mendelssohn ve-Siato* (The Commentary on the Pentateuch of Mendelssohn and His Followers) (Jerusalem, 1940), 2–6; Edward Breuer, "In Defense of Tradition: The Masoretic Text and Its Rabbinic Interpretation in the Early German Haskalah," Ph.D. diss., Harvard University, 1990, pp. 64–70.

ECCLESIASTES

1. The rabbi of Courland identified the central themes in his approbation; see JubA 14:318. Hayim Sheli pointed out the relationship to the *Phaedon*; see *Mehkar ha-Mikra be-Sifrut ha-Haskalah* (Biblical Scholarship in Haskalah Literature) (Jerusalem, 1942), 3–4.

2. BMK, JubA 14:161 (Eccles. 1:1). Notations in parentheses in this section are to the chapter and verse of Ecclesiastes unless otherwise noted.

3. Otto Eissfeldt, *The Old Testament: An Introduction* (New York, 1965), 81–88, 124–129; Robert Gordis, *Koheleth: The Man and His World: A Study in Ecclesiastes,* 3d ed. (New York, 1973), 22–38.

4. BMH, JubA 14:28.

5. BMK, JubA 14:206. Mendelssohn here paraphrased and augmented Avot 1:17.

6. BMK, JubA 14:157.

7. Ibid., 14:163 (Eccles. 1:13); 14:164 (Eccles. 1:17).

8. Ibid., 14:154–155.

9. Ibid., 14:190 (Eccles. 8:17).

10. Ibid., 14:192 (Eccles. 9:3) and 14:193 (Eccles. 9:10). See also 14:201–202 (Eccles. 11:9); 14:170 (Eccles. 3:16–17); 14:194 (Eccles. 9:12).

11. Ibid., 14:205 (Eccles. 12:7). See also 14:172 (Eccles. 3:21) and 14:193 (Eccles. 9:5).

12. Ibid., 14:187 (Eccles. 8:1). See also 14:185 (Eccles. 7:24) and 14:194 (Eccles. 9:12).

13. Ibid., 14:169 (Eccles. 3:11–14).

14. Ibid., 14:185 (Eccles. 7:25–26). See also "Book of the Soul," JubA 14:143.

15. Ibid., 14:201 (Eccles. 11:9). See also 14:156.

16. Ibid., 14:201 (Eccles. 11:9).

17. Ibid., 14:201.

18. Wolfgang Martens, *Die Botschaft der Tugend* (Stuttgart, 1968), 264f. Mendelssohn rejected asceticism in the "Rhapsodie," JubA 1:393.

19. Hans-Joachim Kraus, *Geschichte der historisch-kritischen Erforschung des Alten Testaments,* 3d ed. (Neukirchen, 1982), 44–79; Emil G. Kraeling, *The Old Testament since the Reformation* (London, 1955), 43–58; Edward Breuer, "In Defense of Rabbinic Tradition."

20. Breuer, "In Defense of Tradition," 271f. Arguments about the theological ramifications of language played an important role in Mendelssohn's *Jerusalem.*

21. *Guide of the Perplexed,* III, 27 and 32. See Breuer, "In Defense of Tradition," 269.

22. Asher Weiser, ed., *Perush ha-Torah Abraham Ibn Ezra,* 3 vols. (Jerusalem, 1976), 2:129.

23. BMK, JubA 14:148–149. In his distinction between types of speakers ("natural," "inspired") Mendelssohn may have been relying on Halevi, *Kuzari* 5, 20.

24. BMK, JubA 14:150.

25. Ibid., JubA 14:149.

26. Ibid., JubA 14:151. Mendelssohn explicitly rejected such esoteric meanings in his commentary on Genesis and Exodus. See the discussion below ("Practical Knowledge").

27. Ibid., JubA 14:148.

28. Ibid., JubA 14:151. The rabbinic text is probably a paraphrase of b.Sanhedrin 34a. The mystical text is the *Zohar* I:54a. Mendelssohn quotes the *Zohar* on two other occasions in the introduction. See JubA 14:154 and 158. Dubno also cited the *Zohar* in the introduction to the *Alim le-Terufah.* Mendelssohn was not averse to citing mystical sources. He did so in one of his last works; see *Sache Gottes oder die gerettete Vorsehung,* JubA 3,2:221. Mendelssohn also used the argument of one act for many ends in his closing statement to his commentary on Exodus; see JubA 16:405.

29. For Ibn Ezra's use of this idea see Weiser, *Perush ha-Torah* 1:7. For the physicotheology see Wolfgang Philipp, *Das Werden der Aufklärung in theologiegeschichtlicher Sicht* (Göttigen, 1957).

30. BMK, JubA 14:151.

31. Ibid., JubA 14:151.

32. Ibid., JubA 14:150.

33. Gordis, *Koheleth,* 41.

34. BMK, JubA 14:153–154, 14:169 (Eccles. 3:12–14). Saadia Gaon, *The Book of Beliefs and Opinions,* trans. Samuel Rosenblatt (New Haven, 1948), 275 (to Ecclesiastes 9:4–6). Ibn Ezra to 3:19–20, 9:4, 9:7, and 9:8. Maimonides treated Job as a "parable" on providence; see *Guide of the Perplexed,* III, 22–23. In *De sacra poesi Hebraeorum* Lowth had discussed whether Job could be treated as a drama. For Mendelssohn's discussion of this issue see JubA 4:53f.

35. BMK, JubA 14:153.

36. Ibid., JubA 14:151–153 and 188–195 (Eccles. 8:10–9:12). Ibn Ezra suggested a similar division. See his comment to Eccles. 8:14. Mendelssohn also defended the "secondary intention" or homiletical interpretation of the passage. See JubA 14:152–153. The rabbinic view is in bShabbat 30a.

37. BMK, JubA 14:159–160.

38. Ibid., JubA 14:156–159.

39. Ibid., JubA 14:160.

40. Ibid., JubA 14:160.

41. BMH, JubA 14:29. For Maimonides' assertion see *Guide of the Perplexed,* I, 71; Introduction to "Eight Chapters"; and *Mishneh Torah,* book III, chap. 17, para. 24 (Sanctification of the New Moon).

42. Mendelssohn relied on the late compilation of Shlomo ibn Melech, who had derived much of his work from Kimhi. JubA 14:160.

43. For his use of vowels see JubA 14:171 (Eccles. 3:18), for accents 14:192 (Eccles. 9:4).

44. H.-J. Kraus, *Geschichte der historisch-kritischen Erforschung des Alten Testaments,* 3d ed. (Neukirchen, 1982), 48f.

45. For Mendelssohn's discussion of such issues see JubA 4:20–60.

46. For notable examples see JubA 14:192 (Eccles. 9:4) and 14:204 (Eccles. 12:6). In one verse Mendelssohn confessed that he was unable to reach a satisfactory interpretation that agreed with the accents; see 14:199–200 (Eccles. 11:3).

47. Ibid., 14:205 (Eccles. 12:6).

48. *Kuzari* 2:66. This view is based on I Kings 5:9–14.

49. N. Shapiro, "Natural Sciences and Mathematics as Pathfinders for the Haskalah Movement" (in Hebrew), *Koroth* 2 (1958): 326 and 331; David B. Ruderman, *Science, Medicine, and Jewish Culture in Early Modern Europe* (Tel Aviv, 1987) (Spiegel Lectures, no. 7).

50. For nouns and verbs see, for example, JubA 14:161 (Eccles. 1:1, 1:2, and 1:5). For sentences see 14:177 (Eccles. 4:8), 14:184 (Eccles. 7:19), 14:196 (Eccles. 9:4).

51. Arsene Darmsteter, *Les glosses françaises de Raschi* (Paris, 1909).

52. Judah Leib Minden, *Sefer Milim le-Eloah* (A Dictionary on God's Behalf) (Berlin, 1760). My comments are based on the author's introduction, which is unpaginated.

53. *Levanon,* 2 vols. (Amsterdam, 1765–1766), 1:3b, 8b, 10b, 20b. Volume 1 is entitled *Gan Naul.*

54. Ibid., 1:3b, 5b, 6a–6b, 8b.

55. JubA 14:160.

56. These were the editions of 1765 and 1784. After his death *Logical Terms* was reissued in 1795, 1822, 1828, and 1833.

57. See Johann Jacob Rabe, *Der Predige Salomo* (Anspach, 1771). There was also an early Victorian translation into English; see Theodore Preston, *Kohelet: The Hebrew Text* (London, 1845).

PSALMS

1. JubA 4:20–62, esp. pp. 20–21.

2. Letter to Sophie Becker (December 27, 1785), JubA 13:334. Mendelssohn had also made extensive use of Psalms in the two patriotic sermons he wrote in 1757 and 1763. See "Dankpredigt über den Sieg bei Leuthen" and "Friedenspredigt" in JubA 10,1:279–296.

3. Gegenbetrachtungen, JubA 7:95.

4. GS 5:505 (Mendelssohn to Michaelis, November 1770). On another occasion (1777) Mendelssohn argued that Psalm 49 had never been correctly understood. See "Das jüdische Gebet Aleinu," JubA 10,1:309.

5. GS 5:505. For Mendelssohn's other uses of the term "edification" see, for example, JubA 5,2:87, JubA 13:334.

6. UE, JubA 1:64–65.

7. Armand Nivelle, *Kunst- und Dichtungstheorien zwischen Aufklärung und Klassik* (Berlin, 1960), 1–3; Klaus Berghahn, "From Classicist to Classical Literary Criticism, 1730–1806," in Peter Uwe Hohendahl, ed., *A History of German Literary Criticism, 1730–1980* (Lincoln, Nebraska, 1988), 13–99, and on Mendelssohn see pp. 55–56, 59–64.

8. In the *Allgemeine deutsche Bibliothek* Mendelssohn published twenty-one reviews in 1757–1758. From 1759 he was involved in the *Literaturbriefe* with Nicolai and Lessing. For the basic facts see Altmann, MMBS 69–71. For Mendelssohn's activities as a literary critic see the following articles by Eva Engel: "The Emergence of Mendelssohn as Literary Critic," YLBI 24 (1979); "Die Bedeutung Moses Mendelssohns für die Literatur des 18. Jahrhunderts," *Mendelssohn-Studien* 4 (1979): 111–159; "Moses Mendelssohn: His Importance as a Literary Critic," in Ehrhard Bahr, Edward P. Harris, and Laurence G. Lyon, eds., *Humanität und Dialog: Lessing und Mendelssohn in neuer Sicht* (Detroit, 1982), 259–273. On the role of journals in the German Enlightenment see Klaus Berghahn, "Das schwierige Geschäft der Aufklärung: Zur Bedeutung der Zeitschriften im literarischen Leben des 18. Jahrhunderts," in Hans-Freidrich Wessels, ed., *Aufklärung: Ein literatur-wissenschaftliches Studienbuch* (Königstein, 1984), 32–65.

9. Each writer tends to stress one aspect of Mendelssohn's influence. Liselotte Richter focused on his understanding of the irrational and his influence on the *Sturm und Drang* and sentimentalism; see her *Philosophie der Dichtkunst: Moses Mendelssohns Ästhetik zwischen Aufklärung und Sturm und Drang* (Berlin, 1948). Nivelle emphasized the influence on Lessing and Kant; see his *Kunst- und Dichtungstheorien, 63–64.* For his influence on Schiller see Klaus Werner Segreff, *Moses Mendelssohn und die Aufklärungsaesthetik im 18. Jahrhundert*

(Bonn, 1984), 111–114. For drama see the recent edition with critical apparatus, Jochen Schulte-Sasse, ed., *G. E. Lessing, M. Mendelssohn, F. Nicolai: Briefwechsel über das Trauerspiel* (Munich, 1972), 168–198. For a brief account in English see Lewis White Beck, *Early German Philosophy: Kant and His Predecessors* (Cambridge, Mass., 1969), 326–329.

10. Joachim Krüger, *Christian Wolff und die Ästhetik* (Berlin, 1980), 72–80; Ernst Cassirer, *The Philosophy of the Enlightenment* (Princeton, 1951), 332.

11. UdH, JubA 1:427. On this point see Frederic Will, Jr., "Cognition through Beauty in Moses Mendelssohn's Early Aesthetics," *Journal of Aesthetics and Art Criticism* 1955 (14): 97–105; Richter, *Philosophie der Dichtkunst,* 32f.

12. UdH, JubA 1:431.

13. Ibid., JubA 1:431–435.

14. UE, JubA 1:94.

15. UdH, JubA 1:433–434, 443. See also Rhapsodie, JubA 1:421, and UE, JubA 1:246. On this point see Segreff, *Mendelssohn und die Aufklärungsaesthetik,* 62–67, and Richter, *Philosophie der Dichtkunst,* 14–17.

16. Rhapsodie, JubA 1:422–423; E&N, JubA 1:491.

17. Von dem Vergnügen, JubA 1:31.

18. Rhapsodie, JubA 1:422–423.

19. Abhandlung, JubA 2:327.

20. Segreff, *Mendelssohn und die Aufklärungsaesthetik,* 30–33; Schulte-Sasse, ed., *Briefwechsel über das Trauerspiel,* 189–195.

21. E&N, JubA 1:457–458. On this point see Segreff, *Mendelssohn und die Aufklärungsaesthetik,* 33–46.

22. E&N, JubA 1:462.

23. Ibid., JubA 1:463–483.

24. Ibid., JubA 1:464–465, 477–478.

25. Von der lyrischen Poesie, JubA 3,1:335–341. He cited Psalms nos. 123, 126, 129, 133.

26. JubA 4:20.

27. JubA 14:206 (Eccles. 12:10).

28. Die Psalmen, JubA 10,1:5. On this point see Simon Rawidowicz, "Mendelssohn's Translation of Psalms" (in Hebrew), in B. Ravid, ed., *Iyunim bemahshevet Yisrael,* 2 vols. (Jerusalem, 1969–1971), 2:131.

29. In his 1768 review of Ramler's *Odes,* JubA 5,2:84–85.

30. Werner Weinberg, "Einleitung," JubA 10,1:xxx–xxxi.

31. Die Psalmen, JubA 10,1:6.

32. Weinberg, "Einleitung," JubA 10,1:xx–xxi.

33. Ibid., xi, xxx.

34. Die Psalmen, JubA 10,1:6–7.

35. Rawidowicz, "Mendelssohn's Translation of Psalms," 135.

36. Ibid., 128. See also Weinberg, "Einleitung," JubA 10,1:xxii–xxiii, and David Friedländer, "Etwas über die 'Mendelssohnsche Psalmenübersetzung,'" *Berlinische Monatsschrift* 8 (1786): 538.

37. Weinberg, "Einleitung," JubA 10,1:xliv, L; Rawidowicz, "Mendelssohn's Translation of Psalms," 137–140.

38. Friedländer, "Etwas über die 'Mendelssohnsche Psalmenübersetzung,'" 524.

39. Hans-Joachim Kraus, *Geschichte der historischen-kritischen Erforschung des Alten Testaments,* 2d ed. (Neukirchen, 1969), 52.

40. Ibid., 100–101; Weinberg, "Einleitung," JubA 10,1:xxxiv. On Michaelis and Mendelssohn see Anna-Ruth Löwenbruck, "Johann David Michaelis und Moses Mendelssohn: Judenfeindschaft im Zeitalter der Aufklärung," in Michael Albrecht, Eva J. Engel, and Norbert Hinske, eds., *Moses Mendelssohn und die Kreise seiner Wirksamkeit* (Tübingen, 1994), 315–332.

41. Johann Gottfried Eichhorn, *Einleitung ins Alte Testament,* 2d ed., 3 vols. (Reutlingen, 1790), 3:439.

42. "Über den Werth der Mendelssohnschen Psalmen-Übersetzung," *Deutsches Museum* 13a (1788): 444–445. The review was anonymous.

43. Rawidowicz, "Mendelssohn's Translation of Psalms," 137.

44. "Über den Werth der Mendelssohnschen Psalmen-Übersetzung," 443.

45. Joel Brill, ed., *Sefer Zemirot Yisrael,* 5 vols. (Berlin, 1785–1790). On subsequent editions see Weinberg, "Einleitung," JubA 10,1:xlviii.

THE PENTATEUCH

1. JubA 14:267. *Book of the Paths of Peace* is also an allusion to Proverbs 3:17; "Light for the Path" is an allusion to Psalm 119:105.

2. JubA 14:243. It was also intended to replace the philosophical endeavors precluded by his debility.

3. The notion that Mendelssohn was opposed to Yiddish was the invention of a subsequent age. For the possible origins of the idea, see Leopold Zunz, *Die Gottesdienstliche Vorträge der Juden* (Berlin, 1832), 451. Mendelssohn's alleged "anti-Yiddishism" is an anachronism that has nothing to do with Mendelssohn but everything to do with those who applauded him (advocates of German, Hebrew, or other vernaculars) or attacked him (advocates of Yiddish). For example, the oft-quoted passage "This jargon has contributed not a little to the immorality of the common man" ("Zur Reform des Judeneides," JubA 7:-279) has been wrenched out of context. Mendelssohn made this comment when discussing a revision of the oath administered to Jews appearing before Prussian courts. He insisted that the oath was unacceptable because it mixed languages in a ludicrous and incomprehensible fashion (JubA 7:257, 261). A rabbi had suggested that because most Jews in Silesia and Prussia did not know sufficient German to understand the oath Hebrew words should be introduced to make the oath stronger (JubA 7:278, Klein to Mendelssohn). Mendelssohn strenuously objected, arguing that the oath should be in one language or another, either "pure German or pure Hebrew," or that it should be read in both languages (JubA 7:279). His objection was to an oath that, by mixing languages, made a mockery of itself. On these issues see Werner Weinberg, "Language Questions Relating to Moses Mendelssohn's Pentateuch Translation," HUCA LV (1984): 197–242, esp. pp. 198–202.

4. JubA 14:242–244. For a comprehensive discussion of the reasons for the translation see Werner Weinberg, "Einleitung," JubA 15,1:xx–xxii.

5. JubA 14:243.

6. OlN, JubA 14:243–244.

7. On the changes in Berlin in this period see Steven M. Lowenstein, *The Berlin Jewish Community: Enlightenment, Family, and Crisis, 1770–1830* (New York, 1994), 10–54.

8. Peretz Sandler, *Ha-Biur le-Torah shel Moshe Mendelssohn ve-Siato* (Jerusalem, 1940), 16–30; Altmann, MMBS 398–405; Werner Weinberg, "Einleitung," JubA 15,1:xxxiii–xxxiv.

9. The surviving fragment of Dubno's introduction is reprinted in JubA 15,1:15–18.

10. JubA 7:75 and 95.

11. JubA 15,2:206. On these concepts in Judaism in general see R. J. Zwi Werblowsky, "Faith, Hope and Trust: A Study in the Concept of Bittahon," *Papers of the Institute of Jewish Studies London*, ed. J. G. Weiss (Jerusalem, 1964), 95–139.

12. JubA 15,2:206.

13. Rhapsodie, JubA 1:420–421; Abhandlung, JubA 2:325.

14. JubA 15,2:245. Mendelssohn used this same idea of truth to argue for the superiority of Hebrew over other languages; see OlN, JubA 14:217.

15. JubA 16:26 (Exod. 3:12).

16. Ibid. For another example see JubA 16:99 (Exod. 12:24).

17. JubA 16:57 (Exod. 7:9). The Hebrew for "sign" is *ot*, for "wonder" *mofeit*. For additional examples see the account of Israel's 430 years in the desert (Exod. 12:40–41; JubA 16:103), Israel's fear of having to reenter Egypt through the desert (Exod. 14:13; JubA 16:119), or the explanation for God's splitting the waters (Exod. 14:15; JubA 16:120).

18. JubA 16:125 (Exod. 14:31).

19. JubA 16:149 (Exod. 16:4). For additional examples see Exodus 16:19 (JubA 16:154) and Exodus 16:27 (JubA 16:156).

20. JubA 16:352 (Exod. 34:10).

21. JubA 16:350.

22. On the calendar see JubA 16:90–91 (Exod. 12:1). In general see JubA 16:108 (Exod. 13:8).

23. JubA 16:99 (Exod. 12:24).

24. JubA 16:178 (Exod. 19:9).

25. JubA 16:186–187.

26. JubA 16:186.

27. Ibid. As early as his 1757 thanksgiving sermon, Mendelssohn had affirmed the universality of monotheism among the "cultured nations"; see JubA 10,1:282.

28. JubA 18:133 (Num. 15:39). This passage is an interpolation of Mendelssohn's in the commentary.

29. For Mendelssohn's views during the Lavater affair see JubA 7:13–14 and 74–76.

30. JubA 16:177. On this passage see Edward R. Levenson, "Moses Mendelssohn's Understanding of Logico-Grammatical and Literary Construction in the Pentateuch: A Study of His German Translation and Hebrew Commentary (The Bi'ur)," Ph.D. diss., Brandeis University, 1972, pp. 120–121.

31. Mendelssohn asserted the importance of Israel's relationship to God as

the basis of the Commandments in other passages. See, for example, JubA 16:193–195 (Exod. 20:14) and JubA 16:16 (Exod. 20:19).

32. JubA 16:226. Mendelssohn made the same point in his explanation of Genesis 26:5; see JubA 15,2:270–271. He had already made this point in his *Logical Terms*; see, for example, JubA 14:95.

33. Isaac Heinemann, *Ta'amei ha-Mitsvot bi-Sifrut Yisrael* (The Reasons for the Commandments in Jewish Literature), 2 vols. (Jerusalem, 1956).

34. JubA 16:226. Mendelssohn also quoted Ibn Ezra's endorsement of this position; see JubA 16:114 (Exod. 14:1).

35. JubA 15,2:13.

36. See *Kohelet Musar* 5:83, p. 176.

37. JubA 15,2:26 (Gen. 2:18). Mendelssohn made this same point in an interpolation in the Book of Numbers (15:31), where he argued that isolation is the greatest failure, connection with others the greatest success, for it alone enables us to enjoy the "spiritual pleasures"; see JubA 18:130.

38. For the German works see the extended discussion in Sendschreiben, JubA 2:81–110, and, for example, Rhapsodie, JubA 1:405–406; for the Hebrew works see the commentary to Ecclesiastes, JubA 14:172 (Eccles. 3:21) and 14:193 (Eccles. 9:12).

39. Mendelssohn had pointed to competition and envy as sources of evil in his commentary on Ecclesiastes; see JubA 14:173 (Eccles. 4:4) and 14:186 (Eccles. 7:29). He would also deem economic competition a positive force; see Vorrede, JubA 8:16. The theme of luxury would reappear in *Jerusalem*, see JubA 8:112.

40. JubA 16:406–407.

41. For early passages against the arrogance of philosophy see, for example, PG, JubA 1:22–25; Abhandlung, JubA 2:296–297; Nacherrinnerung, JubA 7:47.

42. BMH, JubA 14:80. For an illuminating comparison of Halevi's and Maimonides' treatment of this issue see Harry Wolfson, "The Platonic, Aristotelian, and Stoic Theories of Creation in Hallevi and Maimonides," in Harry Wolfson, *Studies in the History of Philosophy and Religion*, 2 vols. (Cambridge, Mass., 1973), 1:234–249.

43. JubA 15,2:4 (Gen. 1:2).

44. JubA 15,2:49.

45. JubA 16:66.

46. JubA 16:150.

47. On the cessation of Creation see JubA 15,2:17 (Gen. 2:2); for subsequent divine intervention see JubA 16:47–48 (Exod. 6:2). Mendelssohn had also argued in earlier works for the possibility of divine miracles. In the *Book of the Soul*, for example, he argued that the creation and destruction of the "soul" is not the result of natural causes but rather "by means of a miracle" because it is an act ex nihilo; see JubA 14:127 (par. 19–21).

48. JubA 16:194 (Exod. 20:14).

49. For Nahmanides' views on these issues see David Berger, "Miracles and the Natural Order in Nahmanides," in Isadore Twersky, ed., *Rabbi Moses Nahmanides (Ramban): Explorations in His Religious and Literary Virtuosity*

(Cambridge, Mass., 1983), 107–128. For Mendelssohn's reliance on Nahmanides see Weinberg, "Einleitung," JubA 15,1:lxiii–liv; and Breuer, "In Defense of Rabbinic Tradition: The Masoretic Text and Its Rabbinic Interpretation in the Early Haskalah," Ph.D. diss., Harvard University, 1990, p. 321.

50. JubA 15,2:15 (Gen. 1:31). For similar passages in his German works see Sendschreiben, JubA 2:87–88, and *Sache Gottes, oder die gerettete Vorsehung,* JubA 3,2:243 (par. 70).

51. JubA 15,2:13 (Gen. 1:26). For similar passages see JubA 15,2:21 (Gen. 2:7) and 15,2:20 (Gen. 2:5).

52. JubA 15,2:15 (Gen. 1:30).

53. *Guide of the Perplexed* I,2. The word for "generally accepted opinions" is *mefursamot.* On this issue see Shlomo Pines, "Truth and Falsehood versus Good and Evil: A Study in Jewish and General Philosophy in Connection with the *Guide of the Perplexed,* I,2," in Isadore Twersky, ed., *Studies in Maimonides* (Cambridge, Mass., 1990), 95–157. Mendelssohn had already taken issue with Maimonides on the subject of the *mefursamot* in *Logical Terms,* contending that since such opinions were not truly universal they were not admissible as truth; see JubA 14:74–75.

54. JubA 15,2:22–23 (Gen. 2:9).

55. JubA 15,2:31 (Gen. 3:6). For passages on this theme see 15,2:39 (Gen. 3:22); 15,2:42 (Gen. 4:7); 15,2:56–57 (Gen. 6:6).

56. JubA 15,2:15 (Gen. 1:30).

57. JubA 15,2:37 (Gen. 3:19). For earlier expressions of this idea see Gegenbetrachtungen, JubA 7:96, and "Sefer HaNefesh," JubA 14:143.

58. JubA 16:56 (Exod. 7:3).

59. For some passages where he agreed with the *Guide of the Perplexed,* see JubA 15,2:32 (Gen. 3:8) and JubA 16:187 (Exod. 20:2). For passages in which he followed the *Mishneh Torah* see JubA 16:216 (Exod. 22:15 and 22:17), JubA 16:231 (Exod. 23:28), JubA 16:284 (Exod. 28:17), and JubA 16:334 (Exod. 32:13).

60. JubA 15,2:4 (Gen. 1:2). This is not to say that Mendelssohn refused to introduce science; rather he only did so to the extent that it was absolutely relevant to the literal meaning of the passage. For examples of his use of science see JubA 15,2:24 (Gen. 2:11) on the geography of rivers; JubA 16:85 (Exod. 10:19) on the Mediterranean; JubA 16:91 (Exod. 12:2) on the lunar calendar; JubA 16:230 (Exod. 23:28) on wasps; JubA 16:336 (Exod. 32:20) on chemistry.

61. JubA 16:28.

62. JubA 16:348. For a similar passage on God as a self-comprehending being see JubA 16:28 (Exod. 3:13). For the undeveloped kernel of the same idea see *Logical Terms,* JubA 14:114. For a later statement see Morgenstunden, JubA 3,2:119–120.

63. JubA 16:26 (Exod. 3:13). For other passages see JubA 15,2:18–19 (Gen. 2:4) and JubA 16:26–27 (Exod. 3:13–14).

64. JubA 16:27.

65. Exodus 3:14.

66. Franz Rosenzweig, "Der Ewige," in *Die Schrift,* ed. Karl Thieme (Frankfurt, 1964), 34–36.

67. Ibid., 34–50.

68. For Creation see JubA 15,2:7 (Gen. 1:6); for the Garden of Eden, where he mentions that "Ibn Ezra recalled the various opinions of the philosophisers among our brethren," see JubA 15,2:30 (Gen. 3:1); for the altar see JubA 16: 405, in his peroration to the book of Exodus.

69. JubA 14:243.

70. Raphael Loewe, "The 'Plain' Meaning of Scripture in Early Jewish Exegesis," *Papers of the Institute of Jewish Studies,* ed. J. G. Weiss (Jerusalem, 1964), 140–185.

71. For an especially lucid exposition see Amos Funkenstein, *Signonot be-Parshanut ha-Mikra be-Yemai ha-Beinayim* (Styles in Medieval Biblical Exegesis: An Introduction) (Tel Aviv, 1990), 18–56.

72. The phrase is *omek peshuto shel mikra.* This phrase had first been used by the medieval exegete Samuel ben Meir (Rashbam, 1085–1174). The phrase seems to have fallen into disuse in the intervening centuries. For Rashbam's use of the phrase see his commentary to Genesis 37:2 in A. I. Bromberg, ed., *Perush ha-Torah la-Rashbam* (Rashbam's Commentary to the Torah) (Tel Aviv, 1964), 47.

For a particularly striking example of the phrase in Mendelssohn's commentary, in which he also discussed accents, see JubA 16:221 (Exod. 23:2); see also JubA 16:184 (Exod. 19:24), and JubA 16:347 (Exod. 33:18). For a passage in which Mendelssohn used the accents to determine his translation and Dubno used the phrase in his comment see JubA 15,2:368 (Gen. 32:18). On this last passage see Edward R. Levenson, "Moses Mendelssohn's Understanding of Logico-Grammatical and Literary Construction," Ph.D. diss., Brandeis University, 1972, pp. 54–55.

73. For Mendelssohn's own understanding of what constitutes the "literal" meaning see OlN, JubA 14:244; his letter to Avigdor Levi (1779), JubA 19:252; and his comments in BMK, JubA 14:150.

74. OlN, JubA 14:244.

75. *Kuzari* 2:67–68, 2:72. On this point see Raphael Jospe, "The Superiority of Oral over Written Communication: Judah Halevi's *Kusari* and Modern Jewish Thought," *From Ancient Israel to Modern Judaism: Intellect in Quest of Understanding. Essays in Honor of Marvin Fox,* 3 vols. (Missoula, 1989), 3:127–136.

76. OlN, JubA 14:218.

77. Ibid., JubA 14:217–218.

78. Ibid., JubA 14:213, 217–218. Mendelssohn here echoes the *Kuzari* 4:25. On this point see Jospe, "The Superiority of Oral over Written Communication," 129.

79. OlN, JubA 14:232.

80. Ibid., JubA 14:232. Dubno had made the same point in the prospectus for the Bible translation, "Alim le-Terufah." See JubA 14:323.

81. OlN, JubA 14:229–230.

82. Ibid., JubA 14:231.

83. bTalmud Kiddushin 49a.

84. OlN, JubA 14:235. There is a similar passage in the prospectus "Alim le-Terufah," JubA 14:327–329.

85. OlN, JubA 14:245.

86. Levenson, "Moses Mendelssohn's Understanding," 14.

87. Ibid., 21–64. Levenson provides a comprehensive survey.

88. JubA 16:25.

89. JubA 16:185–186.

90. Two examples are Genesis 14:24 and Genesis 18:21. On these examples and others see Levenson, "Moses Mendelssohn's Understanding," 48–64.

91. JubA 14:249–267.

92. JubA 14:243.

93. OIN, JubA 14:234; see also 14:255–256, 259.

94. Ibid., JubA 14:250–254.

95. Ibid., JubA 14:254–255.

96. Ibid., JubA 14:256–257.

97. Ibid., JubA 14:257–264.

98. Ibid., JubA 14:266.

99. Ibid., JubA 14:266.

100. JubA 15,2:3 (Gen. 1:1).

101. JubA 16:58 (Exod. 7:14).

102. JubA 16:394 (Exod. 39:28).

103. JubA 16:24 (Exod. 3:8).

104. JubA 16:182–183 (Exod. 19:20).

105. JubA 16:327 (Exod. 31:18).

106. JubA 16:344 (Exod. 33:11).

107. BMK, JubA 14:150.

108. There are, of course, innumerable examples of each. For "connection" see JubA 15,2:50 (Gen. 5:3); for "continuity" see JubA 16:57 (Exod. 7:9) and 16:111 (Exod. 13:17); for "division" see 16:98 (Exod. 12:21); for a "conditional" see 16:174 (Exod. 18:23) and 16:248 (Exod. 25:22). On this issue see Levenson, "Moses Mendelssohn's Understanding," 68–69, 105–115.

109. On this issue see the meticulous analysis in Levenson, "Moses Mendelssohn's Understanding," 68–80.

110. Levenson, "Moses Mendelssohn's Understanding," 34–44.

111. JubA 16:328 (Exod. 32:1). Mendelssohn states at the outset that his account is so indebted to Halevi, Nahmanides, and Ibn Ezra that he will not bother to identify the origins of individual ideas; see JubA 16:327 (Exod. 32:1).

112. JubA 16:329.

113. JubA 16:206–207.

114. The Hebrew is *kelal u-ferat* or, alternatively, *ferat u-kelal*. The source is a *baraita* of Rabbi Eliezer outlining the 32 principles of biblical hermeneutics. Mendelssohn cites this source at Genesis 2:5; see JubA 15,2:18. On this point also see Levenson, "Moses Mendelssohn's Understanding," 23–24.

115. JubA 15,2:19 (Gen. 2:5). Sandler discussed this principle briefly; see his *Ha-Biur le-Torah*, 107–110. Levenson has thoroughly analyzed Mendelssohn's use of it, and my discussion draws on his; see "Moses Mendelssohn's Understanding," 25–34, 93–104.

116. JubA 15,2:3. My account and translation follow Levenson, "Moses Mendelssohn's Understanding," 25–26.

117. JubA 15,2:18–19 (Gen. 2:5).

118. JubA 16:123 (Exod. 14:28); 16:270 (Exod. 27:3).

119. JubA 16:239 (Exod. 24:13–18). My discussion follows Levenson, "Moses Mendelssohn's Understanding," 93–96.

120. JubA 16:171 (Exod. 18:13).

121. JubA 16:50–52. On this point see Levenson, "Moses Mendelssohn's Understanding," 209.

122. JubA 15,2:270–271. See Levenson, "Moses Mendelssohn's Understanding," 28–29.

123. JubA 16:194. I have followed Levenson, "Moses Mendelssohn's Understanding," 210–212.

124. JubA 15,2:47.

125. JubA 16:126. Note that Mendelssohn uses the same image here ("stakes and nails") that he employed in the introduction (OlN, JubA 14: 217–218) when discussing practical knowledge.

126. In this regard see especially the *Phaedon,* JubA 3,1:81 and 119.

127. JubA 16:127.

128. JubA 16:127–128. The excerpt is from chapter 60 of the *Imrei Bina*; see Altmann, MMBS, 410–412.

129. JubA 16:128.

130. JubA 16:131.

131. JubA 16:134. I have modified the translation of this passage in Altmann, MMBS 412.

132. A passage that shows his use and range of sources is JubA 16:163 (Exod. 17:15). A passage that illustrates his use of legal and rabbinic sources is JubA 16:212 (Exod. 22:3). For his use of the Jerusalem Talmud see, for example, JubA 16:115 (Exod. 14:3) and JubA 16:183 (Exod. 19:21).

133. JubA 16:198–199 (Exod. 21:1). For Mendelssohn's use of homily in general see Weinberg, "Einleitung," JubA 15,1:lvi–lvii, and Breuer, "In Defense of Tradition," 290–312.

134. This characteristically apt metaphor was Franz Rosenzweig's. As a collaborator (with Martin Buber) on the last of the line of German Jewish translations of the Bible begun by Mendelssohn, Rosenzweig was well placed to understand the nature of the enterprise. See "Der Ewige," in *Die Schrift,* ed. Karl Thieme (Frankfurt, 1964), 34.

135. For Mendelssohn's 1757 review of Lowth, see JubA 4:20–21.

136. GS 5:184–185 (Mendelssohn to Lessing, 29 November 1770).

137. Gegenbetrachtungen, JubA 7:95.

138. JubA 12,2:22 (letter to Johann Georg Zimmermann, November 1771).

139. JubA 14:199. Mendelssohn employed this same technique in defining the "secondary" intention in the introduction: when reprimanding someone powerful, or reminding him of something unpleasant, the necessity of giving one's message a pleasant form would result in a "secondary" intention; see JubA 14:149.

140. JubA 16:58–59 (Exod. 7:15).

141. JubA 18:133.

142. JubA 16:406–407.

143. Johann Gottfried Eichhorn, *Einleitung ins Alte Testament,* 2d ed., 3 vols.

(Reutlingen, 1790), 1:v–vi, 1:71; Mendelssohn owned this work. For the listing in his library see *Verzeichniss der auserlesenen Büchersammlung des seeligen Herrn Moses Mendelssohn* (Berlin, 1786), 27 (nos. 166–168). The work appeared early enough for Mendelssohn to have used it when writing his introduction, "Light for the Path."

144. Eichhorn, *Einleitung ins Alte Testament,* 1:57–58.

145. Ibid., 2:219, 234–244, 387.

146. Ibid., 1:24.

147. Ibid., 1:133–134.

148. Ibid., 1:259.

149. Ibid., 1:135.

150. Ibid., 1:306–307.

151. Ibid., 2:13–14. Eichhorn thought the Jewish exegetes compared favorably with their Christian contemporaries since the latter naively treated the text as divine and perfect.

152. Ibid., 1:v–vi, 57–58, 275.

153. JubA 12,2:33 (no. 384, 16 February 1773). See also JubA 12,2:41–43 (no. 391, 8 February 1774).

154. OlN, JubA 14:211–218.

155. OlN, JubA 14:224–228. The notations included vowels, pauses, accents, and *keri/ketib.*

156. Eichhorn, *Einleitung ins Alte Testament,* 1:297.

157. OlN, JubA 14:243. In Hebrew this is a pun: *sofrim* vs. *sefarim.*

158. Ibid., 14:213 and 243.

159. Eichhorn, *Einleitung ins Alte Testament,* 2:14.

160. JubA 14:244.

161. Eichhorn, *Einleitung ins Alte Testament,* 1:3, 2:234–244 and 387.

162. JubA 16:12 (Exod. 2:3).

163. Eichhorn, *Einleitung ins Alte Testament* 2:261–262, 300–303.

164. JubA 15,2:18 (Exod. 2:3).

165. On this isssue see the extended discussion in Breuer, "In Defense of Tradition," 102–175.

166. Gegenbetrachtungen, JubA 7:86–88. The phrase Mendelssohn used for "matter of history" is "Geschichtssache." He would use the same term in *Jerusalem* in discussing the veracity of Christianity; see JubA 8:156. In his 1757 sermon of thanksgiving, Mendelssohn had spoken of the Bible as "sacred history" (*heilige Geschichte*); see JubA 10,1:284.

167. JubA 16:176–177.

168. JubA 16:178.

169. JubA 16:187–188.

170. JubA 16:191.

171. This use of history was characteristic of the German Enlightenment at mid-century, especially among those historians born prior to 1720. See Peter Hanns Reill, *The German Enlightenment and the Rise of Historicism* (Berkeley, 1975), 31–47.

172. Breuer, "In Defense of Tradition," 121.

173. Siegmund Jacob Baumgarten, *Evangelische Glaubenslehre,* 3 vols.

(Halle, 1759); for Wolffian method see 1:30, 35–37; for key Wolffian ideas, 1:53, 76–78; for his opposition to scholastic speculation, 1:30–32. These same elements are already developed in Baumgarten's inaugural lecture at Halle (1734): *Siegmund Jacob Baumgartens öffentliche Anzeige seiner dissmaligen Academischen Arbeit, dabei zugleich von den vornehmsten Vortheilen bei Erlernung der Theologie auf hohen Schulen gehandelt wird* (Halle, 1734), 3–4. Baumgarten and Mendelssohn obviously shared an opposition to the Aristotelian contemplative ideal.

174. Martin Schloemann, *Siegmund Jacob Baumgarten: System und Geschichte in der Theologie des Übergangs zum Neuprotestantismus,* Forschungen zur Kirchen- und Dogmengeschichte, vol. 26 (Göttingen, 1974), 97–215.

175. *Unterricht von Auslegung der heiligen Schrift,* 3d ed. (Halle, 1759). The first edition was published in 1742. Baumgarten wanted to correct two ahistorical readings of the Bible: Protestant orthodoxy's unmediated extraction of dogma and Pietism's unmediated extraction of edification. For his opposition to the Pietist reading see pp. 26 and 208; for his opposition to the orthodox one see pp. 220–221.

176. *Mosaisches Recht,* 6 vols. (Frankfurt, 1770–1775), 1:3–5. Mendelssohn possessed a copy of parts of this work. See *Verzeichniss der auserlesenen Büchersammlung* 44 (no. 501).

177. *Mosaisches Recht,* 1:20–21.

178. Ibid., 1:23.

179. Ibid., 1:47.

180. Ibid., 1:59.

181. This was Johann Ignaz von Felbiger (1724–1788). See Richard van Dülmen, "Die Prälaten Franz Töpsl aus Polling und Johann Ignaz von Felbiger aus Sagan," *Zeitschrift für bayerische Landesgeschichte* 30 (1967): 741–743. On Felbiger's pedagogical activities see James Van Horn Melton, *Absolutism and the Eighteenth-Century Origins of Compulsory Schooling in Prussia and Austria* (Cambridge, 1988).

182. This was the reform of Stephen Rautenstrauch (1734–1785). See Josef Müller, "Zu den theologiegeschichtlichen Grundlagen der Studienreform Rautenstrauchs," *Tübinger Theologische Quartalschrift* 146 (1966): 62–97.

183. JubA 15,1:3–7; the quotation appears on p. 7.

184. Altmann gives credence to the incident; see MMBS 383–388, 392–393, 397. Moshe Samet dismissed the incident as Henning's invention; see his "Mendelssohn, Wessely, and the Rabbis of Their Era" (in Hebrew), in A. Gilboa, ed., *Mehkarim be-Toldot Am Yisrael ve-Eretz Yisrael* (Studies in the History of the Land of Israel and the Jewish People) 1 (1970): 236–239. On Raphael Cohen see Jacob Katz, "Rabbi Raphael Cohen, Moses Mendelssohn's Adversary" (in Hebrew), *Tarbiz* 56 (1987): 243–264.

185. For this view see the sermon of Rabbi David Tevele of Lissa, reprinted in L. Lewin, "Aus dem jüdischen Kulturkampfe," *Jahrbuch der jüdisch-literarischen Gesellschaft* 12 (1918): 182–194.

186. Altmann, MMBS 485–486.

187. Samet, "Mendelssohn, Wessely, and the Rabbis of Their Era," 236–242; Altmann, MMBS 382–383.

188. *Netiboth Haschalom,* 5 vols. (Vienna, 1818).

189. Vienna edition: Adalbert della Corre, 1861. Vienna was the center of Hebrew book publishing for the Habsburg lands and to an extent for eastern Europe; see B. Wachstein, *Die hebräische Publizistik in Wien* (Vienna, 1930). For a list of central European editions see Steven Lowenstein, "The Readership of Mendelssohn's Bible Translation," in his *The Mechanics of Change: Essays in the Social History of German Jewry* (Atlanta, Ga., 1992), 36–37.

190. Meir Hildesheimer, "Moses Mendelssohn in Nineteenth-Century Rabbinical Literature," PAAJR 55 (1988): 79–133. Lowenstein shows the penetration of the work into pious circles in the German lands in the first half of the nineteenth century but opposition in eastern Europe. He does not take account of the Viennese editions. See "The Readership of Mendelssohn's Bible Translation," 37–46. A maskilic edition of 1849–1852 (Vilna) edited by Adam Ha-Cohen and Yehudah Bohak added many additional commentaries, including those of the Gaon of Vilna and S. D. Luzzatto.

191. Jacob Katz, "Moses Mendelssohns schwankendes Bild bei der jüdischen Nachwelt," in Michael Albrecht, Eva J. Engel, and Norbert Hinske, eds., *Moses Mendelssohn und die Kreise seiner Wirksamkeit* (Tübingen, 1994), 358. For a fuller explication of Moses Sofer's views see Jacob Katz, "Towards a Biography of the Hatam Sofer," in Frances Malino and David Sorkin, eds., *From East and West: Jews in a Changing Europe, 1750–1870* (Oxford, 1990), 237, 254–257. For Akiva Josef Schlesinger see Michael Silber, "The Emergence of Ultra-Orthodoxy: The Invention of a Tradition," in Jack Wertheimer, ed., *The Uses of Tradition: Jewish Continuity in the Modern Era* (New York, 1992), 23–84, esp. pp. 66–67.

192. For the Vilna edition of 1852 and the opposition to it see Lowenstein, "The Readership of Mendelssohn's Bible Translation," 42–43.

INTRODUCTION TO PART THREE

1. Leonard Krieger, *The German Idea of Freedom: History of a Political Tradition* (Chicago, 1957), 1–85. The three hundred polities included principalities, dukedoms, bishoprics, and free cities.

INTERCESSION

1. A specific Hebrew term *(shtadlan)* first emerged in the fourteenth century to designate the intercessor and his undertaking. See Louis Finkelstein, *Jewish Self-Government in the Middle Ages,* 2d ed. (New York, 1964), 331. On the office of *shtadlan* see Jacob Katz, *Tradition and Crisis: Jewish Society at the End of the Middle Ages* (New York, 1993), 85–86. An overview of the activities of court Jews in the seventeenth and eighteenth centuries is found in Jonathan Israel, *European Jewry in the Age of Mercantilism, 1550–1750,* 2d ed. (Oxford, 1989), 123–144. For an introduction to the principles of Jewish politics in the Middle Ages see David Biale, *Power and Powerlessness in Jewish History* (New York, 1987), 34–86.

2. For these assumptions see the discussion in Eli Lederhendler, *The Road to*

Modern Jewish Politics: Political Tradition and Political Reconstruction in the Jewish Community of Tsarist Russia (New York, 1989), 19–21.

3. BMH, JubA 14:117.

4. Dankpredigt, JubA 10,1:288. In 1783 he would assert that the hope for restoration to Zion had no bearing on the Jews' civic behavior. See his rejoinder to Michaelis in UbV 2:74.

5. BMH, JubA 14:116.

6. BMK, JubA 14:187 (Eccles. 8:2–8:3). See also 14:198 (Eccles. 10:20): "The word of the king is law. Who will tell him how to act?" Chimen Abramsky has cited passages as evidence of Mendelssohn's support for absolutism; see his "The Crisis of Authority within European Jewry in the Eighteenth Century," in Siegfried Stein and Raphael Loewe, eds., *Studies in Jewish Religious and Intellectual History* (University, Ala., 1979), 18–19.

7. Dankpredigt, JubA 10,1:279–288. On the circumstances surrounding the two sermons see Altmann, MMBS 67–69. During the Seven Years' War rabbis in many of the belligerent countries began to give sermons on public holidays. For this development see Marc Saperstein, "War and Patriotism in Sermons to Central European Jews: 1756–1815," YLBI 38 (1993): 3–14.

8. Friedenspredigt, JubA 10,1:289–296.

9. The Jews of the Iberian peninsula had adeptly articulated some of these principles. For a contemporary source see, for example, the commentary of Isaac Abravanel to Deuteronomy 28 in his *Perush al Ha-Torah* (Venice, 1579; reprint, Jerusalem, 1964), and for a scholarly discussion see Yosef Haim Yerushalmi, "The Lisbon Massacre of 1506 and the Royal Image in the Shebet Yehudah," HUCA suppl. 1 (1976).

10. JubA 19:133 (no. 111); this is a paraphrase of Proverbs 21:1. Altmann discusses the incident in MMBS 287–288.

11. The order is reprinted in Siegfried Silberstein, "Mendelssohn und Mecklenburg," ZFGJD 1 (1929): 280.

12. The letter is found in JubA 19:154–155 (18 May 1772).

13. The letter is reprinted in Silberstein, "Mendelssohn und Mecklenburg," 284–286. The quotations are from p. 284.

14. Ibid., 284.

15. Ibid., 285.

16. Ibid., 237–238.

17. The issue reemerged in the 1790s; see ibid., 238f.

18. JubA 19:157–158.

19. JubA 19:157.

20. JubA 19:156–157 and 159. For an important recent analysis of Mendelssohn's views see Michael Edward Panitz, "Modernity and Mortality: The Transformation of Central European Jewish Responses to Death," Ph.D. diss., Jewish Theological Seminary, 1989, pp. 92–118.

21. JubA 19:157.

22. Emden's initial response is published in German translation in Silberstein, "Mendelssohn und Mecklenburg," 282–283. For his letters to Mendelssohn see JubA 19:161–163 and 166–168.

23. For the rabbi of Schwerin, Mordechai Jaffe, see JubA 19:164–166. For

Emden see JubA 19:161–163 and 166–168. Emden also accused Mendelssohn of courting heretical views ("rearing a dog").

24. For informative accounts of the development of Jewish views of death see Panitz, "Modernity and Mortality," 11–77, and Sylvie-Anne Goldberg, *Les deux rives du Yabbok: La maladie et la mort dans le judaisme ashkenaze* (Paris, 1989).

25. On the nature and dating of *pilpul* see M. Breuer, "The Rise of Casuistry in the Ashkenazic Talmud Academies" (in Hebrew), in Azriel Hildesheimer, ed., *Sefer ha-Zikaron le-Moreinu Y. Y. Weinberg* (Jerusalem, 1969), 241–255, and Zalman Dimotrovsky, "The Way of Casuistry," in *Salo Wittmayer Baron Jubilee Volume*, 3 vols. (Jerusalem, 1974–1975), Hebrew section, 3:111–181.

26. JubA 7:9.

27. The phrase is from Mendelssohn's letter to the community of Schwerin, JubA 19:157.

28. Isaac Euchel's introduction cast the correspondence in a somewhat different light: he sharpened the contrast between custom and law and implored his brethren to turn away from customs at variance with "truth and wisdom." He also appealed to the musar, or ethical, literature (e.g., Isaiah Horwitz's *The Two Tablets of the Law*, 1649) typical of the Haskalah in this period; see *Ha-Meassef* (1785), 152–154. On the relationship of the Haskalah to the musar tradition see David Sorkin, *The Transformation of German Jewry* (New York, 1987), 45–53. For the most recent discussion of the correspondence's publication see Steven M. Lowenstein, *The Berlin Jewish Community: Enlightenment Family and Crisis, 1770–1830* (New York, 1994), 98.

29. GS 3:106–107. Altmann has translated the first two paragraphs of the three-paragraph letter; see MMBS 426–427.

30. For an account of the law's origins with full citation of archival sources see Ludwig Ernst Borowski, ed., *Moses Mendelssohns und Georg David Kypke Aufsätze über jüdische Gebete und Festfeiern* (Königsberg, 1791), 19–35.

31. Ibid., 46–51.

32. JubA 10,1:307–309.

33. Georg David Kypke, "Anmerkungen über den vorstehenden Mendelssohnschen Aufsatz," in Borowski, ed., *Aufsätze über jüdische Gebete und Festfeiern*, 71. Kypke tried to dismiss the submission by arguing that its poor style and reasoning suggested that Mendelssohn was not in fact the author. Kypke consequently referred to the author anonymously ("der Concipient"); see pp. 67–86.

34. JubA 10,1:309.

35. Ibid., 10,1:309.

36. Ibid., 10,1:310.

37. The community made its proposal on 17 April 1778. The order was issued on 6 July 1778. See Borowski, *Aufsätze über jüdische Gebete und Festfeiern*, 89–96, 105. The community complained that the law of 1703, in addition to violating the freedom of conscience promised in 1767, was a source of shame and a hindrance to commerce because it awakened "mistrust"; see p. 94.

38. For the letter from Samuel Halberstadt see JubA 19:236–237. For additional information see MMBS 427–428.

39. MMBS 427–428.

40. JubA 12,2:102–103.

41. MMBS 430.

42. This is found in paragraph 31 of the Judenreglement. See Ismar Freund, *Die Emanzipation der Juden in Preussen,* 2 vols. (Berlin, 1912), 2:52–54. For the background to this issue see Selma Stern, *Der preussische Staat und die Juden,* 4 vols. (Tübingen, 1962–1975), 3,1:111–133. See also Simon Rawidowicz, "Einleitung" to *Ritualgesetze der Juden,* JubA 7:cviii–cix.

43. For this development see Selma Stern's classic account, *Der preussiche Staat und die Juden.*

44. Rawidowicz, "Einleitung," JubA 7:cx–cxxviii. The cover letter submitted with the first section of the work had used the misnomer "Ritualgesetze"; see ibid., 7:cxxv.

45. For Mendelssohn's own account see the preface, JubA 7:111. A decade later Mendelssohn referred to himself as the editor; see his letter to Elkan Herz (11 January 1785), JubA 19:296–297. Rawidowicz sees Mendelssohn as the translator, systematizer, and editor; see JubA 7:cxlviii.

46. Rawidowicz, "Einleitung," JubA 7:cxviii–cxix.

47. Ibid., JubA 7:cli.

48. Ibid., JubA 7:cxxviii.

We have restricted ourselves to composing our most humble report in such a manner that a lawyer who is not conversant with Hebrew will be able . . . to form a clear idea on property issues, yet that idea will not be adequate for him to render an independent judgment. Rather, it will enable him to understand and to assess properly the grounds cited in a decision by an author [who is conversant with Hebrew and Jewish law].

49. JubA 7:117.

50. *Mishneh Torah,* ed. Saul Lieberman, 6 vols. (Jerusalem, 1964–   ), 1:1–14.

51. JubA 7:118. The *Shulchan Arukh* was only made normative by "Orthodoxy" a generation or more after Mendelssohn. See Moshe Samet, "The Beginnings of Orthodoxy," *Modern Judaism* 8 (1988): 249–269.

52. For examples in the text see JubA 7:149 and 208.

53. Ibid., JubA 7:119–120. For an example see 7:181.

54. For the numerous examples in the text see JubA 7:130, 135, 144, 151, 176, 181, 186, 195, 198, 199, 200, 206, 207–208, 214, 215, 216–217, 218–219, 229.

55. JubA 7:120–121; for examples see 7:129, 141, 153. The passage in the text and the cover letter are virtually identical; see n. 48 above, this chapter.

RIGHTS

1. That the political public on the whole remained loyal to the state goes without saying. For an elegant overview of these developments see James J. Sheehan, *German History, 1770–1866* (Oxford, 1989), 190–206; also see the recent articles in Eckhart Hellmuth, ed., *The Transformation of Political Culture: England and Germany in the Late Eighteenth Century* (Oxford, 1990), especially Ulrich im Hof, "German Associations and Politics in the Second Half of

the Eighteenth Century," 207–218, and Hans Erich Boedeker, "Journals and Public Opinion: The Politicization of the German Enlightenment in the Second Half of the Eighteenth Century," 423–446. That Mendelssohn belonged to this tradition of political thinking has been argued by Arnold Berney, "The Historical and Political Conceptions of Moses Mendelssohn" (in Hebrew), *Zion* 5 (1940): 107f. For the radical democratic fringe that did question the state see Jost Hermand, ed., *Von deutscher Republik, 1775–1795* (Frankfurt, 1968).

2. MMBS 74–77 and 653f. There is a growing literature on the Mittwochgesellschaft. For a summary see Horst Möller, "Enlightened Societies in the Metropolis: The Case of Berlin," in Hellmuth, ed., *The Transformation of Political Culture*, 219–234; for an important aspect see James Schmidt, "The Question of the Enlightenment: Kant, Mendelssohn, and the Mitwochgesellschaft," *Journal of the History of Ideas* 50 (1989): 269–291.

3. Literaturbriefe, no. 138 (1 January 1761), JubA 5,1:321. On Mendelssohn's preference for republican government, see Arnold Berney, "The Historical and Political Conceptions of Moses Mendelssohn," 106–107.

4. These two features of Mendelssohn's political thought were given fuller exposition in his essays of the 1780s first given at the Wednesday Society. See JubA 6,1:115–119; 123–124; 127–136; 145–148; 151–153.

5. For a useful English-language account of this tradition see Diethelm Klippel, "The True Concept of Liberty: Political Theory in Germany in the Second Half of the Eighteenth Century," in Hellmuth, ed., *The Transformation of Political Culture*, 447–466.

6. Über Freiwilligkeit und Freiheit, JubA 3,1:271. Mendelssohn had mentioned rights and contract in his 1756 discussion of Rousseau, but there the emphasis was on man as a social being and the advantages of society. See Sendschreiben, JubA 2:81–110. The categories of "perfect" and "imperfect" duties were part of the natural law tradition derived from Grotius and Pufendorf and were used by later natural law theorists such as Ferguson (whom Mendelssohn had read in Garve's German translation; see JubA 8:124).

7. Aus Kollektaneenbüchern, JubA 2:8. Mendelssohn translated Rousseau in 1755–1756. See MMBS 48–49. Although undated, the notebook entry probably belongs to this period. The passage ends with the following sentence: "If the party being warred against faces force for which it is no match, then it may resort to cunning." Whether this was a mere fleeting thought (there does not seem to be another occasion on which he said or wrote anything similar) or a reliable guide to an otherwise inarticulate side of Mendelssohn's personality is an important question warranting further examination.

8. JubA 11:338 (letter of 30 May 1762 to Isaak Iselin).

9. JubA 12,1:159 (no. 315, to Johann Bernhard Basedow, April 1768).

10. On the conflicts in Alsace see Arthur Hertzberg, *The French Enlightenment and the Jews: The Origins of Modern Anti-Semitism* (New York, 1968).

11. The exact division of labor remains unclear. MMBS 449–451. The memorandum ("Memoire sur l'État des Juifs en Alsace") is reprinted in UbV 1:155–200.

12. For the historical background see UbV 1:155–164; for the survey of the

Jews' contemporary situation see 1:164–200; for the argument in favor of commerce see 1:157 and 186. I assume the argument for commerce is Mendelssohn's, since Dohm argued for artisanry and agriculture as the most appropriate occupations for Jews in UbV a year later.

13. MMBS 450–461.

14. Not Dohm's arguments but the political framework that unified them was new. On this point see Paul H. Meyer, "The Attitude of the Enlightenment towards the Jews," *Studies on Voltaire and the Eighteenth Century* 26 (1963): 1190. For the public discussion prior to Dohm see Jacob Toury, "Die Behandlung jüdischer Problematik in der Tagesliteratur der Aufklärung (bis 1783)," *Jahrbuch des Instituts für deutsche Geschichte* 5 (1976): 13–47.

15. UbV 1:1–16.

16. Ibid., 1:86.

17. Ibid., 1:28.

18. Ibid., 1:87.

19. Ibid., 2:71.

20. Ibid., 2:152.

21. See the older study by Franz Reuss, *Christian Wilhelm Dohms Schrift, "Über die bürgerliche Verbesserung der Juden," und deren Einwirkung auf die gebildeten Stände Deutschlands* (Kaiserslautern, 1891); and Horst Möller, "Aufklärung, Judentum, und Staat: Ursprung und Wirkung von Dohms Schrift über die Bürgerliche Verbesserung der Juden," in Walter Grab, ed., *Deutsche Aufklärung und Judenemanzipation* (1980), 119–149, Beiheft 3 of *Tel Aviver Jahrbuch für deutsche Geschichte*.

22. The preamble read: "As it is our goal to make the Jewish nation useful and servicable to the State, mainly through better education and enlightenment of its youth as well as by directing them to the sciences, the arts and the crafts . . ." Translated in Raphael Mahler, ed., *Jewish Emancipation: A Selection of Documents* (New York, 1944), 18.

23. For Mendelssohn's attitude to Joseph's edict see his letter to Avigdor Levi, JubA 19:278–279 (no. 248).

24. For this point see Vorrede, JubA 8:5–7. The original tract is reprinted in Lucien Wolff, ed., *Menasseh ben Israel's Mission to Oliver Cromwell* (London, 1901), 107–147.

25. Alexander Altmann, Einleitung, JubA 8:xv. The term Mendelssohn used was not "emancipation" but "civic acceptance" (*bürgerliche Aufnahme*). See Vorrede, JubA 8:4. *Emancipation* came into widespread use much later. On this point see Jacob Katz, "The Term 'Jewish Emancipation': Its Origin and Historical Impact," in Alexander Altmann, ed., *Studies in Nineteenth-Century Jewish Intellectual History* (Cambridge, 1964), 1–25, and David Sorkin, "Emancipation and Assimilation: Two Concepts and Their Application to German-Jewish History," YLBI 35 (1990): 17–22. To describe the social as well as the political process Mendelssohn used the term "civic incorporation" (*bürgerliche Vereinigung*). See Jerusalem, JubA 8:200.

26. Vorrede, JubA 8:3. Mendelssohn used the word "Providence" (*Vorsehung*) five times in the first two pages of the preface.

27. Ibid., JubA 8:4. Mendelssohn expressed a similar sentiment in the letter in which he rejected the suggestion of a return to Zion; see JubA 12,1:211–212 (26 January 1770). On this incident see Altmann, MMBS 424–425.

28. Vorrede, JubA 8:6.

29. In his essay "On the Principles of Government" Mendelssohn would argue that since freedom is necessary for man's vocation, it should also be at the center of politics and the state. See Über die Grundsätze der Regierung, JubA 6,1:127–136.

30. Vorrede, JubA 8:7–10. The quotation appears on p. 10.

31. Ibid., JubA 8:6. I have translated the term *Kultur* as "applied knowledge" in keeping with Mendelssohn's definition in his essay, "Über die Frage: Was heisst Aufklären?" JubA 6,1:115–119. To translate the German as "culture" would be misleading for an English-speaking audience. Mendelssohn's phrase "They tie our hands" was more than just an apt metaphor—though it was that as well—since he was discussing manual labor.

32. Ibid., JubA 8:11. See *Menasseh ben Israel's Mission to Oliver Cromwell*, 139–142.

33. Vorrede, JubA 8:11.

34. Ibid., JubA 8:13.

35. Ibid., JubA 8:16.

36. The possible sources for this argument are multiple. Mendelssohn's own experience was crucial. An expert on silk manufacture and trade policy, he was consulted by the Prussian government on more than one occasion. As early as 1771 he had advocated measures that would lessen government control, and in 1782 he wrote a memorandum on the silk trade in which he advocated the greatest possible freedom of trade. On this point see Max Birnbaum, "Moses Mendelssohn, der Seidenfabrikant," *Gemeindeblatt der jüdischen Gemeinde zu Berlin* 19 (1929): 452–454. I am indebted to Derek Penslar for bringing Birnbaum's article to my attention. Systematic arguments for the Jews' contribution to commerce date from Simone Luzzatto's *Discorso circa il stato de gl' hebrei et in particolar dimoranti nell'inclita citta di Venetia* (1638), which might have influenced Menasseh ben Israel—though Mendelssohn seems not to have had direct knowledge of Luzzatto's work. Physiocratic arguments for free trade began to appear in the German states in the 1770s and may have influenced Mendelssohn. On the impact of physiocratic theory see Keith Tribe, *Governing Economy: The Reformation of German Economic Discourse, 1750–1840* (Cambridge, 1988), 119–132.

37. UbV 1:124–127.

38. Ibid., 1:124. On this point: Vorrede, JubA 8:23. In terms of ecclesiastical law, Dohm would permit the use of the "minor ban," which excluded the excommunicant from religious functions (like the sacrament), but would not permit the "major ban," which aimed to ostracize the offender from the community.

39. Vorrede, JubA 8:17.

40. Ibid., JubA 8:17.

41. Mendelssohn understood this insight to be his contribution to natural

rights theory; see Jerusalem, JubA 8:151, and Altmann, Einleitung, JubA 8: xxxiv. Mendelssohn first developed the idea in his notebook essay of 1781, Von Vollkommenen und Unvollkommenen Rechten und Pflichten, JubA 3,1:280–282. See also, Über die Grundsätze der Regierung, JubA 6,1:131–132.

42. Vorrede, JubA 8:21. Some commentators have taken this passage ("reason's house of devotion") to imply that Mendelssohn believed in an ideal religion of reason. This interpretation is incorrect insofar as Mendelssohn understood religion to arise from a combination of reason and history, as he would argue in *Jerusalem*. On this point see Eliezer Schweid, "The Attitude toward the State in Modern Jewish Thought before Zionism," in Daniel J. Elazar, ed., *Kinship and Consent: The Jewish Political Tradition and Its Contemporary Uses* (Ramat Gan, 1981), 130–131.

43. UE, JubA 1:64–65.

44. Vorrede, JubA 8:18.

45. Ibid., JubA 8:22.

46. Ibid., JubA 8:24. For the government's ruling see Günter Marwedel, ed., *Die Privilegien der Juden in Altona* (Hamburg, 1976), Hamburger Beiträge zur Geschichte der deutschen Juden, 5:339–341. For an analysis of Rabbi Raphael Cohen and his role see Jacob Katz, "Rabbi Raphael Cohen, Moses Mendelssohn's Adversary" (in Hebrew), *Tarbiz* 56 (1987): 243–264. Katz sees the case as part of Rabbi Cohen's assertion of authority in the face of two challenges: (1) individuals who wished to remove themselves from the jurisdiction of the Jewish community, and (2) the culture of the Haskalah, especially Mendelssohn's translation of the Pentateuch.

47. For the growing limitation of the ban see Selma Stern, *Der preussische Staat und die Juden,* 4 vols. (Tübingen, 1962–1975), 1,1:113–114; 3,1:120–126. For the last ban issued in Berlin (1770) see Josef Meisl, ed., *Protokollbuch der jüdischen Gemeinde Berlin (1723–1854)* (Jerusalem, 1962), no. 256, pp. 260–261. For the complaint of a Christian scholar of ecclesiastical law (ca. 1760) who pointed out the odd situation of some Jewish courts having the power of the ban that Protestant courts lacked, see Johann Lorenz von Mosheim, *Allgemeines Kirchenrecht der Protestanten* (Helmstädt, 1760), 407.

48. Katz, "Rabbi Raphael Cohen," 247.

49. Marwedel, *Die Privilegien,* 339–340; for the editor's discussion see p. 87.

50. Alexander Altmann, "Moses Mendelssohn on Excommunication: The Ecclesiastical Law Background," in his *Essays in Jewish Intellectual History* (Hanover, 1981), 170–189.

51. Vorrede, JubA 8:4.

52. Ibid., JubA 8:12.

53. JubA 19:292 (to Avigdor Levi, 22 April 1784). Simon Rawidowicz identified the change in Mendelssohn's conception of the translation; see his "Mendelssohn's Translation of Psalms" (in Hebrew), in B. Ravid, ed., *Iyunim be-Mahshevet Yisrael,* 2 vols. (Jerusalem, 1969–1971).

54. "Über den Werth der Mendelssohnschen Psalmen-Übersetzung," *Deutsches Museum* 13a (1788): 444–445.

55. On the pamphlet and its author see J. Katz, "To Whom Did Mendelssohn Reply in His *Jerusalem*," *Scripta Hierosolymitana* 23 (1972): 214–243, and Altmann, MMBS 502–513.

56. *Das Forschen nach Licht und Recht in einem Schreiben an Herrn Moses Mendelssohn, auf Veranlassung seiner merkwürdigen Vorrede zu Manasseh ben Israel* (Berlin, 1782), JubA 8:76.

57. Ibid., JubA 8:80.

58. Ibid., JubA 8:81 and 85.

59. Ibid., JubA 8:83.

60. Ibid., JubA 8:83–84. For a close analysis of Cranz's pamphlet see Edward Breuer, "Politics, Tradition, History: Rabbinic Judaism and the Eighteenth-Century Struggle for Civil Equality," *Harvard Theological Review* 85, no. 3 (1992): 369–376.

61. Nachschrift, JubA 8:91–92.

CREDO

1. Jerusalem, JubA 8:103–109 (Arkush, pp. 33–40). In quoting *Jerusalem* I have usually followed Allan Arkush's excellent English rendition: *Jerusalem, or On Religious Power and Judaism* (Hanover, N.H., 1983). Citations to this edition appear in parentheses.

2. The concepts of *perfection* and *felicity* were also central to Wolff's theory of natural law. See Hanns-Martin Bachmann, *Die naturrechtliche Staatslehre Christian Wolffs* (Berlin, 1977), 78–96. For the concept of *felicity* see Ulrich Engelhardt, "Zum Begriff der Glückseligkeit in der kameralistischen Staatslehre des 18. Jahrhundert (J. H. G. v. Justi)," *Zeitschrift für historische Forschung* 8 (1981): 37–79.

3. Jerusalem, JubA 8:109 (Arkush, p. 39). The quotation is from Mishnah Avot, 4:16.

4. Jerusalem, JubA 8:116 (Arkush, p. 47). For sociability in Wolff's theory of natural law see Bachmann, *Die naturrechtliche Staatslehre Christian Wolffs*, 86–89. Mendelssohn had used the concept of benevolence early on; see Rhapsodie, JubA 1:405. This notion was prevalent in the more optimistic tradition of the Scottish, English, and German Enlightenment; see Altmann's comment to Moses Mendelssohn's *Anmerkungen zu Abbts freundschaftlicher Correspondenz,* JubA 6,1:222–223. Mendelssohn stated in a letter of 1764 that his understanding of natural law and political theory was derived largely from Wolff; see JubA 12,1:44 (1 May 1764, to Abbt).

5. Jerusalem, JubA 8:110–111, 116 (Arkush, pp. 40–41 and 47). For Mendelssohn's concept of benevolence see Nathan Rotenstreich, "On Mendelssohn's Political Philosophy," YLBI 11 (1966): 28–30, and Michael Albrecht, "'Nunmehr sind Sie ein preussischer Untertan': Moses Mendelssohns Staatstheorie," in Friedrich Rapp and Hans-Werner Schuett, eds., *Philosophie und Wissenschaft in Preussen* (Berlin, 1982), 26–27.

6. Jerusalem, JubA 8:110 (Arkush, p. 40).

7. Ibid., JubA 8:111 (Arkush, p. 42): "Under all circumstances and conditions . . . the infallible measure of excellence of a form of government is the ex-

tent to which it functions through morals and convictions, the extent to which it is governed exclusively through education."

8. Ibid., JubA 8:112 (Arkush, p. 43).

9. Ibid., JubA 8:110 (Arkush, p. 41). Emphasis in the original. Mendelssohn uses the term "Bildung" for "formation of man."

10. Ibid., JubA 8:141 (Arkush, p. 74). Emphasis in the original.

11. Ibid., JubA 8:114 (Arkush, p. 45).

12. For earlier uses of "edification" see UE, JubA 1:64–65; Vorrede, JubA 8:21.

13. Jerusalem, JubA 8:112–113 (Arkush, p. 43).

14. Ibid., JubA 8:113 (Arkush, p. 44).

15. Ibid., JubA 8:118 (Arkush, p. 49). Cf. 8:120–121 (Arkush, pp. 52–53).

16. Ibid., JubA 8:118–119 (Arkush, pp. 49–50).

17. Ibid., JubA 8:122–125 (Arkush, pp. 53–55).

18. Ibid., JubA 8:127 (Arkush, p. 58).

19. Ibid., JubA 8:129 (Arkush, p. 61).

20. Ibid., JubA 8:129 (Arkush, p. 61)

21. Ibid., JubA 8:128 (Arkush, pp. 59–60).

22. Ibid., JubA 8:130 (Arkush, p. 62).

23. Ibid., JubA 8:131 (Arkush, p. 63). See also Alexander Altmann, "The Philosophic Roots of Moses Mendelssohn's Plea for Emancipation," in his *Essays in Jewish Intellectual History* (Hanover, 1981), 160. The language recalls Mendelssohn's commentary to Ecclesiastes 8:17; see JubA 14:190.

24. Jerusalem, JubA 8:132 (Arkush, p. 64).

25. Diethelm Klippel, "The True Concept of Liberty: Political Theory in Germany in the Second Half of the Eighteenth Century," in Eckhart Hellmuth, ed., *The Transformation of Political Culture: England and Germany in the Late Eighteenth Century* (Oxford, 1990), 452–456. In the technical language of the tradition the individual repudiated "natural liberty" for a "civil liberty," which was understood through the concept of felicity (*Glückseligkeit*) and defined by the state (*Polizeiwissenschaft*).

26. Thinkers influenced by the physiocrats' ideas, for example, began to insist on freedom of property and trade. Klippel, "The True Concept of Liberty," 456–458.

27. Mendelssohn's emphasis on state authority is evident in the fragment of 1769, "Über Freiwilligkeit und Freiheit"; see JubA 3,1:271.

28. This account is based on Klaus Schlaich, *Kollegialtheorie: Kirche, Recht, und Staat in der Aufklärung* (Munich, 1969). The difference between the two schools emerges in regard to the adiaphora (secondary religious observances): territorialists gave control to the state whereas collegialists gave it to the church.

29. For the Dutch origins of collegialism see Andrew C. Fix, *Prophecy and Reason: The Dutch Collegiants in the Early Enlightenment* (Princeton, 1991). In England the argument is found in Locke's *A Letter Concerning Toleration* (1689) and William Warburton's *The Alliance of Church and State* (1736). For German Protestants and Catholics see Schlaich, *Kollegialtheorie*.

30. David Sorkin, "Jews, the Enlightenment, and Religious Toleration— Some Reflections," YLBI 37 (1992): 12–16.

31. *Theologisches Bedenken von gewissenhafter Duldung der Juden und ihres Gottesdienstes unter den Christen und über Christian Wilhelm Christliebs kurzen Auszug aus den Selichoth oder jüdischen Busgebeten* (Halle, 1745). This tract was Baumgarten's response to a debate provoked by a convert over the propriety of a Jewish prayer. Johann David Michaelis also responded to the debate, advocating toleration on the grounds that Protestants respect freedom of conscience but also because it was the best means to convert the Jews. See *Vertheydigung des wegen der jüdischen Selichoth gestelleten Bedenckens seines Vaters des D. Christian Benedikt Michaelis gegen die in den Regenspurger Gelerhten Zeitungen befindliche ungütige Beurtheilung solches Bedenckens* (Halle, n.d.).

32. The major exponents of collegialism were prominent religious Enlighteners though not specifically theological Wolffians. One example is Christoph Matthaeus Pfaff (1686–1760), professor at Tübingen, who was a committed follower of the Enlightenment and an irenicist who favored the union of Lutherans and Calvinists as well as religious toleration; for his major work on collegialism see *Academische Reden über das so wohl allgemeine als auch Teutsche Protestantische Kirchen-Recht* (Tübingen, 1742). Another example is Johann Lorenz Mosheim (1694–1755), professor at Helmstädt, the architect of the new theology faculty at the University of Göttingen; for his important exposition of collegialism see *Allgemeines Kirchenrecht der Protestanten* (Helmstädt, 1760). On Pfaff and Mosheim see D. A. Tholuck, *Geschichte des Rationalismus: Geschichte des Pietismus und des Ersten Stadiums der Aufklärung* (Berlin, 1865), 149–164.

33. Alexander Altmann, "Moses Mendelssohn on Excommunication: The Ecclesiastical Law Background," in his *Essays in Jewish Intellectual History* (Hanover, 1981), 182–184. For the example of a prominent collegialist who endorsed the ban see Johann Lorenz von Mosheim, *Allgemeines Kirchenrecht der Protestanten,* 395f.

34. Jerusalem, JubA 8:140 (Arkush, p. 73). Altmann mistakenly argued that Mendelssohn believed the church was not a "moral person." See Altmann, "Moses Mendelssohn on Excommunication," 174.

35. Simon Rawidowicz pointed out that Mendelssohn understood the issue of Judaism to be subordinate to the question of church-state relations. See "The Philosophy of the *Jerusalem*" (in Hebrew), *Sefer Hayim Nahman Bialik* (Tel Aviv, 1934), 106.

36. Jerusalem, JubA 8:119–121 (Arkush, pp. 50–52).

37. For a brief account of these developments see David Sorkin, *The Transformation of German Jewry* (New York, 1987), 54–62. The role of enterprising individuals in the emergence of the Haskalah should not be underestimated. On this point see Shmuel Feiner, "Isaac Euchel—Entrepreneur of the Haskalah Movement in Germany" (in Hebrew), *Zion* 52 (1987): 427–469.

38. See the striking passage in regard to Joseph II:

> May the name of God be with this great king, reward him well, defend him from all evil; may the house of wisdom which he is building be a model of wisdom for all rulers of the earth to increase peace in the world, may his name be increased and nations praise him.

Naphtali Herz Wessely, *Divrei Shalom ve-Emet* (Warsaw, 1886), 17. For a comparison of Wessely's and Mendelssohn's political views see Sorkin, *The Transformation of German Jewry,* 66–73. For a complementary comparison of Mendelssohn's views of history with those of other *maskilim* see Shmuel Feiner, *Haskalah ve-Historyah: Toledoteha shel Hakaras-Ever Yehudit Modernit* (Haskalah and History: The Emergence of a Modern Jewish Awareness of the Past) (Jerusalem, 1995), 21–103.

39. *Akten-Stücke, die Reform der Jüdischen Kolonieen in den Preussischen Staaten betreffend* (Berlin, 1793). For an analysis of Friedländer see Sorkin, *The Transformation of German Jewry,* 73–78.

40. Mendelssohn had used this term in the preface to the *Vindiciae Judaeorum*; see JubA 8:4.

41. Mendelssohn pointed to this fact. Jerusalem, JubA 8:170 (Arkush, p. 104). Cf. ibid., 8:157.

42. Ibid., JubA 8:157 (Arkush, pp. 89–90). Emphasis in the original.

43. Ibid., JubA 8:166 (Arkush, p. 100).

44. Ibid., JubA 8:165–166 (Arkush, p. 99).

45. Ibid., JubA 8:166 (Arkush, p. 99).

46. JubA 8:157–158 (Arkush, pp. 90–91). This typology is a reworking of Leibniz's categories which shows Mendelssohn's characteristic independence. On this point see Berney, "The Historical and Political Conceptions of Moses Mendelssohn" (in Hebrew), *Zion* 5 (1940): 251; Alexander Altmann, "Moses Mendelssohn's Concept of Judaism Reexamined," in his *Von der mittelalterlichen zur modernen Aufklärung: Studien zur jüdischen Geistesgeschichte* (Tübingen, 1987), 234–235.

47. Jerusalem, JubA 8:158 (Arkush, p. 91).

48. Ibid., JubA 8:165 (Arkush, p. 98). Emphasis in the original.

49. For Halevi's position see *Kuzari* I,25. Harry Wolfson has characterized Halevi's position as the "single faith theory of the authoritative type, according to which the teachings of . . . Scripture are to be accepted primarily as self-evident truth" and Maimonides' position as the "single faith theory of the rationalistic type, according to which the teachings of . . . Scripture are to be accepted primarily as demonstrated truths"; see "The Double Faith Theory in Saadia, Averroes, and St. Thomas," in *Studies in the History of Philosophy and Religion,* 2 vols. (Cambridge, Mass., 1973), 1:583–584, 597. On the contrast between Maimonides and Halevi see also Wolfson, "Hallevi and Maimonides on Design, Chance, and Necessity," in *Studies in the History of Philosophy and Religion,* 2:57–58. Arkush points out that Mendelssohn's views are closest to those of Halevi; see Arkush, *Moses Mendelssohn and the Enlightenment* (Albany, N.Y., 1994), 170–179.

50. Jerusalem, JubA 8:191 (Arkush, p. 126).

51. JubA 8:160–161 (Arkush, pp. 94–95). Mendelssohn discussed whether salvation or eternal life was universally available in his correspondence with Emden. Mendelssohn took issue with Maimonides because he was unwilling to concede that non-Jews must recognize the Noahide laws as divine in order to achieve eternal life. For Mendelssohn morality was sufficient; see JubA 19:178.

On this point see Altmann, "Moses Mendelssohn's Concept of Judaism Re-examined," 239–240.

52. Jerusalem, JubA 8:192–193 (Arkush, p. 127).

53. Ibid., JubA 8:193 (Arkush, p. 128).

54. Ibid., JubA 8:166 (Arkush, p. 99).

55. Since Mendelssohn did not offer a detailed explanation of the relationship between the acts and the doctrines they recall, scholars have speculated about it. See, for example, Michael Morgan, "History and Modern Jewish Thought: Spinoza and Mendelssohn on the Ritual Law," *Judaism* 30 (1981): 467–478.

56. Jerusalem, JubA 8:153 (Arkush, p. 86). He made the same point in the Morgenstunden; see JubA 3,2:137.

57. Jerusalem, JubA 8:156 (Arkush, p. 89). For a similar argument see JubA 7:13–14, 74 and 76.

58. Jerusalem, JubA 8:161–162 (Arkush, pp. 95–96). Mendelssohn's examples include prominent Enlightenment philosophers: thinkers such as Helvetius and Hume had gone astray in attempting to correct crude conceptions of nature with more complicated ones that virtually deified it. For similar arguments in Mendelssohn's early works see Abhandlung, JubA 2:311–312, 328–329, and Rhapsodie, JubA 1:413–423.

59. Jerusalem, JubA 8:182 (Arkush, p. 116).

60. Ibid., JubA 8:162–163. This passage echoes earlier ones; see, for example, Orakel, JubA 6,1:21. For an account of Lessing's and Mendelssohn's views of history see Hans Liebeschütz, "Mendelssohn und Lessing in ihrer Stellung zur Geschichte," in Siegfried Stein and Raphael Loewe, eds., *Studies in Jewish Religious and Intellectual History* (University, Ala., 1979), 167–182.

61. Jerusalem, JubA 8:184 (Arkush, p. 118).

62. Ibid., JubA 8:166 (Arkush, pp. 99–100). Emphasis in original.

63. Ibid., JubA 8:166–167 (Arkush, p. 100). Emphasis in original.

64. Ibid., JubA 8:183 (Arkush, p. 118). Emphasis in original. See his commentary to Exodus 19:5–6, JubA 16:177.

65. *Kuzari*, I,79, I,98, II,49, III,23.

66. JubA 16:406–407.

67. Jerusalem, JubA 8:160 (Arkush, pp. 93–94).

68. Ibid., JubA 8:160 (Arkush, p. 93).

69. BMH, JubA 14:71–72. For an analysis of Mendelssohn's views see Edward Breuer, "Of Miracles and Events Past: Mendelssohn on History," *Jewish History* 9 (1995): 1–26. I am grateful to Edward Breuer for allowing me to read his manuscript.

70. Gegenbetrachtungen, JubA 7:90.

71. Ibid., JubA 7:87–89.

72. The relevant passages are *Kuzari* I,87, and *Guide* II,33. Halevi understood obedience to the law, Maimonides intellectual perfection, as the prerequisite for prophecy. On this point see Harry Wolfson, "Hallevi and Maimonides on Prophecy," *Studies in the History of Philosophy and Religion*, 2:97, 103, 112.

73. Jerusalem, JubA 8:165 (Arkush, p. 99). For an early fragment on the nature of miracles which confirms this point see Über Wunder u[nd] wunderbar,

JubA 6,1:4–5. For a similar passage see his commentary to Exodus 19:9 in JubA 16:178. On this issue see Alexander Altmann, "Moses Mendelssohn on Miracles," in his *Die Trostvolle Aufklärung: Studien zur Metaphysik und politischen Theorie Moses Mendelssohn* (Stuttgart, 1982), 152–163.

74. Mendelssohn drew on the categories of his earlier essays on this subject. See "Über die Sprache," JubA 6,2:3–25.

75. Jerusalem, JubA 8:179 (Arkush, p. 113). On the idolatry of written language see Amos Funkenstein, "The Political Theory of Jewish Emancipation," in Walter Grab, ed., *Deutsche Aufklärung und Judenemanzipation* (Tel Aviv, 1980), 18–21. Altmann suggests that Mendelssohn derived this theory from William Warburton; see Altmann, "Moses Mendelssohn's Concept of Judaism Reexamined," 244.

76. Jerusalem, JubA 8:168 (Arkush, pp. 101–102).

77. Ibid., JubA 8:168 (Arkush, p. 102). I have modified Arkush's translation, rendering "lebendig" as "vital" rather than "living." For an analysis of Mendelssohn's understanding of Judaism which emphasizes the notion of a "living script," see Arnold Eisen, "Divine Legislation as 'Ceremonial Script': Mendelssohn on the Commandments," *Association for Jewish Studies Review* 15 (1990): 239–267.

78. Jerusalem, JubA 8:184 (Arkush, p. 119).

79. On this point see the classic essay by Leo Baeck, "Does Traditional Judaism Possess Dogmas?" in Alfred Jospe, ed., *Studies in Jewish Thought: An Anthology of German Jewish Scholarship* (Detroit, 1981), 41–53.

80. Jerusalem, JubA 8:132 (Arkush, p. 64).

81. Ibid., JubA 8:167 (Arkush, p. 101).

82. Ibid., JubA 8:134–135 (Arkush, pp. 66–67).

83. Ibid., JubA 8:193 (Arkush, pp. 127–128).

84. Ibid., JubA 8:184 (Arkush, p. 119).

85. Ibid., JubA 8:185 (Arkush, pp. 119–120).

86. Mendelssohn used these terms ("Leben und Lehre") in a number of key passages. See JubA 8:170, 185, 193 (Arkush, pp. 104, 119, 128).

87. Ibid., JubA 8:193–194 (Arkush, pp. 128–129).

88. On this point see Julius Guttman, "Mendelssohn's *Jerusalem* and Spinoza's *Theological-Political Treatise*," in Alfred Jospe, ed., *Studies in Jewish Thought: An Anthology of German Jewish Scholarship*, 361–386.

89. Rhapsodie, JubA 1:407.

90. Jerusalem, JubA 8:194–195 (Arkush, pp. 129–130).

91. Ibid., JubA 8:188–189 (Arkush, pp. 123–124). For earlier passages see Book of the Soul, JubA 14:143; Gegenbetrachtungen, JubA 7:96; and his commentary to Genesis 3:19 in JubA 15,2:37.

92. Jerusalem, JubA 8:187 (Arkush, p. 122).

93. JubA 16:348.

94. Jerusalem, JubA 8:190 (Arkush, p. 124).

95. The Psalms are nos. 62 and 103. See ibid., JubA 8:190–191 (Arkush, p. 125).

96. Ibid., JubA 8:195, 197 (Arkush, pp. 130, 132).

97. Ibid., JubA 8:195–196 (Arkush, p. 130). Emphasis in the original.

98. Ibid., JubA 8:200 (Arkush, p. 135). He also used the phrase "personal commandments." See 8:199 (Arkush, p. 134).

99. Ibid., JubA 8:198–199 (Arkush, pp. 133–134). Emphasis in the original.

100. Mendelssohn might have been criticizing the historicist side of Maimonides' treatment of the law in the *Guide of the Perplexed*. On this aspect of Maimonides see Amos Funkenstein, "Gesetz und Geschichte: Zur historisierenden Hermeneutik bei Moses Maimonides und Thomas von Aquin," *Viator* 1 (1970): 147–178.

101. Jerusalem, JubA 8:198 (Arkush, p. 133).

102. Ibid., JubA 8:200 (Arkush, p. 135). "Civil union" is the translation of "bürgerliche Vereinigung."

103. For the development of such a quid pro quo through the radicalization of the Haskalah into an ideology of emancipation see Sorkin, *The Transformation of German Jewry*, 79–104.

104. For the important example of Johann Joachim Spalding see Joseph Schollmeier, *Johann Joachim Spalding: Ein Beitrag zur Theologie der Aufklärung* (Gütersloh, 1967). For the central process by which dogma was supplanted by a new Christian "sensibility" (*Gesinnung*), thus paving the way for a nonconfessional Protestantism, see Walter Sparn, "Vernünftiges Christentum: Über die geschichtliche Aufgabe der theologischen Aufklärung im 18. Jahrhundert in Deutschland," in Rudolf Vierhaus, ed., *Wissenschaften im Zeitalter der Aufklärung* (Göttingen, 1985), 18–57.

105. Joseph II's Edict of Toleration provoked a debate (1781–1782) on toleration in which the desire for reunification found expression. A major proponent of reform leading to reunification was Marc Anton Wittola, whose main work appeared in 1781; see his *Schreiben eines österreichischen Pfarrers über die Toleranz nach den Grundsätzen der katholischen Kirche* (Vienna, 1781). On his ideas of reunification see Peter Hersche, *Der Spätjansenismus in Österreich* (Vienna, 1977), 267, and Charles O'Brien, *Ideas of Religious Toleration at the Time of Joseph II*, in *Transactions of the American Philosophical Society*, n.s. vol. 59, part 7 (Philadelphia, 1969), p. 57. Another proponent of reunification in the same debate was Bishop Auersperg of Gurk. See O'Brien, *Ideas of Religious Toleration at the Time of Joseph II*, 46–47. Additional examples are Beda Mayr (see Wilhelm Forster, "Die kirchliche Aufklärung bei den Benediktinern der Abtei Banz . . . ," in *Studien und Mitteilungen zur Geschichte des Benediktiner-Ordens und seiner Zweige* 64 [1952]: 178–185), and Benedikt Werkmeister (see August Hagen, *Die kirchliche Aufklärung in der diozese Rottenburg* [Stuttgart, 1953] 175f.).

106. Jerusalem, JubA 8:200 and 202 (Arkush, pp. 135 and 138).

107. Ibid., JubA 8:201–203 (Arkush, pp. 135–138).

108. JubA 13:134 (from a letter to Herz Homberg, 22 September 1783).

109. JubA 12,1:225 (from a letter to an anonymous correspondent, 20 August 1770).

110. His distance on this issue from the medieval philosophers comes out clearly in regard to the Noahide laws. See Steven S. Schwarzschild, "Do Noahites Have to Believe in Revelation," *Jewish Quarterly Review* 52 (1962): 297–308 and 53 (1962): 30–65; David Novak, *The Image of the Non-Jew in Ju-*

daism: An Historical and Constructive Study of the Noahide Laws (New York and Toronto, 1983); and Arkush, *Mendelssohn and the Enlightenment,* 200–207.

111. A prominent Protestant example is Johann Joachim Spalding. See Schollmeier, *Johann Joachim Spalding,* 67–68. A prominent Catholic is Beda Mayr: see his *Vertheidigung der natürlichen, christlichen und katholischen Religion: Nach den Bedürfnissen unsrer Zeiten,* 3 vols. (Augsburg, 1787–1789). Altmann identified this aspect of Mendelssohn's thought with deism: see his "Einleitung," JubA 8:xliii–li. Guttmann suggested that Mendelssohn, "wanted to defeat the deistic critique of Judaism with its own weapons": see his "Mendelssohn's *Jerusalem* and Spinoza's *Theologico-Political Treatise,*" 374. All of the religious Enlighteners were responding to the deist critique of religion.

112. Altmann has pointed out the extent to which Mendelssohn's stress on Israel's election departed from medieval precedents: see his "Mendelssohn's Concept of Judaism Reexamined," 244–245.

113. Jerusalem, JubA 8:203 (Arkush, pp. 138–139).

114. Mendelssohn reported such a charge in one of his letters; see JubA 13:179 (1 March 1784, to Herz Homberg).

115. Jerusalem, JubA 8:196–197 (Arkush, pp. 131–132).

116. On this point see Sorkin, *The Transformation of German Jewry,* 70–71.

117. David Sorkin, "From Context to Comparison: The German Haskalah and Reform Catholicism," *Tel Aviver Jahrbuch für deutsche Geschichte* 20 (1991): 41–55.

CONCLUSION

1. These essays are in JubA 6,1.

2. These works include the *Morgenstunden, An die Freunde Lessings* (1786), and *Sache Gottes oder die gerettete Vorsehung.* For his emphasis on the practical in the *Morgenstunden* see, for example, his identity of common sense and reason (JubA 3,2:33, 50); his introduction of the third faculty of appreciation (3,2:61); his understanding of the function of the exposition of natural religion (3,2:72); and his assertion that there was no practical difference between a refined pantheism and true religion and morality (3,2:133). His preference for practical over speculative reason also comes out clearly in *An die Freunde Lessings;* see JubA 3,2:197–199.

3. The brief discussion of Judaism in *An die Freunde Lessings* merely summarizes ideas presented in *Jerusalem;* see JubA 3,2:196–197, 218.

4. The conventional view is of two periods of activity, the first centered around the *Kohelet Musar,* the second commencing after the Lavater affair and continuing until *Jerusalem.* I mistakenly asserted this view in *The Transformation of German Jewry* (New York, 1987), 67.

5. The greater the distance from the living Mendelssohn, the more were the *maskilim* able to disregard his differences with them—the fundamental political differences we saw in chapter 9 above—and to claim him as one of their own. See Moshe Pelli, "Mendelssohn's Image in the Literature of the Early Hebrew

Haskalah in Germany" (in Hebrew), *Fifth World Congress of Jewish Studies* (1969): 1–14.

6. Gotthold Salomon, *Licht und Segen oder auf welchem Wege können Völker wahrhaft erleuchtet und beglückt werden* (Hamburg, 1829), 18. The centenary of Mendelssohn's birth (1829) and death (1886) as well as the bicentenary of his birth (1929) became public occasions for the affirmation of his importance. See Ernst G. Lowenthal, "Vor fünfzig Jahren—Das erste grosse Mendelssohn-Gedenken/Versuch eines Rückblicks," *Mendelssohn Studien* 4 (1979): 235–275.

7. Leopold Zunz, *Rede gehalten bei der Feier von Moses Mendelssohns hundertjährigen Geburtstage* (Berlin, 1829), 7.

8. "Die Construction der jüdischen Geschichte," *Zeitschrift für die religioesen Interessen des Judenthums* 3 (1846): 81–97, 121–132, 361–368, 413–421; now available in English in Ismar Schorsch, ed., *Heinrich Grätz: The Structure of Jewish History and Other Essays* (New York, 1975), 63–124, esp. pp. 119–121.

9. *History of the Jews,* 6 vols. (Philadelphia, 1895), 5:292–293. The German original, in eleven volumes, appeared between 1853 and 1876.

10. For Mendelssohn and the subculture see David Sorkin, *The Transformation of German Jewry* (New York, 1987). For Mendelssohn and the religious changes of the nineteenth century see Max Wiener, "Moses Mendelssohn and the Religious Forms of Judaism in the Nineteenth Century," in Alfred Jospe, ed., *Studies in Jewish Thought: An Anthology of German Jewish Scholarship* (Detroit, 1981), 404–415, and Jacob Katz, "Moses Mendelssohns schwankendes Bild bei der jüdischen Nachwelt," in Michael Albrecht, Eva J. Engel, and Norbert Hinske, eds., *Moses Mendelssohn und die Kreise seiner Wirksamkeit* (Tübingen, 1994), 349–362.

11. Quoted in Arnold Springer, "Enlightened Absolutism and Jewish Reform: Prussia, Austria, and Russia," *California Slavic Studies* 11 (1980): 261–262.

12. Smolenskin, "Eit la-Ta'at" (Planting Season), in *Ma'amarim* 2:10. Cited in Shmuel Feiner, "Smolenskin's Repudiations of the Haskalah and the Roots of Nationalist Jewish Historiography" (in Hebrew), *HaTsiyonut* 16 (1991): 10. Jews in eastern Europe were influenced as much by Hebrew translations of Mendelssohn's works as by the German originals. Euchel's 1788 biography used Mendelssohn's life and thought as a means to propagate the Haskalah. The volume of Mendelssohn's writings published in 1794 added to this heroic image by choosing letters that displayed Mendelssohn's towering personality yet also his criticisms of tradition and suggestions for renewal. Moreover, the editor made Mendelssohn the father of the Haskalah: "Your sons are not orphans": *Igrot Ramad,* ed. Avigdor Glogau (Vienna, 1794), 23a. An example of the direct impact of Mendelssohn's Hebrew works is the Lithuanian *maskil* Mordechai Aaron Günzburg. He credited Mendelssohn's commentary on Ecclesiastes with persuading him of the necessity of a Haskalah in which intellect would be subordinate to faith; see Israel Bartal, "Mordechai Aaron Günzburg: A Lithuanian Maskil Faces Modernity," in Frances Malino and David Sorkin, eds., *From East and West: Jews in a Changing Europe, 1750–1870* (Oxford, 1990), 129–130.

13. Cited in Steven J. Zipperstein, *The Jews of Odessa: A Cultural History, 1794–1881* (Stanford, 1986), 44.

14. Michael Stanislawski, *Tsar Nicholas I and the Jews: The Transformation of Jewish Society in Russia, 1825–1855* (Philadelphia, 1983), 97.

15. Trans. A. B. Gottlober (Zhitomir, 1867). There was also an edition in 1876 (Vienna) of the translation of Vladimir Feodorov, a convert to Christianity. See Lederhendler, *The Road to Modern Jewish Politics*, 106.

16. *Transactions of the Parisian Sanhedrim, or Acts of the Assembly of Israelitish Deputies of France and Italy*, trans. Diogène Tama (London, 1807), 20–21, 159. The textbook was Louis Cottard's *Souvenirs de Moise Mendelssohn, ou Le second livre de lecture des écoles israélites* (Paris, 1832), cited in Paula Hyman, *The Emancipation of the Jews of Alsace: Acculturation and Tradition in the Nineteenth Century* (New Haven, 1991), 111.

17. Isaac D'israeli, "A Biographical Sketch of the Jewish Socrates," *The Monthly Magazine, and British Register* 6 (1798): 39. I am indebted to Todd Endelman for this reference.

18. M. Samuels, *Memoirs of Moses Mendelssohn, the Jewish Philosopher, including the Celebrated Correspondence, On the Christian Religion, with J. C. Lavater* (London, 1825), vii.

19. Gabriel Riesser, *Einige Worte über Lessings Denkmal: An die Israeliten Deutschlands gerichtet* (Frankfurt, 1838).

20. Dr. Moritz Brasch, *Zwei Freunde: Vortrage, gehalten am Todestage Lessings (15 Februar) im "Verein für jüdische Geschichte und Literatur" zu Leipzig* (Leipzig, 1893), 16. Emphasis in the original.

21. Gustav Frank, *Das Toleranzpatent Kaiser Joseph II: Urkundliche Geschichte seiner Entstehung und seiner Folgen* (Vienna, 1882), 4. For additional examples of Mendelssohn as the hero of an "integrationist" politics see Ezra Mendelssohn, *On Modern Jewish Politics* (New York, 1993), 13–14.

22. Michael Meyer, *The Origins of the Modern Jew* (Detroit, 1967), 85–101. The very popular history of the Mendelssohn family, S. Hensel, *Die Familie Mendelssohn*, 2 vols. (Berlin, 1908)—which was reprinted many times—treated Mendelssohn's life as an exemplary story of self-formation (*Bildung*) (1:4–5, 7, 11) and the conversion of his children as a harmonious mix of the races, the Jew with the "Christian German" (1:133).

23. It should not be overlooked that in the Zionist movement Mendelssohn's negative image was often mitigated by his effort to revive Hebrew as a vernacular—the example always cited being the *Kohelet Musar*—and by his discussion in his correspondence of the idea of a Jewish state (even though he dismissed it as impractical). See Julius Schoeps, "Assimilant oder Präzionist? Zur Moses Mendelssohn-Rezeption im Zionismus," *Deutsche Aufklärung und Judenemanzipation*, Beiheft 3 of *Jahrbuch des Instituts für deutsche Geschichte* (Tel Aviv, 1979), 295–309. For an example of Mendelssohn's relationship to Hebrew see Ahad Haam, "Le-Shealat Ha-Lashon" (The Language Question), *Kitvei Ahad Haam*, 8th ed. (Tel Aviv, 1965), 95. On Ahad Haam's relationship to Mendelssohn in general see Steven Zipperstein, *Elusive Prophet: Ahad Ha'am and the Origins of Zionism* (Berkeley, 1993), 292.

24. Simon Dubnow, *A History of the Jews*, 5 vols. (South Brunswick, N.J.,

1967–1973), 4:498. This passage is discussed by Jonathan Frankel, "Assimilation and the Jews in Nineteenth-Century Europe," in Jonathan Frankel and Steven Zipperstein, eds., *Assimilation and Community: The Jews in Nineteenth-Century Europe* (Cambridge, 1992), 7–8. Also see H. I. Bach, "Moses Mendelssohn and His Followers in Dubnow's Presentation," in Aaron Steinberg, ed., *Simon Dubnow: The Man and His Work* (Paris, 1963), 112–123. Bach observed that Dubnow failed to treat Mendelssohn as a figure of the eighteenth century.

25. Raphael Mahler, *A History of Modern Jewry, 1780–1815* (London, 1971), 162.

26. The phrase is borrowed from Michael Meyer, *The Origins of the Modern Jew: Jewish Identity and European Culture in Germany, 1749–1824* (Detroit, 1967), 29f.

27. *Morgenstunden oder Vorlesungen über das Dasein Gottes*, JubA 3,2:3. The German is "die Werke . . . des alles zermalmenden Kants."

28. Immanuel Kant, *Die Religion innerhalb der Grenzen der blossen Vernunft* (Hamburg, 1958), vol. 45 of *Philosophische Bibliothek*, 134–143. On this topic see Nathan Rotenstreich, "Kant's Image of Judaism" (in Hebrew), *Tarbiz* 27, nos. 2–3 (1957–1958): 388–405.

29. *Leviathan, oder über Religion in Rücksicht des Judenthums* (Berlin, 1972). Ascher attacked Mendelssohn on two counts: first, laws that were only a means were dispensable; second, laws could not be based on external truths presented in symbolic form (see especially pp. 159–160). On Ascher see Michael Grätz, "A New Jewish Consciousness in the Making in the Generation of Mendelssohn's Students" (in Hebrew), *Mehkarim Be-Toldot Am-Yisrael Ve-Eretz Yisrael*, vol. 4 (Haifa, 1978), 219–237; Ellen Littmann, "Saul Ascher, First Theorist of Progressive Judaism," YLBI 5 (1960): 107–121. For general works on Jewish thought in the age of emancipation see Max Wiener, *Jüdische Religion im Zeitalter der Emanzipation* (Berlin, 1933), Eliezer Schweid, *Toldot He-Hagut Ha-Yehudit Be-Ait Ha-Hadasha* (A History of Modern Jewish Thought) (Jerusalem, 1977), and Nathan Rotenstreich, *Jewish Philosophy in Modern Times: From Mendelssohn to Rosenzweig* (New York, 1968).

30. For those who claimed Mendelssohn's heritage but were not true to it see Sorkin, *The Transformation of German Jewry*, 79–104. For one of the more important figures see David Sorkin, "Preacher, Teacher, Publicist: Joseph Wolf and the Ideology of Emancipation," in *From East and West: Jews in a Changing Europe, 1750–1870*, 107–125. For Mendelssohn and the reformers see Michael Meyer, *Response to Modernity: A History of the Reform Movement in Judaism* (New York, 1988), 10–99.

31. *Die Offenbarung nach dem Lehrbegriffe der Synagoge*, 4 vols. (Frankfurt, Leipzig, Altona, 1835–1865). An English abridgment is now available: see Joshua O. Haberman, *Philosopher of Revelation: The Life and Thought of S. L. Steinheim* (Philadelphia, 1990).

32. See Michael Grätz, "'Die Erziehung des Menschengeschlechts' und jüdisches Selbstbewusstsein im 19. Jahrhundert," *Wolfenbütteler Studien zur Aufklärung* 4 (1977): 273–295.

33. "Über den Begriff einer Wissenschaft des Judentums," *Zeitschrift für die*

Wissenschaft des Judentums, 1–24; available in English translation as "On the Concept of a Science of Judaism," YLBI 2 (1956): 194–204. On the relationship between essence and development see S. Ucko, "Geistesgeschichtliche Grundlagen der Wissenschaft des Judentums," in Kurt Wilhelm, ed., *Wissenschaft des Judentums im deutschen Sprachbereich* (Tübingen, 1967), 325–326.

34. The *Guide* was published posthumously in 1851. The standard edition is Simon Rawidowicz, ed., *Kitvei Rabbi Nahman Krochmal* (Waltham, Mass., 1961). On Krochmal and Mendelssohn see Jay Harris, *Nachman Krochmal: Guiding the Perplexed of the Modern Age* (New York, 1991), 100–101, 140–141, 161–162.

35. Krochmal seems to be one of the exceptions: he discussed the *Biur Le-Megillat Kohelet,* the *Book of the Paths of Peace,* and *Jerusalem.* On this see Harris, *Nahman Krochmal.*

36. For the excerpts from the introduction "Light for the Path" see GS 7:xvii–lv; for the translation in Latin characters see 7:1–489.

37. *Igrot Tsafon: Neunzehn Briefe über Judenthum* (Altona, 1836), 87–102 (letter no. 18).

Select Bibliography
in English

WORKS BY MENDELSSOHN

Jerusalem and Other Jewish Writings. Ed. Alfred Jospe. New York, 1969.
Jerusalem, or On Religious Power and Judaism. Trans. Allan Arkush. Hanover, 1983.
Moses Mendelssohn: Selections from His Writings. Ed. Eva Jospe. New York, 1975.

SECONDARY WORKS

Altmann, Alexander. *Essays in Jewish Intellectual History,* 119–189. Hanover, 1981.
———. *Moses Mendelssohn: A Biographical Study.* University, Ala., 1973.
———. "Moses Mendelssohn as the Archetypal German Jew." In *The Jewish Response to German Culture,* ed. Jehuda Reinharz and Walter Schatzberg, 17–31. Hanover and London, 1985.
Arkush, Allan. *Moses Mendelssohn and the Enlightenment.* Albany, N.Y., 1994.
Beck, Lewis White. *Early German Philosophy: Kant and His Predecessors.* Cambridge, Mass., 1969.
Breuer, Edward. "In Defense of Rabbinic Tradition: The Masoretic Text and Its Rabbinic Interpretation in the Early Haskalah." Ph.D. diss., Harvard University, 1990.
———. "Politics, Tradition, History: Rabbinic Judaism and the Eighteenth-Century Struggle for Civil Equality." *Harvard Theological Review* 85, no. 3 (1992): 357–383.
Eisen, Arnold. "Divine Legislation as 'Ceremonial Script': Mendelssohn on the Commandments." *Association for Jewish Studies Review* 15 (1990): 239–267.

Engel, Eva. "The Emergence of Mendelssohn as Literary Critic." *Yearbook of the Leo Baeck Institute* 24 (1979): 61–82.

Guttman, Julius. "Mendelssohn's *Jerusalem* and Spinoza's *Theological Political Treatise.*" In *Studies in Jewish Thought: An Anthology of German Jewish Scholarship,* ed. Alfred Jospe, 361–386. Detroit, 1981.

Hildesheimer, Meir. "Moses Mendelssohn in Nineteenth-Century Rabbinical Literature." *Proceedings of the American Academy for Jewish Research* 55 (1988): 79–133.

Jospe, Raphael. "The Superiority of Oral over Written Communication: Judah Halevi's *Kuzari* and Modern Jewish Thought." In *From Ancient Israel to Modern Judaism: Intellect in Quest of Understanding: Essays in Honor of Marvin Fox,* 3:127–156. Missoula, 1989.

Katz, Jacob. "To Whom Did Mendelssohn Reply in His *Jerusalem.*" *Scripta Hierosolymitana* 23 (1972): 214–243.

———. *Tradition and Crisis: Jewish Society at the End of the Middle Ages.* New York, 1993.

Levenson, Edward R. "Moses Mendelssohn's Understanding of Logico-Grammatical and Literary Construction in the Pentateuch: A Study of His German Translation and Hebrew Commentary (The Bi'ur)." Ph.D. diss., Brandeis University, 1972.

Lowenstein, Steven M. *The Berlin Jewish Community: Enlightenment, Family, and Crisis, 1770–1830.* New York, 1994.

———. "The Readership of Mendelssohn's Bible Translation." In *The Mechanics of Change: Essays in the Social History of German Jewry,* ed. Steven M. Lowenstein, 29–64. Atlanta, 1992.

Meyer, Michael. *The Origins of the Modern Jew: Jewish Identity and European Culture in Germany, 1749–1824.* Detroit, 1967.

Rotenstreich, Nathan. "On Mendelssohn's Political Philosophy." *Yearbook of the Leo Baeck Institute* 11 (1966): 28–41.

Schmidt, James. "The Question of the Enlightenment: Kant, Mendelssohn, and the Mitwochgesellschaft." *Journal of the History of Ideas* 50 (1989): 269–291.

Sorkin, David. "The Case for Comparison: Moses Mendelssohn and the Religious Enlightenment." *Modern Judaism* 14 (1994): 121–138.

———. "From Context to Comparison: The German Haskalah and Reform Catholicism." *Tel Aviver Jahrbuch für deutsche Geschichte* 20 (1991): 23–58.

———. *The Transformation of German Jewry, 1780–1840.* New York, 1987.

Wiener, Max. "Moses Mendelssohn and the Religious Forms of Judaism in the Nineteenth Century." In *Studies in Jewish Thought: An Anthology of German Jewish Scholarship,* ed. Alfred Jospe, 404–415. Detroit, 1981.

Will, Frederic, Jr. "Cognition Through Beauty in Moses Mendelssohn's Early Aesthetics." *Journal of Aesthetics and Art Criticism* 1955 (14): 97–105.

Index

Designer: U.C. Press Staff
Compositor: Prestige Typography
Text: 10/13 Sabon
Display: Sabon
Printer: Thomson-Shore
Binder: Thomson-Shore